*I have tried to recreate events, locales and conversations
from my memories of them.
Some names and identifying characteristics have been
changed to protect the privacy of individuals.*

Preface

"*Who is today?*"

My mother has asked this sometimes playful but always serious question countless times since dementia robbed her of the ability to remember the day of the week. She needs my help to remember something that is important to her, and she asks in such a silly way because of her lively spirit and sense of fun. When I hear her question, no matter how many times it is asked, I smile. I am reminded that despite being diagnosed with dementia (most likely Alzheimer's disease) more than eight years ago, my mother has not only survived, but, at the time of writing, was thriving and living a happy life.

I wrote this book out of a desire to share my journey with my mother into the darkness of her dementia. I chose to write about our victories over a formidable enemy, rather than succumbing to the overwhelming sense of helplessness, anger, and frustration I felt toward a disease that I had no control over and a healthcare system that failed us at every turn. Although our story is tragic, it is one of triumph, and it's my greatest hope that it may help illuminate a path for those whose lives have been profoundly affected by dementia. By sharing our experiences, along with our successes and failures, I hope to initiate a broader conversation on how the healthcare system can be changed to better serve dementia patients and their caregivers.

It wouldn't be presumptuous of me to assume that we are very far from a cure for Alzheimer's disease. Too many more will be afflicted before it is found. Alzheimer's is predictably unpredictable and doesn't manifest in the same way for everyone, but if our story helps even one person find some measure of comfort or success, I can think of no better way to celebrate and honor the life of my mother. I would rather open our imperfect lives for all to see than watch my mother slip into the vast, cold sea of Alzheimer's without doing something to change the tide for those who will come long after it has washed the memory of my mother away.

I am not an expert and this book is not intended to be a substitute for appropriate medical, legal, or professional advice, though my experiences have taught me that good advice and professional help is hard to come by. I can only share my experiences from my own perspective, and I do so with appreciation for those who have loved my mother and who have helped us cope with the ravages of this merciless disease. Please forgive me if you feel that I have treated you unfairly or have not given you just recognition.

I almost didn't write this book for fear that by telling just one side of a very personal story, I might cause further pain to those I love. I hope that you won't rush to judge my family as I show how my mother's dementia exposed us all.

Contents

1 *The Beginning of Our Journey*

The last time our lives were blissfully ordinary and relatively uneventful was in the early 1990s. My mother, Barbara, was in her sixties and was in reasonably good health for someone who had smoked most of her adult life and had been raised on a diet of meat, potatoes, gravy, and all things rich, sweet, salty, and deep-fried. Except for the occasional awkward sit-up, she didn't go out of her way to get physical exercise. Tall for her generation at 5'7", she wasn't overweight and, despite her diet and bad habits, was seldom ill. In her youth, she was considered attractive because of her naturally thin build and long, slender legs. Her deep brown eyes were framed by dramatic, dark eyebrows, which matched her rich brunette hair. Although her hair was naturally straight, she had a regular permanent so she could maintain a neat, curly style. When she turned sixty, her hair started to change to shiny silver-gray. The skin on her face has always been soft, pale, and without blemish. She has an intelligent, kind, and open face, one that invites strangers to strike up a conversation with her, as if they somehow know she is trustworthy and interesting.

My name is Anita, and I am the youngest of Mother's three daughters. During the 1990s, I was newly divorced, independent, and quite self-centered. I'm pretty much a carbon copy of my mother, just taller and not quite as good looking. I inherited my father's long face and straight, fine hair.

My father died when I was eleven years old, and Mother had been without a partner for several years when she met her second husband, Joe. I wasn't overly fond of Joe, but I liked him well enough. They eloped sometime in the early eighties, but I never remembered or celebrated the exact date of their marriage. They were inseparable. I was grateful that Joe truly loved my mother and always seemed to be looking out for her best interest. To be honest, their marriage served me well because it relieved me of any responsibility of worrying about my mother's welfare. Although she and I had always been close, our relationship was far from perfect. Joe's presence allowed me to feel free and unfettered by concern for my mother. I was able to pursue my own dreams, comfortable in my role as a daughter. I didn't know how fleeting my idyllic life would be or that I would one day find myself in the unexpected and alien role of parent to my mother.

In 1993, I got my first glimpse of the nightmare to come. At the time, both Mother and Joe were still working, and on this particular day, she had arrived home from work well before him. When Joe arrived home, he found her in the living room, confused, agitated, and disheveled. Dirt was smudged on her cheek, hands, and the knees of her pants, as if she had been crawling in her vegetable garden, and her normally pristine hair stood out in all directions. She angrily accused him of cheating on her while pointing to a box of new shoes she had purchased and left on the floor the night before. Joe was concerned and afraid because she was unable to remember anything for more than a few minutes and didn't recognize her own belongings, including her shoes or the new car they had recently bought. It took a long time for her to believe that the strange shoes were her own, and even longer for him to convince her that she should get into an unfamiliar car and go to the emergency room. He finally told her that the owner of the strange car wouldn't mind if they borrowed it, and she hesitantly got in. Once they reached the hospital, he called me and asked me to come.

I don't remember much about the hospital itself. To me, it was just a hospital – a place for the sick to get well, clinical and nondescript with doctors and nurses bustling about. Perhaps the years have faded my memory, or maybe my lack of impression was due to my role of concerned daughter, rather than watchful advocate. When I walked into Mother's room, I found Joe holding her hand, the lines of worry creasing his face not matching the smile he wore for her. She was sitting up in bed, dressed in a hospital gown with the covers pulled tight against her waist. She looked just fine to me, although her eyes seemed a bit wide and unnaturally bright as she smiled and laughed. She turned to Joe and said, "Sweetheart, don't worry. I feel just fine. I can't understand why I'm here. I feel so good! This is just crazy. I don't need to be in the hospital!" As soon as Mother caught sight of me, her smile faded a bit. "You shouldn't have bothered to come. I'm just fine!" I was immediately relieved, but as I searched for a chair, she asked, "Why am I in the hospital? I don't understand. I feel just fine. You really shouldn't have bothered to come. I'll be going home soon."

Worry replaced my momentary relief. I glanced at Joe and

could see the tension in his face deepening the lines already there. He patted her hand and said, "The doctors think you've had a little stroke. They're going to run some routine tests to find out what to do next. I love you, and I promise I'll stay with you until we figure out what's going on."

She continued to laugh nervously. "Don't worry, I feel fine." Looking over at me, she repeated, "Why am I in the hospital? I feel fine. You really shouldn't have bothered to come!" Now, I was really worried. It seemed as though she was stuck behind an invisible barrier that prevented her from moving forward and forced her to repeat the same questions. I found a folding chair and sat by her bedside, opposite Joe. We took turns answering her repeated questions, and eventually, she just started asking, "Have I had a little strokie?" She continued to laugh and giggle nervously, perplexed about why we were so worried. An icy hand gripped my heart.

When she grew tired of not getting an answer that she could remember; she became angry. "I only live across the street, after all. There's no reason why I shouldn't be able to go home and you can't stop me!" Knowing she lived almost 20 miles away but had lived in a house less than a block away from the hospital many years before (the house I had been raised in) I was struck with a cold sensation of dread that she had forgotten much more than just the reason for her hospital stay.

My sister Marie came to visit and I think my sister Lee did, too. The only strong memory I have is of my concern over what had caused her short-term memory to falter. What was causing her to believe that she still lived in the home she raised us in? I didn't sleep well that night, worried that she would remain stuck in the strange and debilitating state Joe had found her in that day, cursed to ask the same questions over and over, unable to remember what she had just been told. I prayed hard to God for a miracle and fell into a troubled sleep.

When I arrived at the hospital early the next morning, my prayers had been answered. As soon as I walked into her room, she proudly held up the MRI they had taken of her brain. "Now I can prove to everyone that I really do have a brain!" I laughed at her joke, relief slowly replacing the fear and dread I felt just prior to entering the room. To me, she seemed restored to her normal self. She looked alert and oriented and did not ask me why she was in the hospital. Humor was a familiar coping mechanism for my mother, so her joke was music to my ears. Still laughing, I hugged her and gave her a kiss on the cheek. I sat on her bed and listened with great relief as Joe updated me on her condition. He said that she had regained her memory, with the exception of a few hours shortly before he found her. The diagnosis was that she'd had a small stroke, or transient ischemic attack (TIA), but was expected to make a full recovery. It seemed we all had just avoided a life-altering tragedy.

To prevent another stroke that she may not recover from, her doctor warned her to stop smoking. She rose to the occasion and quit for good shortly after her release from the hospital. When life returned to normal for Mother, it didn't take long for me to push her ordeal to the back of my mind and happily retreat into my own self-centered life. Little did I know, this event was just a glimpse of things to come.

Shortly after her stroke, Mother and Joe retired. They spent their well-earned free time traveling, enjoying each other's company, and doing anything their hearts desired. Once again, life seemed blissfully uneventful for our family. Everything changed on April 19, 1998, when we lost Joe to a massive heart attack. He literally dropped dead at the home he shared with my mother after mowing the lawn on a beautiful, spring morning. His death, although sudden, was not wholly unexpected. Joe had a heart condition that both he and Mother were well aware of, and although she had successfully quit smoking, Joe was a chain smoker and didn't have as much success. His death had a profound and lasting effect on my mother.

When she called to tell me that Joe had died, I raced over to offer my support. I knew how much she loved Joe and how dependent on him she had been for the past eighteen years. The magnitude of grief written on her face was horrible to see. I felt an overwhelming urge to protect my heartbroken mother and help her through this painful time. She no longer had her love, her protector, and her advocate. Worry and deep concern crept into my mind about how she was going to cope with being truly alone for the first time in her life.

Once the immediate shock of Joe's sudden death faded, I was taken aback by the condition of their home. I was unprepared and horrified by what I saw when I opened her front door, but my brain was slow to process the chaos. Their house was stuffed to the gills with clutter, stacked everywhere I looked. The knee-high mess had clearly defined paths running through it, like a rat's maze woven throughout the house. Stacks of magazines, paper bags, newspapers, sacks of old lottery tickets, and boxes of new shoes were piled everywhere. Empty cans and pill bottles crowded the counters and kitchen table. It felt crowded, claustrophobic, and was clearly a fire hazard. A dirty, narrow pathway ran from the front door to their two easy chairs in front of the TV, which was the only place to sit. Even the sofa was full of shoeboxes. I knew that Mother had a difficult time finding comfortable shoes due to her chronic foot problems, but I still couldn't understand why she'd bought so many pairs or why she stacked them on her sofa. I chuckled to myself when I thought that Imelda Marcos must have been hiding out in their home. I struggled to breathe without gagging because the walls, windows, carpets, and mess were all sticky and stained with nicotine residue from the years of Joe's chain smoking. The air reeked of stale cigarette smoke. It made me sick to think that my mother had been living in these conditions. I knew they both had a difficult time throwing away anything that might be of use later, but I couldn't understand why they would hold onto what was clearly garbage. My childhood home was frequently cluttered, but it had always been clean. This behavior seemed incomprehensible for my mother.

I tried to remember when I had last been inside their house, and realized I hadn't been to visit since her stroke. They always seemed to have a good excuse for not inviting me, or anyone else for that matter. The list of excuses had been long: they were traveling, they were ill, or just weren't up for company. For the last several years, we always met at restaurants to share time and meals together, and our relationship had largely taken place over the phone. She and Joe were usually out of town for the holidays, but occasionally were willing to meet at a restaurant for Thanksgiving or Christmas dinner. I resented them a little for not wanting to spend more time with me, especially during the holidays. Often, I found myself wishing for a more traditional family, and I suspect Marie and Lee felt the same.

Once I saw the state of her home, I understood why she'd kept everyone away. Perhaps Mother had not fully recovered from her stroke, as we had all been led to believe. I couldn't help but think that Joe had been hiding this from us. I quickly pushed that thought from my mind and focused my energy on coping with this sudden and abrupt change to our lives.

I had called my sister Marie, and she arrived shortly after I did. Her expression revealed that she was just as shocked and appalled by the condition of their home as I was. Together, we packed a suitcase with essentials, bundled up our grief-stricken mother, and took her to my house. We began working on a plan to help her cope with the death of her husband and to address the awful state in which we found her living. From that day forward, our lives were joined and our feet set upon an unavoidable path.

2 *Two Years In Limbo*

I was living in a small, one-bedroom duplex when Mother came to stay. I gave her my bedroom and relegated myself to sleeping on the sofa for the duration of her visit. She was adamant about not sleeping alone in the house that Joe had died in, and was obviously ashamed and embarrassed that we'd seen the state of their home. Marie and I didn't press her about how things had gotten so bad. Instead, we concentrated on making arrangements and providing as much comfort as we could to help her deal with her overwhelming grief.

Lee, my eldest sister, lived a good distance away, worked nights as a nurse at a local hospital, and wasn't as close to Mother as Marie and I were. The true reason for estrangement was kept between Lee and Mother. I don't know what the unforgiven sin was or who was most at fault. Lee is ten years my senior, so we have very little in common; we are polar opposites in personality and don't look anything alike. The only thing we have in common is that we share the same parents. Marie and I, however, are only sixteen months apart and look very much alike. Despite our dramatically different personalities, we have always been close. For as long as I can remember, I have sensed the animosity Lee felt toward not only Mother, but Marie and me as well. All I truly know is that since I was young, I gave Lee a wide berth or suffered the consequences. There seems to be nothing I can do to change our relationship and I gave up trying a long time ago. She always seemed to harbor some unspoken resentment that I could never breach.

Despite their estrangement, Lee did come to Joe's funeral and offered her support to our grieving mother. After the service, while I loitered around the tables of food at the reception, Lee approached me and pulled me aside. Quietly, so no one could hear, she whispered, "Mother will not survive this. She will die without Joe."

I just stared at her blankly. "She's a lot stronger than you realize." I excused myself and made a hasty retreat before I said something I would later regret. Lee and her husband, Allen, left the funeral shortly after our encounter and faded back into their busy lives. As I had done so many times before, I tried not to let Lee's words bother me, but I was disturbed by her lack of faith. How could my sister know so little about our mother's strength of character? How could she believe such a thing? Our mother was strong and had endured worse than this. Although I had my own doubts about how Mother was going to get through this, I quickly chased them away. I was sure of one thing: she would weather this storm. I focused on getting her back on her feet and home again to rebuild her life so that I could return to mine.

A few days after Joe's funeral, Mother and I had breakfast at Denny's. While we were discussing her upcoming appointment with an attorney regarding Joe's will, a thought crossed my mind: with Joe gone, who would take care of her if she became ill? What would become of her if she had another stroke and didn't fully recover? In between bites of hash browns, I asked, "Do you have a living will or power of attorney?"

She looked a bit surprised, but remained calm. "No, I don't." With a catch in her voice, she said, "Joe had my power of attorney. I didn't think I would ever need an alternate."

"What about a living will? Do you have one of those?"

"I can't remember. Why do you ask? I have more important things to worry about right now."

I, however, thought it very important. Since she had not named an alternate person to hold power of attorney, she no longer had a legal advocate. The memory of her hospital stay flashed into my mind, and I envisioned her stuck repeating the same questions over and over. "Mother, you need to name an attorney-in-fact right away. At the very least, you should have a living will in place. You need to be proactive and do this now. Don't wait until something bad happens. You're going to see your attorney next week; why don't you take care of it then? That way, you won't have to worry about it later."

She seemed a bit annoyed as she gazed at me through narrowed eyes. She held her coffee cup near her lips, taking occasional sips. I could see by the look on her face that she knew I was prepared to get up on my high horse and ride. Used to me speaking my mind, her expression changed from irritation to resignation as she realized that I wouldn't back down until she heard me out. She continued to sip her coffee and looked me in the eye. She let out a long, heavy sigh. "I'm glad you love me and I know you won't let this go, but I don't see why the damn power of attorney is so important right now!"

She listened patiently as I pled my case. "You need to give someone you trust power of attorney and draft a living will right away, in case you have another stroke you can't recover from. It's especially important now with all the stress you're under. I know we've joked about how funny it was when you couldn't remember, but what if you hadn't come out of it?" I went on to paint a graphic picture of what could happen if her brain was once again addled by a stroke. "You'd have no voice in your care if you couldn't remember what someone just said to you." I described a long list of possibilities – hospitals, tubes, ventilators, nursing homes, unpaid bills – all made worse because her family would be powerless to make medical or financial decisions on her behalf. "Even if you don't care what happens to you, it wouldn't be fair to me, Marie, or Lee."

Her expression softened. "I'll definitely think about it. Can we talk about something else now?" I had done all I could. The rest was up to her.

When I picked Mother up on the day of her appointment with the attorney, she said, "I spoke to Marie and asked if she would be OK if I gave you power of attorney. She agreed with my decision, so if you are willing, I'd like to name you the executor of my will and give you power of attorney."

Relieved, I said, "Of course I'm willing!" I gave her a hug, and together, we went to her appointment. The attorney agreed with Mother's decision and the papers were drawn up and signed that day. I breathed a sigh of relief, knowing she was protected. If I hadn't witnessed the mental impairment even a small stroke

could cause, I would never have thought to encourage her to have
a living will and power of attorney in place. I wanted to ensure
that she always had someone who loved her able to advocate on
her behalf and make sure she had a voice in her care, even if she
lost the capacity to speak for herself. I could never have guessed
what the future held in store for us or how important this decision would be. Having the power of attorney in place gave me the
ability to advocate for my mother when she needed me most.

It was strange to live with my mother after so many years
apart, and it took some time to adjust. Mother needed me, and
my life had to slow down to a pace that was comfortable for her.
After the shock of Joe's death, she wasn't comfortable driving for
several weeks, and so my days were filled with work and driving
her to countless appointments. We spent our evenings together
watching Colombo or Antiques Road Show and grooving to the
sound track from the original Hawaii Five-O series. Normally, I
would have gone to the gym or met friends for drinks or coffee
after work. I missed my daily workouts and alternative rock music. I was recovering from a knee injury, so the relaxed pace wasn't
too much of a hardship, but I put my life on hold to care for her.

She stayed with me for a little over three weeks until she was
feeling stronger, felt ready to drive, and had resigned herself to
putting her house in order. Sleeping on the sofa was getting old
and I was glad to get my bed back. I offered my help and support,
and together, we cleaned the shoes off her couch and converted it
into a bed, as she felt uncomfortable sleeping in the bed that she
had shared with Joe. We widened the pathways so that she could
once again get around her home safely. There was a lot of work

ahead of us. Her home, including the garage, was packed full of a mind-boggling amount of crap and was in an unimaginable state of neglect. The roof leaked and the floors, carpets, walls, and fixtures were all in desperate need of repair, replacement, cleaning, or a fresh coat of paint. When I finally asked her how things had gotten so bad, she said, "Joe never could throw anything away. He wasn't feeling well toward the end and had been under a lot of stress. I was so worried about him. He'd been trying so hard to quit smoking, poor dear. I didn't want to add to his stress by nagging him about the house. I guess I just gave up cleaning his messes." Regardless of what she told me, I knew it had taken both of them to create such chaos.

Embarrassed by my mother's home, I told few people about it. Instead, I committed myself to getting the house in order before anyone else discovered her terrible secret. Years later, when the TV program Hoarders aired, I realized how many people live this way. We were far from alone. I realize now that this could have been an early manifestation of her current condition, but at the time, I was happy to accept her explanation and concentrated on making the problem disappear so my life could return to normal. Other than the despicable condition of her house, Mother seemed to be just a normal, grieving widow who found herself alone and needed a little help to regain her independence. I was determined to help her do just that. I couldn't have known that this project would take up almost every Saturday and countless weekdays for the next two years. I understood that it wasn't going to be easy to get rid of the hoard and make the necessary repairs to her house, including the removal of years of sticky nicotine residue, but I never imagined it would take so long.

Once she recovered from the shock and profound grief of losing Joe, she mustered her energy and focused on slowly repairing her house so that she could sell it and close the door on the painful memories. Every Saturday morning, dressed in old clothes with a scarf covering my hair, I picked her up and she would buy me breakfast. After we ate, we went back to her house and began the Herculean task of boxing, bagging and sorting the good from the bad. Unfortunately, what I considered garbage always seemed to be worth keeping to Mother. If I found an open bag of old paper plates stained with nicotine, I would throw them in the trash bag. She would protest, fish them out of the garbage, and say with a huff, "You can't throw those away. They haven't even been used yet!"

"You've got to be kidding me! The package is open and the plates are all stained. It's disgusting garbage!"

She didn't care. "They're mine and I don't want to throw them away. You can leave if you don't want to help." This scenario played out over and over again with paper plates, old magazines that Joe had collected, crushed boxes of plastic forks they had taken on a camping trip, and sacks of lottery tickets Joe had been saving for tax purposes in case he hit the big one. There was a mountain of empty pill bottles that had to be saved for some unknown reason. I couldn't understand why she wanted to save empty pill bottles, but there must have been over one hundred of them crowding the kitchen table, shelves, and countertops. It was a sea of endless, dirty crap. In my frustration, I would sneak the indisputable garbage into the bags she had already approved to be thrown away.

We made at least one run to the city dump in Joe's red pickup truck almost every Saturday.

From time to time, we took a break from the monotony of sorting through the muck. We spent some days shopping or going for a drive after our routine Saturday breakfast. Occasionally, Marie would join us, and once, even took us on a road trip to Portland, Oregon. We stayed in an old, historic hotel and spent our time shopping at the local boutiques and malls.

One day, Mother decided that she wanted to buy a new car, so instead of our normal weekend trip to the dump, we went car shopping. It didn't take long for her to set her sights on a cherry-red Mercury Cougar. It was a two-door sporty car, sleek and low to the ground. She fell in love with it the moment she saw it, and we drove it off the lot right away. She loved that car and named it "Cougee." She seemed brighter, younger somehow, now that she had a vehicle she enjoyed and had chosen on her own. I was grateful that she was starting to show signs of life after losing Joe. I had high hopes that things would return to normal and we all could be happy again.

The new car's appeal didn't last very long. Suffering from arthritis in her hip, Mother had difficulty getting in and out of the car. Each time she drove, she said, "If I come home drunk, I won't have to worry about getting out of this car. I can just roll out!" She would laugh at her joke and that would make me laugh, too. Eventually, she decided to get a more practical car and traded Cougee in for a Subaru Forester.

Except for her unnatural attachment to the trash in her house, her memory seemed intact and her behavior was normal. She wasn't exhibiting any physical or mental problems that might indicate dementia. She could be irrational and irritating, but I wasn't worried; angry and disgusted, maybe, but not worried. We enjoyed each other's company and I understood that grief was the reason she had trouble getting rid of Joe's things. Except for the occasional fit of exasperation, I tried my best to be patient. Slowly, the tide was turning and I was winning the battle, one trash bag at a time. It didn't help matters that Marie had long since gotten bored with cleaning out Mother's house. Instead of joining us on our Saturday adventures at the city dump, she spent her time concentrating on her career, living life to the fullest, and going out with friends. I began to battle the unattractive emotions of self-pity and jealousy. I can't say that I blamed Marie for moving on with her life. I wished I could have done the same, but I had made it my mission to get Mother out of the mess that she and Joe had created. I longed for more help, which certainly would have expedited my arduous task, but I also understood that I had made my own choice and Marie was free to make hers. I resolved to follow through on my promise to my mother. I wasn't dating anyone special at the time, had no children, and held a steady, well-paying job, so I had the freedom to help her through this difficult time. After all, I told myself, she had always been there for me when I needed her.

Slowly but surely, all was getting accomplished. Professional roofers, cleaners, plumbers, carpet installers, and painters were hired. Mother bribed me during my weekday lunch hours to come supervise the work by making her homemade soups, which I must admit were heavenly. She was a very good cook and soup had always been her specialty. I had no reason to complain, although I sometimes wished for a sharp stick to blind myself with when the occasional workman bent over to expose a large, hairy butt crack. I began to worry when I had the frightening realization that the employees at the dump were starting to look like potential mates. Still, I took great satisfaction in the strides we were making at her house.

Marie was a trained interior designer, so she helped with choosing the color palette, selecting new fixtures, and shopping for all things bright, new, and beautiful, while I was in charge of the countless trips to the dump and ridding the house of its toxic nicotine goop. I began to feel like Nicorella; instead of cinders, I was covered in nicotine and was left behind to clean up while Marie was invited out to the ball. My fairy godmother was nowhere to be found. Taking pity on me, Marie lent me her fiancé and his massive, old army truck to make the final dump runs, saving me at least a month of Saturdays. Using her considerable organizational skills, we held a garage sale to whittle down the pile of salvageable items.

Then one day, everything was done. I looked around in amazement after putting the finishing touches of paint on the trim around the front picture window that was now bright and clean. Sunshine streamed in to highlight the clean, soft, beige carpeting. No one would ever be able to imagine the horror this house had once been, I thought. It looked brand new and had an open, clean, warm feeling without a hint of clutter. It smelled of fresh paint and new furniture, and it looked as if the owners had taken great care in maintaining the house. That thought made me snort and laugh aloud. Mother came from the kitchen to see what was so funny. I looked at her pristine, beautiful home and said, "Can you believe it?"

She smiled. "It looks so good I don't want to move anymore!" It was too late for that. The house had been listed the previous weekend and a young couple was due to view it that very day. As soon as the couple laid eyes on the house, they made an offer for the full asking price, and just like that, the house was sold. Now we were faced with another challenge: finding Mother a new home and quickly.

As luck would have it, there happened to be a lovely single-story home for sale across the street from Marie. It was a well-built wood and brick structure with an open floor plan and large picture windows in the front and back. It had a small, level yard and a large, covered patio in the back that led to a detached garage. The floors were unfinished and the appliances were old and outdated, but otherwise, it was perfect. Marie and I loved walking through the neighborhood; it was well-established and tranquil, with level sidewalks and tree-lined streets. All the homes, although older, were well-kept with manicured lawns and beautifully landscaped yards. It was an idyllic location, close to where Mother had lived for many years and where Lee, Marie, and I had grown up. It would have been difficult not to feel at home in that neighborhood.

Mother fell in love with the house as soon as she laid eyes on it and was overjoyed that we had found it. It wasn't often that a house came up for sale in that neighborhood, as the homes there were very much in demand. Mother quickly made an offer, and before long, her old home was sold and the new one was purchased. The neighbors were friendly, the area familiar, and she soon settled in with a stray cat she adopted and named Honey. I was overjoyed and finally felt free to pursue my own interests.

Things settled down into a predictable routine. I felt confident that she was in a good place mentally and physically, and I finally was able to spend more time focusing on my life. She regained her self-confidence and drove herself wherever she needed to go. She filled her time with weekly trips to the hairdresser, trips to the mall with her friend Nancy, reading books, and doting on her kitty. With Marie's help, she renovated the interior of her new home with plush carpeting, elegant window coverings, and new appliances, all of which contributed to a pleasant and welcoming atmosphere. She hired a landscaper to maintain her yard, and soon, the neighbors welcomed her as one of their own, inviting her to the neighborhood barbecues and progressive dinners.

I called Mother almost daily to check in and visited on my free Saturdays. Lee called from time to time and came by shortly after the move, taking the furniture and household items that were left over from the garage sale. I got the impression she thought we were withholding things that were rightfully hers. She had no idea how Mother had been living prior to Joe's death or how difficult it had been to clean up her old house so that it could be sold. Mother loved Lee very much and I knew that the strain and distance between them caused her a great deal of pain and regret. She once said, "I can never meet Lee's expectations of me. I can't change how she feels, but it still makes me sad."

3 *The Telltale Signs*

In the year 2000, Mother turned seventy-one years old. Her health was good, but she had been steadily gaining weight and refused to exercise. For the most part, she seemed to have adjusted to her life alone and was content. I didn't spend as much time with her once we completed the monumental task of selling her old house and moving her to the new one. Free at last to invest some time in myself, I fell in love with my future husband, Lyle, a long-time friend and not an employee of the city dump.

She had lived in her new home for less than a year when I started to notice that her health was declining. She had gained weight and was wearing plus sizes, something she'd never had to do before. She was tired all the time and complained more than usual. I knew that she'd been avoiding going to the doctor since Joe died, and one day, I felt compelled to say something. Delicately and without trying to make her feel fat or old, I said, "I know you haven't been feeling well lately and I'm worried about you. I think you should make an appointment for a physical. It's been more than two years since you've been to see your doctor." She agreed to go, but I had to pester her about it several times before she actually went.

After the appointment, she called me and sounded upset.

"Well, you were right. I'm glad I went because apparently I have high blood pressure and type 2 diabetes. Damn it to hell, anyway! I guess I'll have to give up candy and pasta, if you can believe it! The doctor said that the carbs in pasta are worse than the sugar in candy. I'm going to have to take blood pressure medication, and the doctor warned me that if I don't lose weight and start cutting down on carbs, I'll have to take meds for the diabetes, too!"

"Thank God you went to the doctor. You could've had a heart attack! Aren't you glad you found out you have diabetes before you had to take medication to control it?"

She agreed. "I promise I'll see the doctor more regularly and try to keep my diabetes under control. I can still have candy and pasta in moderation; I sure as hell don't want to give them up altogether, so I'll behave. If you really want to help, you'll come over and take my candy so I'm not tempted to eat it. Marie can have some, too."

To our surprise, Marie and I were given sacks and sacks of chocolates, so many that I had to take most of what she had given me to work and set it out in the break room. It seemed that Mother had been trying to commit suicide by chocolate. Perhaps she wasn't doing as well as we all thought and used sweets to fill the awful void that Joe's death left in her life.

I kept a closer eye on her after that, and for a short while, she gave up candy and carbs, checked her blood sugar regularly, lost weight, complained a lot, and was grumpy. Although she saw her doctor regularly, whenever I asked what the doctor had to say, she replied, "I don't remember. It must not have been very important or I would've remembered. Right?" The first time this happened,

I agreed that her appointment must not have been noteworthy or worth remembering. However, when this became a pattern, I became very concerned. Surely, the doctor said something important once in a while, but it seemed that the appointment was completely forgotten as soon as she returned home. It was as if she had never gone.

Unfortunately, her regular doctor had moved away, and she saw a series of doctors at her clinic. None of them picked up anything unusual about her symptoms or behavior, but without continuity of care, it would be hard for them to notice troubling patterns. I was eventually concerned enough that I intervened. "Mother, the next time you go to the doctor, why don't I drive you?" I thought my presence would help her remember at least the highlights. Perhaps the doctor was frequently in a hurry and Mother failed to write something down that she needed to remember. It was difficult enough for me to remember my own doctor's instructions. I wanted to give her the benefit of the doubt. "Taking you to the doctor is a good excuse for me to take a few hours off work. We could go to lunch after your appointment. Wouldn't that be fun? I'll be your secretary and write anything down that you think is important."

Mother liked the idea of having her own personal secretary, so she agreed. She was happy for me to drive her, and when I attended her appointments, she seemed better able to remember the doctor's instructions. I wrote down what she needed to know and reminded her if she forgot something, such as picking up a new prescription.

Everything was fine until I realized one day that she had

stopped reading. Mother was an avid reader and read at least one or two novels each week. One of our favorite pastimes was perusing the paperbacks together at the drug store or bookstore. Although she was still buying the same number of books, they just piled up next to her easy chair, unread. One sunny Saturday afternoon, I settled myself onto her living room sofa after an afternoon of shopping. I watched as she placed several new novels on top of the accumulating pile, a pile that almost reached the arm of the chair. Frowning, I asked, "Why are you buying more books when you haven't read the ones you have?"

Mother instantly became defensive. "I don't think what I buy is really any of your business! If you must know, I have read so many books over the years and I'm just taking a little break. Do you have a problem with that?"

I didn't feel that her explanation was rational, so I couldn't let it go. "That doesn't make any sense. If you don't want this house to become a disaster like your last one, you should wait to buy more books until you have read the pile you have!" My tone was probably condescending and a bit sarcastic because she shot me a deadly look, the same one I received as a child shortly before she thumped me in the mouth for being sassy. I knew if I said another word, things were going to get ugly. I took the easy way out. "Have it your way, then!"

The fact that she had stopped reading had a chilling effect on me. I knew her eyesight was perfect with her glasses, so I wondered what this sudden change in behavior was signaling. I had noticed that she was starting to forget things, such as her doctor's instructions, and she was having a harder time remembering a familiar name or finding the right words in conversation. She had started to insert placeholder words such as thingamabob or whatchamacallit when she blanked on a word or name. Sometimes, she even forgot what day of the week it was and asked me, "Who is today?" Mother always enjoyed phrasing questions in a funny or nonsensical way. It wasn't how she asked the question but what she had forgotten that disturbed me. I wondered if her memory loss was tied to the reason she had abruptly stopped reading.

Whenever an opportunity presented itself, I would say, "I'm a little concerned that you're forgetting too many things. You really need to let your doctor know."

She would just smile and laugh dismissively. "I have a selective memory and only remember things that I want to. Now that I'm retired, why should I be bothered to remember what day it is? Every day is Saturday to me anyway!"

Shortly after she stopped reading, she also stopped going to the hairdresser. For as long as I can remember, Mother had gone to the salon at least once a week for a wash and set. I knew she hated to wash her own hair because she cursed and complained when she had to do it herself. She would only wash her hair in the kitchen sink, as she had done since she was a child before every home had a shower. I asked her about it one day, and she said, "I hate the way the water feels when it strikes my head. I would rather wash my hair in the sink." However, when she did wash her hair in the sink, she always complained. The water was too hot or too cold, she got water on the floor, or she was unable to get it to look right when she was done.

I had grown tired of her nonstop complaints. I rolled my eyes and sighed with exasperation. "If it's so much trouble to do your own hair, why'd you stop going to the hairdresser?"

She snapped at me. "The person who has been doing my hair for over ten years moved to another city. I don't know anyone else at that salon and it's too far for me to drive anyway. I guess it's just too damn bad and tough shit for me, isn't it?" Put off by her negative attitude and bad language, I kept my mouth shut but thought, unkindly, that it was her own damn fault. I dropped the subject.

I would be sorry for my unkind thought, because not long after that encounter, Mother suffered another small stroke while washing her hair. I felt badly that I hadn't been more helpful. In my defense, her angry and hostile outbursts were nothing new, just different. She had always been prone to complaining and angry outbursts, throwing an occasional fit if crossed, pounding her fists against the wall in fury or frustration. Her excuse for these outbursts had always been that they were her way of not carrying anger around or holding a grudge, letting it all go at once so it wouldn't fester inside of her. If we complained about her treatment of the walls, she would reply, "Would you prefer I pound on you?"

The second stroke was different from the first. I was at work when Marie called, and I could tell right away that something was wrong. "I'm with Mother right now. She called me earlier and said that she'd gotten really upset while washing her hair. All of a sudden, she was having trouble moving her arms and legs. When she tried to lie down, she couldn't swing her legs up onto the bed and that really scared her, so she called me. I told her to call 911 right away, but she refused, so I rushed over."

I interrupted her. "How is she? How does she look?"

"When I got here, she was sitting in her chair and so far, she seems fine but kind of shaky. She refuses to go to the hospital to get checked out."

"I'm coming right over. If you're worried or she gets worse, call 911 whether she wants you to or not."

"Of course I will, but she seems fine right now and I don't want to force her to go to the hospital if she doesn't need to." I agreed, we hung up, and I made my way to Mother's house. I arrived approximately twenty minutes after Marie's call and found Mother just as Marie had described: she was alert, speaking clearly, and had regained control of her limbs, but was still a little shaky. I was convinced that we should take her to the hospital immediately because we didn't know what had caused the sudden loss of motor function. Marie agreed, and although Mother protested, it was two against one now. We took her to the local emergency room, which was just a few blocks away from her home. We described her symptoms to the person checking us in and a nurse came out immediately to determine the urgency of the situation. As soon as she took Mother's blood pressure, she rushed us back to a treatment room.

When we were settled, a doctor came in and explained that her symptoms and her blood pressure indicated a high probability she'd had a stroke or was experiencing a heart attack. He attached her to a heart monitor and started her on oxygen, and although she was worried, Mother was feeling much better and trusted that the doctor would know what to do. Her heart rate was regular, so blood tests were run to determine if she'd had a heart attack and an MRI was ordered to determine if she'd had a stroke. It took hours for the tests to be completed, but Mother was comfortable and we were thankful she was receiving the care and attention she needed. After waiting for hours, the doctor informed us that Mother was not having a heart attack, but that the MRI showed some indication she might have had a small stroke. Her vital signs had stabilized, so she was ready to be released from the hospital. She was instructed to follow up with her regular doctor, prescribed a blood thinner, and told to call 911 immediately if her symptoms returned. Fortunately, her symptoms didn't return. Her follow-up visit determined that she'd had another TIA, but she was again expected to make a full recovery. Her doctor added low-dose aspirin to her regimen and changed her blood pressure medication, and Mother was eventually given a clean bill of health.

To avoid future anxiety over her hair, Marie found a hairdresser nearby that she liked. We learned an important lesson from this experience: stress had a direct and potentially devastating effect on Mother's physical well-being. This knowledge served us well when we were later faced with a more formidable enemy.

As time when on, she exhibited increasingly odd behavior that I didn't understand. Once, when I stayed overnight with her, she came into my room after I was asleep. Awakened by her presence, I opened my eyes and could see her standing next to my bed holding her wind-up alarm clock watching me silently in the dark. It was a little spooky to see her night-gowned silhouette standing over me and to hear the tick, tick, tick of her wind-up clock. I was annoyed. Tired of waiting for her to say something, I finally asked, "Is there something you need? Is something wrong?"

She seemed glad that I had asked. "I want to set my clock for when you need to get up."

"Oh, is that all?" I sighed with relief. "It's Saturday. I don't need to get up at any particular time. You don't need to set your clock for me. I'll just wake up when I do."

She seemed satisfied. "I just wanted to make sure you woke up when you needed to. I won't bother you anymore." She retreated to her bedroom, but came back a short time later, again just watching me silently and holding onto her clock. I had a sinking feeling that she would keep coming back until I let her set the damn clock. My eyes had adjusted to the darkness and I could see her better; she looked so childlike standing over me dressed in her favorite purple satin nightgown, clutching her clock with an expectant look on her face. The nightgown only came to her knees and her pale white legs looked like twigs stuffed into her worn, fuzzy slippers.

I instinctively knew not to be cross with her. Instead, I drew in a deep breath and said, "I'd love to get up at seven o'clock. It would be really nice of you to set your clock for me."

She smiled and set the alarm. "I'm really glad I asked you. I just want to make sure you get up when you need to."

Desperate to sleep, I said, "I love you, Mother. Now, goodnight! OK?"

"I love you, too." She shuffled out of the room. I could hear her as she settled into her own bed and, thankfully, she didn't return. I was more annoyed than alarmed by her behavior, and because it was late and I was tired, I simply made a mental note not to spend the night with her anymore if I wanted to get any rest.

Then, the constant phone calls began. She would call to complain that someone had stolen her newspaper or that she couldn't find her purse. One day, she even called to tell me that the furnace repairman had stolen all of her jewelry. "I'm sure that repairman took it! It was here before he came, and now it's all gone! I'm going to call the police as soon as I hang up with you. This is just terrible!"

Suspecting that she'd just misplaced it, I managed to calm her down. "I'm sure you've just put it in a safe place. Let me help you look for it before you call the police. You don't want to falsely accuse that poor man unless we are sure." I dropped what I was doing and went to her house, afraid she really would call the police. After an extensive search, I found all of her jewelry in one of her favorite hiding places. Paranoid about having a stranger in the house, she'd stashed it away in an odd location and then forgot that she'd hidden it. Whenever this happened, the lost items were always found in one of her strange hiding places. I began to cringe whenever my phone rang, convinced that it was Mother and wondering what was I going to have to find for her this time.

Our relationship started to feel like an unending tug-of-war. If I questioned a change in behavior, she always had a good reason or excuse to explain it away. When I didn't accept her explanation, she became angry and told me to mind my own business. It was always much easier to just back off and let her be. No matter how reasonable the explanation or how resolute she seemed, I couldn't shake the feeling that something was wrong. I took great care to tiptoe around touchy subjects, stayed alert, and paid attention to the telltale signs that something wasn't right. She did everything she could to pretend that things were exactly as they'd always been. She was very good at hiding things she didn't want others to see.

No one else seemed to picking up on the signs that were causing me such concern, not even my sisters or Mother's doctor. I thought that perhaps I was seeing things no one else could see because of the closeness of our relationship. I was willing to face her unpleasantness, and always questioned her behavior in an attempt to put my finger on what was wrong. I had an eerie sense that she also knew something was wrong, and every now and then, she let her guard down just enough for me to get a glimpse of the life-and-death battle she was waging against an unknown enemy.

Even though her home was in a quiet, low-crime, residential neighborhood, she became increasingly paranoid and fearful. She kept her curtains closed because she was convinced that others were looking in. At night, she peeked out of the curtains to make sure no one was lurking about, and then complained about the dark shadows on the side of her house. "Anyone could be hiding there and I would never know it!" She also complained that it was too quiet in the neighborhood during the day, since most of the neighbors worked. It was clear that she no longer felt safe living in a house by herself. She refused to visit a neighbor or attend one of the neighborhood events unless Marie or I escorted her.

Mother eventually started looking for what she called, "a room with a view." Without my knowledge, Marie and Mother began to look for a condominium with a waterfront view with the help of their friend, Cathy, a real estate agent. Marie hoped that living in a condo would help Mother feel more secure while also satisfying a lifelong dream to live on or near the water. I'm sure they didn't want to tell me about their plans because I had been questioning Mother's every move. They were right. Knowing she was becoming increasingly forgetful, I would have wanted to ensure this move was safe and financially prudent. I had always been the practical child, responsible and levelheaded. They sometimes saw me as a Debbie Downer when it came to cutting loose, having fun, and enjoying the good things in life whether you could afford them or not.

However, I didn't get the opportunity to weigh in on the matter. One day, Mother called out of the blue and said, "Anita, I have found my room with a view! I'm here at my new condo with Marie and Cathy and I just signed the papers! It's perfect. I can't wait for you to see it. It has the most spectacular waterfront view and floor-to-ceiling windows. And I mean it is right on the waterfront."

Shocked and suspicious, I asked, "Is Marie with you? If she is, can you give her the phone for a minute? I have a question I'd like to ask her."

She passed the phone to Marie. "You heard the good news?"

"Yeah. Is it true? Did she really just buy a condo?" I was thinking it had to be expensive. What the hell did she just get herself into?

"She got it at a great price. Cathy found it for us. It just came on the market and wouldn't be available for long, so we made an offer and they accepted it. It's perfect, Anita, although it does need a lot of work. Mother and I can work together to get the place into shape."

I really didn't know what to say. Sure, I could have argued and thrown a fit about being left out of the loop, but what good would that do? Mother seemed over the moon and the papers had already been signed. "I don't know what to think, but if it's such a great deal and it makes Mother happy, I guess I'm happy for her. It would have been nice if you'd given me a heads up on your plans, though." I was pissed off and Marie heard it in my tone.

"Well, it really is a great deal and one she couldn't pass up. It's an investment and she loves it. She always wanted a room with a view and now she has one!" There was fire in her voice.

I backed down. "OK, I'll talk to you both later. I'll look forward to seeing Mother's investment." After I hung up, I decided to hope for the best, as I really had no say in the matter. Mother may have given me power of attorney, but that power could only be used if she wasn't competent to manage her own affairs due to illness or advanced age. She was neither too old nor too sick to make her own decisions. Who was I to stand in the way of her life and her happiness just because I thought she was forgetful or acting oddly?

Due to its desirable location, it didn't take long to sell her home. Mother's new investment was on Puget Sound near a busy ferry landing and had a spectacular waterfront view. With Marie's help, Mother threw herself into remodeling it. I loved her new place, and even though it was a fixer-upper, you felt as if you'd arrived at a vacation destination as soon as you saw the building. The white brick building was on a beach adjacent to a ferry landing, and Mother's unit was on the third of four floors. Her new home was large enough to feel comfortable, but not so large that she felt lonely. She had a large kitchen and her own laundry machines – all the comforts of home. Within walking distance were a beach front park, a historic lighthouse, and a variety of restaurants. The best feature was the floor-to-ceiling windows that overlooked Puget Sound. You could see sky, water, the ferry landing, and Whidbey Island in the distance. Beneath the patio was a small beach with clear, deep green water full of Dungeness crab and the occasional salmon or harbor seal.

Mother had a bird's eye view of the ferry as it landed to load and unload at all hours of the day and night. Thankfully, her condo was well insulated from the sounds outside. The building had thick walls and soundproof windows, so the hubbub outside was barely audible. Occasionally, you could hear the piercing sound of the ferry's horn on a foggy day. The first time I visited, I wanted to drink in the view for hours. On her patio, savory smells wafted up from the restaurants and mixed with the smell of salty seawater, filling my nostrils. I closed my eyes and focused on the sound of the surf breaking on the rocks and the cries of hungry gulls.

The interior, however, was in dire need of renovation. The condo hadn't been updated since the 1970s, and the green and gold décor was dark, depressing, and outdated. The dingy, mustard-yellow laminate countertops strained to be released from the hold of the glue that had held it fast for so many years, gaps showing where it had successfully come away. The appliances showed their age and seemed barely functional. There was an enormous amount of work to be done, but as bad as it was, nothing could overshadow the magic of the location. Perhaps this move is what Mother needed, I thought. Mother's new home was thirty minutes away from mine, a bit farther away than I would have liked, but Marie lived less than five miles from her and that gave me some comfort.

4 *The Disease That Shall Not Be Named*

Mother was seventy-three years old when she moved into her condo, and she seemed better for a time. I was grateful to see her spirits improve and tried not to worry. I hoped that the change in scenery and the magic of her new home would somehow make everything better, that all the forgetfulness and odd behavior would disappear.

Unfortunately, not long after she settled into her condo, her memory started to slip again. On the way home from a shopping trip, Mother ordered a cup of coffee and placed it in the cup holder of my car for the trip home. A few miles into our drive, she looked at the coffee in the holder and innocently asked, "Is that your coffee?"

"No, it's yours. I didn't have any coffee."

"Are you sure?" she said with an odd look on her face.

Oh my God, I thought, she must be having another stroke. "Mom, are you all right? How do you feel?"

She laughed at me, picking up on the concern in my voice. Sarcastically, she said, "I feel fine. How do you feel?"

I wasn't pleased with her teasing when I was so worried. "I'm very concerned that you don't remember buying or drinking that coffee. What if you've had another stroke? This is serious and I'm worried!"

The smile faded from her face. "I would know if I were having a goddamn stroke! You don't know what you're talking about. Drop it!"

"Are you sure you're OK?"

She rolled her eyes as she summoned her most deadly voice. "I'm fine and I don't want to discuss this with you anymore." I was uneasy, but she was getting angry so I decided to let it go.

After I dropped her off, I called Marie to tell her about the newest worrisome incident. "I think Mother might've had another stroke or has something even more sinister wrong with her."

Since Mother has been known to pull my leg in an effort to help me relax, Marie wasn't concerned. "Mother was just teasing you! Why don't you lighten up? God, you're just too damn easy to tease."

I was angry with Marie for not taking my concern seriously, and felt frustrated that no one seemed to see what I was seeing. I knew something was wrong and finally decided to do some investigation. I was worried that she'd had yet another small stroke or was suffering the side effects of her previous attacks. I was slowly starting to realize that she might be struggling with something so insidious that I didn't even want to name. I hoped and prayed that I was wrong. Perhaps if I didn't think it, if I didn't speak its name aloud, it wouldn't be so. After all, I seemed to be the only one who noticed a problem.

I did some research on the Internet – what harm could that do, I thought. I searched for information on memory loss and stumbled across the Alzheimer's Association website, which would eventually become my lifeline and an important source for information and counseling. Through the site, I learned a lot about dementia and its many causes, and the symptoms of Alzheimer's. As I studied the information that day, my heart sank as I realized that she was exhibiting many of the symptoms listed. Even then, I was convinced that she couldn't possibly have this dreadful and terminal disease. I decided that her symptoms had to be caused by something else, something such as medication, her thyroid, or her history of strokes, anything that could be identified and treated. I thought her doctor was the best person to advise us and provide the help I knew my mother needed. I couldn't have been more wrong.

Mother's clinic seemed to be a revolving door for doctors, and her newest doctor recently moved out of state. She was forced to see a nurse practitioner who didn't notice Mother's forgetfulness and prescribed a new blood pressure medication she was allergic to. Unfortunately, Marie and I didn't discover the allergy until the nurse practitioner increased her dosage from half a pill to a whole pill each day, despite the fact that we'd brought the reaction to her attention. We were told the occasional facial swelling must be caused by something in her diet.

The day that Mother began taking the increased dosage, Marie picked her up for a day of shopping and found her lying on the couch, complaining that she wasn't feeling well. Marie was shocked. Mother's face was grotesquely swollen, her lips double their normal size, and her eyes were nearly swollen shut. Marie said that she looked like Yoda. She called the clinic and scheduled an emergency appointment. Apparently, the medication she had been prescribed for her blood pressure had an ingredient that she was allergic to. I wondered if Mother had simply forgotten to tell them about her allergies. I noted the drug allergy and updated her pharmacy to avoid any future exposure to that particular medication. She didn't seem to have any continuity of care at the clinic, and so because of my increasing concerns about her memory, I decided that she needed to find a new primary care doctor. Luckily, she agreed.

The new medical group I found for her comprised four doctors that shared a common waiting room. I selected a doctor from the list and made her an appointment. This time, I told her, "I'll not only drive you to your appointment, but I'll also go into the exam room with you to take even better notes. That way, I can write everything down and be a better secretary."

She didn't think that was a good idea at all. "I'm just fine on my own. I don't need you in there with me. Do you think I'm a child?"

"Of course not! No one knows better than I do how capable you are. With all the damn doctors you've seen, this has all become so confusing. I just want to be able to back you up and write things down. You know how little time doctors spend with each patient. Everything happens so fast, I'm surprised anyone can remember what the doctor says. To be honest, I wish I had a secretary sometimes. I promise I won't interfere, I'll just write things down."

She seemed convinced. "You're right, I'm lucky to have you. You've been a very good secretary. As long as you know that I'm in charge and you won't interfere, you can come in with me."

While we waited for her appointment and the transfer of her medical records, my concern grew. No longer able to control her diabetes by diet alone, the nurse practitioner had prescribed medication to control it. It was imperative that she tested her blood sugar several times a day, but she often forgot to do it. She also had frequent bouts of diarrhea, was quick to anger at the slightest provocation, and became very unpleasant to be around.

At about this time, she stopped cleaning her house. Every time I came to visit, her condo was just a little more cluttered. The carpet was stained and blackened from the dirt being tracked in that was never vacuumed up. Dishes accumulated in her sink and she seemed to have forgotten how to operate her dishwasher. Rather than cooking, which was something she'd always loved to do, she ate frozen dinners, snack foods, and ice cream. I was looking forward to discussing my concerns with her new doctor, as no one else seemed to notice the growing list of odd behaviors.

When we met with her new doctor, I brought a list of her abnormal behaviors, when they had started, and my questions and concerns. Along with the power of attorney document, I quietly slipped this information to the receptionist in a plain envelope with instructions to give it to the doctor. I did this when Mother's head was turned so she wouldn't question me.

As we sat in the busy waiting room, I reminded her of our plan. "Don't forget, I'll be going back into the exam room with you when they call your name."

Looking perplexed, she tightened her lips and furrowed her brow. "Why do you think it's necessary to come back with me?"

"Because I love you and you've gone through too many doctors. I was unhappy with the nurse practitioner who gave you a medication you were allergic to and then didn't notice, even though we reported your allergic reactions. Doctors are in too big of a hurry these days. Won't it be nice to have someone on your side?"

Her face relaxed. "I see your point. I'll be lucky if the doctor gives me fifteen minutes. I never can remember what to ask. They always seem to be in a hurry to rush me out the door. I suppose you think I should buy you lunch for helping me?" The last bit she said with her eyebrows raised and an impish smile.

I smiled back. "Of course. I work for food!"

When the nurse called her name, we both stood up. She smiled at us and said, "Hello, which one of you is Barbara?"

Mother spoke up. "I'm Barbara, and this is my daughter Anita. She's my personal secretary."

Mother smiled at me. I said, "That's right. Not everyone has an assistant."

The nurse smiled back and looked directly at Mother. "That's the truth. We all sure could use one, though. You're a very lucky lady!" Glad that the nurse seemed to be in my corner and had reinforced the importance of my presence, I gave her a grateful look. She led the way to an exam room, checked Mother's vital signs, made some notes in the chart, and left us to wait for the doctor.

Mother seemed genuinely glad that I was there. She was smiling and we made idle conversation while we waited. It wasn't long until Dr. C came in and introduced herself. "I've reviewed the information provided and feel we should start by doing a complete physical, take some blood and urine for testing, and then I will perform a mini-cognitive test so we have a baseline in your file."

Mother seemed to warm to her and listened intently as the doctor explained the procedure for the physical exam. She asked Mother to undress and put on the exam gown.

"I'll wait outside for this bit," I said. Looking at the doctor, I asked, "When you're done, will you let me know?"

She nodded. "I'll have my nurse get you when I've completed the physical. You can join your mother then."

After a short time in the waiting room, the nurse called my name and I went back to see Mother. When I entered the exam room, Mother was alone, dressed, and sitting in one of the chairs next to the exam table. She smiled as I came in. "I like this new doctor. She's funny and gets my sense of humor." I was happy to hear this.

As I sat down next to Mother, Dr. C returned to perform the mini-cognitive test. She started by giving her three words to remember: apple, table, and penny. She gave Mother a moment to memorize them before she started her interview and said, "I need you to tell me those three words after I finish my interview." The doctor proceeded to ask Mother some simple memory questions, followed by a short written test. Mother did well on the cognitive portion of the test, but struggled with a large percentage of the memory questions. She was obviously uneasy with these questions, and shot me pleading looks for help. Not knowing any better, I gave in and helped with some of the responses by signaling to her or nodding my head whenever the doctor looked away. This, of course, was the last thing I should have done, but I couldn't resist the desperate look in her eyes. My natural response was to help her, but my help actually did more harm than good.

Dr. C concluded that Mother did not have dementia. I couldn't understand this diagnosis because when asked to recall the three words from the beginning of the interview, Mother had just looked blankly at her. "You didn't ask me to remember any words. If you had, I would've remembered them, right?"

Mother and I both liked her new doctor. She was personable, funny, pleasant, took her time, and laughed at Mother's jokes, which made her feel at ease. Mother had already been to several different doctors and a nurse practitioner, all of whom seemed less capable than Dr. C. I didn't know of anywhere else we could go. Mother happily accepted that she didn't have dementia but was simply suffering the normal effects of aging. I, however, was not completely satisfied with the diagnosis. I knew my mother well and was convinced that something was truly wrong, but who was I to argue with a doctor? I didn't want her to have dementia, so I grudgingly accepted the diagnosis. Deep down, I knew that things were not right. The new doctor seemed to be managing Mother's hypertension and diabetes well, so I continued to accept her opinion about Mother's cognitive state.

Even if she were just getting older, I didn't want to sit by and watch my mother fail, so I began taking steps to help her how I could. I couldn't stand to see her lovely home in filth and disarray. One Saturday at breakfast, I said, "Mother, you really should hire someone to clean your house for you."

"I don't need any help, and I don't feel comfortable having a stranger in my home. I can take care of myself."

I knew that I would be unable to change her mind, so I decided to accept responsibility for the task myself. I arrived early every Saturday and just began to clean. When she protested, I said, "I'm here every Saturday anyway. I don't mind coming a little earlier because I love to clean your place and make it sparkle. It's such a special place!" This was the first of many lies I would tell my mother, just to get things done while maintaining an uneasy peace between us. I didn't need the extra work and hated that I felt compelled to do her housework. I had my own house to keep and a full-time job. I was dating my future husband, Lyle, at the time and resented the fact that I had to take time away from this important relationship to help my mother. I was fortunate that my future partner was understanding and supportive and encouraged me to do what I felt was right: take care of my mother.

In addition to cleaning her house, I reminded her to take her blood sugar readings. As soon as I arrived each Saturday, I asked, "Have you tested your blood sugar today? What's your number?"

If she had done it, she would go to the log she kept on her counter and tell me. If she'd forgotten, she would say, "I must have been distracted. I was just going to do it when you interrupted me!" Sometimes, she seemed to have trouble remembering how to set her meter or insert the test strip. She often refused my help. "I don't know why the hell I have to bother with this. It's just too much trouble."

I couldn't just let her skip such an important task. I set it up for her and guided her through the steps. If she became angry and refused, I waited an hour for her to forget her anger. I always made sure to write down the test results so we could report them to her doctor.

Since I was spending more time with her at her condo, I began to notice that she wasn't taking her medications as prescribed. While cleaning, I often checked her pill bottles and started looking through drawers and cupboards. I found too many loose pills where they didn't belong. Mother's blood sugar readings were high, indicating that she wasn't taking her diabetes medication faithfully. When confronted, she said, "I take all my pills and it's none of your business if I do or not!"

In frustration, I bought her a pillbox with the day and time compartments, filled it weekly, and checked to make sure she was taking her meds. She resisted and was angry at first. "I can take my own goddamn pills! I don't need your help. If I did, I would ask for it!" It took a lot of convincing before she accepted my help without arguing, but it was important that she take her pills, so I intervened no matter how much she complained. I quietly set up her pills as she pounded her hands against the walls and screamed at me. It was unpleasant and I felt sorry for myself that I had to put up with such an unpleasant and ungrateful parent. Sometimes, I made a snarky comment on how ridiculous she was acting, which only made her angrier and caused her to pound the walls even harder.

After I began setting up her medications and checking that she was taking them correctly, she started feeling better and her blood sugar was back under control. She also seemed less angry and had fewer bouts of diarrhea. If I hadn't taken these early steps, her condition would have worsened, she would have become ill, and would have suffered needlessly.

Lyle and I began to have Mother over for dinner a couple of times a week to make sure she was eating better. I kept her doctor updated about my concerns and her symptoms, which the doctor continued to ignore. It didn't help that Mother still had periods of unusual clarity and was able to convince her doctor (and almost everyone else) that nothing was wrong. I was frustrated with Marie because she refused to recognize that Mother had a problem, but nonetheless, I kept her informed when I noticed something troublesome. I was starting to feel resentful that I was the only one doing the dirty work: cleaning house, grocery shopping, and constantly nagging her to take her pills and eat better.

Tired of being solely responsible for Mother's well-being, I reached out to Marie. "I really think it would be helpful if you had Mother over for a home-cooked meal once a week. I've been having her over on Mondays and Wednesdays, and we go out for breakfast every Saturday. It would really help if you could pick a day that works for you and have her over for dinner. That way, we both can make sure she's eating right. I'm worried about her diabetes and that she's become so forgetful. We really need to be keeping a closer eye on her."

Marie didn't think that there was anything to worry about but wanted to spend more time with Mother, so she agreed. I hoped that she would begin to observe some of the uncharacteristic behaviors I had seen. Marie invited her over for dinner a few times, but she was inconsistent and only followed through when she didn't have better plans. Eventually, she stopped altogether, and once again, it was up to me to pick up the slack.

As time went on, I could no longer ignore the signs that Mother was suffering from something beyond normal aging. Although she had been a meticulous bookkeeper professionally, I began to notice unopened overdue notices scattered around her home. I searched for bills that she may have forgotten or had put away without opening, but any time I rifled through her drawers and files, she would get angry and suspicious, demanding to know what I was doing. "What the hell are you looking for? Are you stealing something? Tell me, damn it! That's my goddamn drawer and you have no business in it!"

I tried to restrict my searches to times when she wasn't looking, but in case she caught me, I always had a good excuse handy. "Of course I'm not stealing from you. I lost my keys and thought I may have put them in one of your drawers because I always keep my keys in a drawer at home." Or, "I'm looking for a cat toy for Honey and thought I saw one in this drawer." I said anything I thought she would believe that was nonthreatening. I learned quickly not to tell the truth, that I was looking for unpaid bills, because that would only start a fight I couldn't win.

Not only did she hide her mail and pills, but she also started stuffing drawers with used paper towels. When I asked about it, she said, "They can be used again, and I don't want to throw them away." Soon, her drawers became so full of paper towels that I couldn't close them. There were also neatly folded stacks of them on her kitchen counter. I would wait until she wasn't looking and threw as many of them away as I could. I hid them at the bottom of her trash can because if she saw them, she would throw a fit. I thought back to her old house and all the empty pill bottles and mountain of trash. Perhaps Mother had been deteriorating for quite some time.

I became even more alarmed when she started to hide soiled cat litter in her kitchen cupboards. That is not normal behavior for anyone. When she cleaned the litter box, she put the soiled litter in a plastic bag. Then, for some unknown reason, she hid the bag in her cupboard rather than throwing it away. Marie suggested that we get her a Litter Locker, a litter disposal system with a continuous blue plastic bag. All Mother had to do was open the lid, place the soiled litter in the top, and rotate a dial that made the bag wrap around the soiled litter. When she closed the lid, presto! Problem solved. I emptied the locker every Saturday when I cleaned her house, but if it became too full or the bag needed replacing, she hid the soiled litter in the cupboards again. If this happened, I had to smell out the hiding place and air out her condominium.

When it became apparent that she wasn't paying her mortgage or other bills on time, I took early steps to help manage her finances. I first needed to convince her to make Marie or me a cosigner on all of her accounts, so that we could pay her bills if something bad happened. I felt this was an important step, in case someone challenged my authority to access her money or pay her bills. Her denial of her diminished capacity made it more difficult to help. I feared that if Mother believed that I had overstepped my authority, she could revoke the power of attorney or do something crazy. She was, after all, acting pretty crazy lately.

The conversation was difficult but necessary. First, I called Marie to ask if she and her husband, Tom, would be willing to manage Mother's finances. "Tom has so much financial expertise.

Do you think he would be willing to help you manage Mother's finances? I'm already doing so much and don't think I'm the best person to manage her investments. This would be a way for you to help while I try to figure out why she's becoming so forgetful. We can't ignore the fact that she's not paying her mortgage or HOA dues on time. She only pays her bills when I find them hidden away, put her checkbook in front of her, and nag her until she's finished. One of us needs to be a cosigner on her account so that if she gets worse, there is never a lapse in her payments. She has already been receiving a lot of overdue notices. Mother has a near-perfect credit score. I'd hate to see it ruined."

Marie agreed to help. "I know Mother respects Tom. I'll talk to him about it and let you know. Don't worry so much; I'm sure things will be all right."

I was relieved, but soon, Marie and Tom left on an extended vacation. When they returned, they always seemed to have an excuse for not getting back to me. It was as if our conversation had never happened. Since Marie didn't believe that something was wrong, I suspect she didn't see this as an urgent matter. I believed that Mother's finances were indeed a very urgent matter, I decided to take action.

At breakfast one Saturday, I approached Mother. "I think that you should make me a cosigner on your bank accounts. Before you answer, let me tell you why. I may have power of attorney, but it isn't useful until you are too ill or too old to do things on your own. It's not automatic; it'll have to be reviewed and accepted by the bank, depending upon how it's written. What if something happens before then? If a bill needs to be paid right away, I'll have to use my own money. You know that I don't have a lot of money set aside, so paying your bills might be a problem for me. If I'm unable to pay them on time, it could wreck your credit score. I would hate for that to happen. I love you very much and wouldn't ask this if I didn't think it was important. Would you please consider it for my sake?"

She must have been having a clearheaded day because she didn't seem surprised or offended. Instead of the fight I expected, she calmly said, "I think that's a very good idea, but I'm still in charge! I only want you to step in if I'm unable to take care of something myself. It's my money to do with as I please. Are you clear on that?"

I was delighted with her response. "Crystal clear! I'll act as your secretary just like I do when you go to the doctor, and only when you truly need me." I gave her a hug, a kiss on her cheek, and a smile. We set a date for the following week and I accompanied her to her banks to become a cosigner on all of her accounts. We also left each institution with a copy of the power of attorney, which paved the way for me later. Once this was done, I was able to pay her bills for her.

I started slowly and with her cooperation. Initially, I gathered her bills together each month and filled out the checks for her to sign. I claimed that I wanted to spare her hands from the pain of her arthritis, and she was grateful for the help. I kept her in the loop and always told her that things were being done exactly as she instructed. Taking over gradually gave her a sense of control over her own finances. To this day, she will proudly state, "I know who, where, why, and how much!" even though her disease makes it impossible for her to know the details of her income, savings, or expenses.

We had been having lunch together almost every Saturday since Joe died, but what used to be a pleasant afternoon was fast becoming a dreaded chore. She started eating certain foods, like salad, with her fingers, and showed me her chewed food and asked me if I wanted to play See Food. When I got upset or tried to scold her, the bad behavior escalated. I was stunned into an angry silence one day when she shot water at me through her straw after I asked why she was eating with her fingers. I started to feel very sorry for myself and wondered why I was putting so much effort into helping someone who was so ungrateful and difficult.

Eventually, even Marie recognized that something was wrong and shared my concern. We both grew frustrated as Mother's behavior became more erratic and unpredictable. With Marie as an ally, we confronted Mother's doctor and insisted that something was definitely wrong. Dr. C referred us to a clinical psychologist who specialized in dementia. I suspect she thought the psychologist would prove that Marie and I were the ones with the problem.

After sharing Mother's symptoms with the psychologist, she agreed to see us all. Although she'd agreed to go, Mother was on her game the day of the interview and refused to take any of the tests. When the psychologist tried to guide her through the first test, Mother snapped, "I took my last test in high school and I will not participate in any tests. There's nothing wrong with me and I'm only here to satisfy my daughters." She looked defiantly in our direction and crossed her arms over her chest.

The psychologist, a pleasant young woman with a kind face,

smiled at Mother. "Well, I couldn't agree with you more! But since you're already here and I've set aside several hours just for you, would you mind if I just ask you a few questions instead of my normal battery of tests?"

Mother seemed to relax a little, warming to the psychologist's agreeable manner. "I don't mind answering a few questions, as long as you realize that there is nothing wrong with me and I'm only doing this to please my daughters."

The psychologist's smile broadened. "Of course. I'll keep it short, and then you all can get on with your day. Will that suit you?" The psychologist proceeded to ask her simple memory and cognitive questions, such as the name of the current President of the United States.

Mother was in a sassy mood. "Would you be offended if I told you 'an asshole?' "

The psychologist couldn't hide her smile. "Not at all, as long as you can tell me the asshole's name."

Mother grinned. "George W. Cranberry Bush!" (Mother was a staunch Republican and voted for George W. twice, so I was a bit surprised by her answer.) She was proud of herself that she found the right answer, but failed many of the other questions. The psychologist determined that Mother did indeed have some memory deficits, but her resistance limited the amount of information we learned.

Mother's doctor received the psychologist's report, but maintained her opinion that my mother did not have dementia. I was desperate for answers, but felt that we had reached a dead end with Dr. C, so I asked for a referral to a neurologist. Surprisingly, she said, "I will not recommend or refer you to a neurologist because I don't think she needs one. However, I won't prevent you from going to a neurologist if that's what you choose to do."

I couldn't wrap my brain around the doctor's unwillingness to recommend a neurologist. The only explanation I could come up with was that she was so certain of her diagnosis that she couldn't justify the recommendation professionally. I was disappointed and confused about why she continued to dismiss my concerns and the information I provided. Was she misguided or just inept? Unfortunately, Mother liked her doctor, and when I tried to suggest that we find a new one, she resisted. "She's my doctor, not yours. I like her just fine and it's not your decision to make!"

5 *Expectation and Reality*

For a long time, Mother seemed to be in a holding pattern, with no additional troubling behaviors surfacing. During her next routine doctor's visit, I mentioned that Mother was looking very pale and had recently become inactive, even for her. Mother, of course, protested. "I feel just fine! My daughter doesn't know what she's talking about." However, once I brought it to her attention, the doctor noticed that Mother looked like she was wearing an ashen gray mask. She looked under Mother's eyelids and at her nail beds and said, "I think I should do a quick blood test to make sure you're not becoming anemic. Anita, I'll call you if there's anything abnormal in her blood work." After the blood was drawn, I took her home. Marie picked her up a short while later to eat lunch and go shopping.

Later that day, the doctor called me at work. "Your mother's blood count is very low. In fact, it's so low that she may need a transfusion. If she becomes more lethargic, short of breath, or has any pain in her arms or shoulder, please call me immediately. We may need to admit her to the hospital for a transfusion. I don't think she needs one at this point, but I'll monitor her status. I'll prescribe a high dose of iron and she should be fine, but do call if she feels any worse." I arranged a follow-up appointment to discuss long-term solutions for her anemia, and then called Marie to pass along the new information.

Marie sounded frantic. "Oh no! Mother has complained about pain in her shoulder and she is so tired she can hardly function. What should I do?"

I wasn't sure what to do, so I called the doctor, who said, "You need to get your mother to the emergency room right away. I'll call the hospital and let them know to expect her. Please bring her into my office on Monday and we'll discuss how to treat her anemia."

I thanked her and called Marie back. "The doctor said to take her to the emergency room. I'll meet you there!" I met them in the same emergency room we had visited just a few years earlier when Mother suffered her most recent stroke, but it didn't seem like the same place at all. The changes were dramatic; there was a new entrance, a much smaller waiting area, and just one window to check in patients. It felt small, overcrowded, and chaotic. There was a long line at the window, and the waiting room was full of people holding broken or sprained limbs and mothers cuddling their coughing and feverish children. It looked more like a busy free clinic than an emergency room. I found a seat for Mother and stood near her while Marie waited in line to check in.

After a short wait, we were ushered to an exam room. The hallways were far from sanitary. I spotted a bloodstain on the rail of a gurney, and the floors were littered with discarded bits of paper, tubing, and soiled bandages. I avoided touching anything and felt dirty as we sat in the exam room. Chaos swirled around us. Several policemen stood guard at other exam rooms, and inside, the patients were tied to their beds, yelling, swearing, and struggling to get free. All this happened in full view of the other patients coming in for emergency treatment. I assumed the wildly flailing patients were suffering from drug overdoses. Mother was afraid, weak, hungry, and confused. I could only imagine how she would have felt if she had been alone. Actually, had she been alone, I'm sure she would have taken one look at the place and walked right back out the door.

It was a very busy Friday night and we waited for over an hour before the ER doctor came in. With a withering look in Mother's direction, he said, "I'm not going to waste a precious resource on someone who might not need it!"

I could hardly believe that a doctor had just said such a thing. I was dumbstruck by the magnitude of his thoughtless words. Marie and I both were so shocked that we could only numbly advise him of Mother's symptoms and tell him how low her blood count was earlier that day. Marie and I exchanged wide-eyed looks of disbelief. I asked, "Did her doctor not call ahead? I don't understand."

"Yes, her doctor did call. I've been trying to reach her to verify the blood work and find out why she sent you here." He seemed frustrated and overworked. "I'll have to do my own blood work because I will not give blood to someone that I cannot confirm needs it. It's too precious a resource to give away to just anyone!"

I wondered if his attitude would have been different if the patient were a younger person. I was horrified by how my mother was being treated. Were only the young worthy of precious resources? Was her value so diminished simply because of her age?

I didn't question his need to verify her blood work, but his attitude was deplorable. I tried to give him the benefit of the doubt. Perhaps he was just having a bad day, which was highly likely considering the chaos around us.

After the blood had been taken for testing, the surly doctor returned. "Your mother's blood count is dangerously low. She will require a transfusion. I'll admit her and she will be given the transfusion after she's been transferred to the hospital floor. We're not set up to give transfusions in the emergency room." I couldn't shake the feeling that he felt it still was a waste to give the precious, lifesaving blood to an elderly person. He told us that tests would be run the next day to determine the cause of her anemia and to rule out any internal bleeding, and then mercifully, he left.

Mother was uncomfortable, tired, and anxious. She picked up on our anxiety and frustration, but hadn't really understood the severity of what the doctor had said. She wanted to go home. "Damn it to hell. If they don't want to do anything, why can't I go home to my own bed? I don't like it here."

A nurse came in to take more blood. Reading the concern on my face, she said, "I need to type and cross-match her blood so I can ensure she receives the correct type." After the nurse drew the blood, she put a band on Mother's arm and left.

Soon, a different nurse came in and started drawing more blood. I was concerned about why they were taking more of that which she had so little. "Why are you taking more blood?"

Annoyed by my question, this nurse quickly said that she had to type and cross-match Mother's blood in order to band her arm.

I pointed to the band on Mother's opposite arm, and the nurse said, "That's not the correct arm to be banded and I was not told it had been done already!" She angrily stomped out of the room. No effort was ever made to comfort Mother; she wasn't even offered a blanket or pillow but was left to lay in cold discomfort, flat on a gurney in the exam room, pure torture for someone with arthritis in the neck and shoulder.

After more than four hours in that awful room, I became insistent that something needed to be done to make her more comfortable. She was becoming increasingly agitated, even in her weakened state. A nurse told me that all the pillows were gone because the nurses on the patient floors never returned them like they were supposed to. Disgusted with their excuses and resigned to finding a solution myself, I located a blanket in a cabinet in our exam room and covered our cold mother. Marie rolled up her coat and placed it under her head. It had been hours since Mother had last eaten, and because she was diabetic, I was concerned. I got the attention of a nurse in the hall and expressed my worry, but she just shrugged her shoulders and kept walking.

After five long hours, they finally admitted Mother and moved her to a patient floor for a transfusion. Marie and I agreed that one of us needed to stay to comfort and reassure her. After our bad experience in the emergency room, leaving her alone was not an option. The nurses were opposed to one of us staying the night, and claimed that they had no beds or chairs available for us to sleep on. Marie was a resourceful person and took it upon herself to search the floor; she found a rollaway bed, and the nurses couldn't find a reason why she shouldn't use it. Marie stayed with

Mother the first night, and I came the following day to give her a break.

The next day, two very disturbing things happened. First, a student nurse came in with a cup of pills. She cheerfully placed them in Mother's hand and then handed her some water. "You need to take your pills now."

Mother smiled up at the cute nurse with a trusting look. I reached over and stopped her from taking them. I asked, "What are those pills for?"

"They're her blood pressure medications."

I was perplexed. I'd been watching the blood pressure monitor all day, and the readings had been extremely low due to her lack of blood volume. Knowing her blood pressure was already low, I took the pills out of Mother's hand and gave them back to the student nurse, who seemed surprised. "I don't understand why my mother is being given medication to lower her blood pressure when it's already dangerously low. I don't have a problem with you giving her medication, but someone needs to explain why it's necessary first. Can you do that for me?"

The student nurse had lost her smile. "I'm not sure why, but I'll ask the charge nurse and let you know." She turned and left with the pills in her hand.

A short while later, a middle-aged, dark-haired nurse came. With a stern voice, she said, "I have contacted the doctor about the medication orders, and your mother's blood pressure medications are to be held due to her low blood pressure readings."

I was exasperated, disappointed, and wanted to scream. What would have happened if I hadn't been there to refuse the medications? Mother would have taken the pills from the pretty nurse without question. Like a child, she trusted that those charged with her care would know what to do. I kept a very close eye on all the nurses after that. There was an endless stream of nurses and I don't recall ever seeing the same nurse return to care for Mother. Wouldn't it be better to have some continuity of care, so a nurse could become familiar with her patients rather than just relying on what was in the chart? Then again, what did I know?

The second incident, which caused even greater concern, occurred when there was a delay in the delivery of Mother's second bag of blood. It was getting late and I was concerned that Mother had not yet received her second transfusion so that she could be released. The transfusion process should only take one day. When the next nurse came into Mother's room, I asked, "Why hasn't my mother been given her second transfusion yet? I was told that her transfusion would be complete today. What's the holdup?"

"We wanted to train the nursing student on how to perform a transfusion. Unfortunately, her instructor must be present for the training and she never arrived. The second transfusion will be started too late for your mother to be discharged today, so she'll need to stay another night." Disappointed, I stayed with her that second night and I will never forget the experience. It opened my eyes to how poorly the elderly with dementia are treated. The emergency room may have been traumatic, but the hospital stay was unbelievable torture.

I settled in on the rollaway bed. It was Saturday, and Lyle had brought me a change of clothes that I could sleep in and still feel comfortable walking around the hospital in. Lyle left us in the early evening when we started to watch Mother's favorite TV shows, beginning with Wheel of Fortune. We didn't watch much of the program because I had to explain over and over why she was in the hospital. I held her hand and assured her that I wouldn't leave. She was very disoriented, weak, and pale. She repeatedly asked, "Why am I here? What happened to me? Are you going to stay with me?" When I tried to reassure her, she said, "Oh, good! I don't want you to leave because I'm afraid. I don't like it here. Please, please, don't leave me in this awful place!"

Mother shared the room with another patient, whose bed was close to the window. A curtain separated the beds, and every time a nurse came in to attend to Mother's roommate, I could see a large elderly woman with wild, white hair, snoring loudly. Mother was given a potty chair, which was left by her bedside. The nurse never seemed to be around when Mother needed to use it. I was forced to help her use the potty chair, sometimes multiple times before a nurse would come to empty it.

During the evening, an elderly gentleman with dementia was admitted to the room across the hall. The door to Mother's room was usually open, so I had a clear view into his room. At first, his family members were there and seemed genuinely concerned for his welfare, but I could tell that they were eager to leave him in the hospital's care. I don't know their circumstances, nor do I fault them for leaving him. I think we all assume that our loved ones are in good hands with doctors and nurses.

Shortly after his family departed, the man began to cry. He wailed, "Why can't I go home? Where's my wife?" He got up many times during the night and when he tore out his IV, his arm would bleed and a bed alarm would play an odd electronic version of "Mary Had a Little Lamb." The nurse would rush in, bandage up his bloodied arm, and try to get him back into bed. She would remind him why he was in the hospital and that his family would be back in the morning. Not able to remember what he had been told, the process would start again. Throughout the night, I repeatedly heard, "Why can't I go home? Where's my wife?"

The nurse had several patients that night who got up and sounded their alarms. The elderly gentleman continued to tear the IV out of his arm, which always led to profuse bleeding. It was a surreal experience, as the eerie version of "Mary Had a Little Lamb" played all around us. The man wandered into the hall several times with blood dripping down his arm and onto the floor. I felt like we were unwilling actors in a low-budget horror movie.

The nurse was overwhelmed to the point of tears, and I was glad that I was there to keep Mother calm and help her use her potty chair. I only pressed the call light when it was absolutely necessary, trying to relieve a little of the nurse's burden. It didn't help that her roommate woke up periodically, spewed a tirade of abusive and foul language, and then fell back asleep and snored loudly.

Mother didn't understand why she was there and was very fearful and confused. "Is this where the crazy people go? Am I crazy? Is that why I'm here?" She was convinced we had put her in an insane asylum. She was also suffering the side effects of the anesthesia from her tests that day and was much more confused and forgetful than normal.

I patiently answered her repeated questions. "You're here for a transfusion because you're terribly anemic. You should be better by tomorrow and will be able to go home. I promise I'll stay the night with you!" Her eyes wide with fear, she held my hand tightly all night. She relaxed her grip each time I reassured her I wouldn't leave, only to clutch it tighter each time she forgot my promise. She only stayed in bed because I was there to keep her calm and answer her questions.

There were always several nurses gathered at the nurses' station while the overwhelmed nurse ran from room to room. They seemed to be having a good time, laughing and talking loudly. I'm sure there was some protocol that prevented them from helping the overwhelmed nurse, but it certainly didn't benefit the patients on that floor.

The morning couldn't arrive quickly enough, but eventually, Mother's transfusion was complete. The previous day's tests were all negative for bleeding, and she was cleared for release. The hospital doctor told me that "anemia of an unknown cause" is common for the elderly. He prescribed supplemental iron and told us to have her primary care doctor monitor her for anemia in future. If anemia is so common in the elderly, why hadn't Dr. C been checking for it all along? I planned to ask. If she had, it may have saved us from this traumatic experience.

This was my first experience with Mother in the hospital, and I hoped it would be our very last. I expected to receive a certain level of care and consideration from the hospital staff, but my expectations were far from the reality of our experience. I had always felt that hospitals were a safe and clean environment for the sick to get well, regardless of age, and that those who worked within those hallowed halls were held to the highest professional standards. We were not in a third-world country and this was not a charity hospital. It was the largest and only public hospital in our community of over one hundred thousand people. My mother had Medicare and private insurance, and the means to pay. I could find no excuse for the substandard level of care we received. After her release, I pondered the disparity between my expectations and the reality of the care we received.

From that day on, I was determined to make every effort to keep her out of the hospital. Based on what I witnessed that awful night, I realized that it was cruel to leave a dementia patient alone in the hospital. Most hospitals are not equipped to handle their special needs. Even if that poor man forgot what had happened to him that night, it just was not right. It seemed cruel and unfair to drop him in an environment he had no hope of understanding or navigating without any support.

If a patient has two ailments, a competent doctor would not treat one and ignore the other. The doctors may have treated her anemia, but they completely disregarded her dementia, and without my presence, she would have been lost. I knew I could never leave Mother alone if she were hospitalized again. Even though Dr. C continued to tell me that she didn't have dementia, I knew that she would be unable to advocate for herself, monitor her treatment, or protest about the care she received.

6 *The Awful Truth*

After our experience at the hospital and still unable to convince Mother to change doctors, Marie and I decided to make another appointment with the neurologist she had seen years earlier. I had her medical records sent to the neurologist, and true to her word, Dr. C didn't stand in our way; the records were transferred soon after we requested them. Getting Mother to agree to go to the neurologist was not as easy. She needed coaxing. "Mother, you're going to a neurologist because your brain, just like the rest of your body, needs checkups from time to time as your body ages."

"I'm not crazy, and no damn psychiatrist is going to prove that I am!"

Countless times, I said, "You're going to a neurologist, not a psychiatrist, the same guy you saw when you had your stroke. I know you don't need a psychiatrist!" I finally was able to convince her that the neurologist wasn't going to prove she was crazy or forgetful, but just wanted to make sure her brain was healthy and would help us prevent strokes or other brain illnesses. I took special care not to mention Alzheimer's disease or dementia, or she would never agree to see him. Even when she seemed to accept my logic without argument, I still had to reassure her and repeat the explanation many times. By this time, Mother's short-term memory had gotten very short indeed.

Again, I wrote up a list of odd behaviors, onset dates, and my specific concerns. I called the neurologist ahead of time to inform him that although I was desperate for answers, I didn't want him to scare or stress my confused mother with a label. I said, "Unless you feel it's in my mother's best interest, please don't say anything in front of her that she may not be able to process or that might cause her unnecessary stress." I explained her unwillingness to accept that anything was wrong with her. I was convinced that if she had dementia (or worse, Alzheimer's), she would fight us with all that she had if we discussed the diagnosis with her. After all, I couldn't even get her to admit she was forgetful without her becoming angry and belligerent.

Marie and I were hopeful for answers, but were equally afraid of what those answers might be. The day of the appointment, Marie met us at the neurologist's office, which was located in a renovated home in an older but upscale residential neighborhood. When we arrived, I handed a letter and my list of concerns to the receptionist and asked her to pass them along to the neurologist. Even though we had already discussed my concerns over the phone, I wanted to ensure he had the information beforehand so he wouldn't ask me about Mother's memory problems in front of her. I had already learned to avoid anything that would cause her to think that I doubted her abilities.

We sat in the cozy waiting area, which was actually the living room of the home, and it felt more like we were visiting friends instead of waiting to see a doctor. Every few minutes, Mother asked, "Who is today? Why are we here? What kind of doctor

am I seeing, anyway?" When our turn came, the receptionist took us back to a large but comfortable exam room, which
had probably once been the master bedroom. Half of the room
was set up for consultations, with three chairs for patients and
their families, a large desk, and the doctor's chair behind it. The
other end of the room was arranged for exams, with a scale, an
exam table, and a large chart of the brain and nervous system. We
sat down and waited in uncomfortable silence for the neurologist. When he joined us, he politely introduced himself and said,
"Every question I will be asking will be a test. I only want Barbara
to respond." He looked pointedly at Marie and me as he said, "You
are not to reply or respond in any way. Please let your mother do
all the talking, unless I ask you a question directly."

Marie and I nodded, but his instruction immediately made
Mother very uncomfortable. She knew he was going to ask her
to remember things, and she became angry and uncooperative.
"I'm done taking tests. There is nothing wrong with me and I
don't see why I should answer any of your questions!" She looked
a bit like a cat preparing for a fight, and I hoped and prayed she
would behave herself. I assume that neurologists are experienced
with many forms of dementia, because he was able to complete
his interview with relative ease. Agitated, she kept looking at us
and pleading for help with her eyes when she was confused or
couldn't remember what she had been asked. She shot Marie and
me very dirty looks when we refused to respond. It was upsetting
to watch her flounder, unable to remember what floor we were
on or what city we were in. I learned from my previous experiences that it was in her best interest to allow her to complete the

interview on her own. I just averted my eyes and looked down at the floor, wishing it were over. He continued his interview for the next half hour, asking many simple memory, cognitive, and math questions.

When the interview was mercifully over, he performed a physical examination, which included testing her reflexes and balance. After Mother was done, Marie escorted her to the bathroom. The moment they were out of the room, the neurologist scribbled a note on a small piece of paper and handed it to me. "I would recommend that you and your sister read this book, *The 36-Hour Day*. Unfortunately, the most likely diagnosis is Alzheimer's. All the other physical causes for her symptoms such as a stroke, vascular issues, a thyroid imbalance, or medication interactions have already been ruled out. Your mother definitely has dementia, most likely caused by Alzheimer's disease. I'm going to order an MRI and the receptionist will help you schedule that when you leave. I'll compare it to her past MRI to determine if there have been any changes in her brain that would indicate or rule out Alzheimer's. Although I'm confident in this conclusion, there can be no definitive diagnosis until a patient dies and an autopsy is done."

From that point forward, he would always refer to Mother's disease as a chronic, progressive, irreversible neurologic decline. To me, it was like Lord Voldemort from the Harry Potter series – everyone knew what you were talking about, but the name was so terrible you couldn't say it aloud. So, to me, my mother's Alzheimer's became the disease that shall not be named.

The neurologist prescribed a medication called Aricept to

hopefully slow the progression of the disease. He explained, "There are no known drugs that can cure Alzheimer's, and the drug I am prescribing doesn't work for everyone. It only offers the possibility of slowing down the progression of the disease." He started her out at five milligrams, the lowest dose, and said, "If there are no adverse side effects and her symptoms warrant it, we can increase it to ten milligrams per day." I asked him if he could recommend a doctor in our area that specialized in elder care, but he said, "I don't know of any one." A bit disappointed, I thanked him and joined Mother and Marie in the waiting area. As we were leaving and Mother's back was turned, I passed the slip of paper with the book title to Marie and silently mouthed, "Alzheimer's."

This was a nightmare, and I knew I would never awaken. The awful truth was that my mother had just been diagnosed with a cruel, progressive, and incurable disease, a disease that would slowly rob her of her memory and everything that she had worked so hard for, the same disease I had researched and prayed that she did not have. This happened to other people, not us! All the hope that I had desperately been holding onto shattered into a million pieces the moment he had spoken the name: Alzheimer's. I struggled with the reality that this was a problem I couldn't fix. My mind was racing. How could I handle this? What was I going to do? My mother lived alone, I worked, and I didn't have extra time or unlimited resources to spend. I wanted my life back. I was already resentful of all the time I had to invest caring for my increasingly difficult mother. I was devastated. Even though I now had a diagnosis, I felt no relief, just dread. The horror that lurked in my future was more than my brain could handle. Mother was just happy that she could finally leave the neurologist's office. In her mind, there was nothing wrong with her. The entire visit was forgotten by the time we reached the car. She was hungry and asked, "Who is today? Have we eaten lunch?"

After lunch, Marie went home to process the new information and I took Mother back to her condo and got her safely settled in. I went home to Lyle and told him what had happened as we sat outside in our peaceful backyard and drank a chilled bottle of Chardonnay on a late summer afternoon. Tears streamed down my face as I listened to the birds singing and the hum of traffic in the distance. I focused on the steady drone of a lawn mower a couple of backyards away, bitter that the world was going on as normal even though I had been thrown into inescapable darkness. Although I finally had a diagnosis, I was angry that it had taken such a long time. This was just the beginning, and I was having a hard time understanding why none of the medical professionals we had seen had provided us with more guidance or information. I was utterly and totally lost, left alone to feel my way in the profound darkness in which I found myself. This felt like being given a terminal cancer diagnosis and then being sent home with nothing more than a recommendation for a book, a medication that held little hope, and a "Good luck with that!" on our way out the door.

I'm not sure what I had expected from the neurologist. He had been professional, clinical, and matter-of-fact, and he gave me what I needed most: a diagnosis. I could move forward into the great unknown armed with a speck of information. However, a little empathy or an acknowledgment of the pain that came with such a devastating diagnosis would have been welcomed. I started to sob and Lyle gathered me into his arms, saying nothing. There really was nothing he could say to make any of it better.

Eventually, I recovered from the shock and was able to control the endless river of tears that sprang up at the slightest provocation, but it took time for me to fully accept and process the terrifying diagnosis. I was afraid for our mother and for how this was going to change all of our lives. Any hope of my life returning to normal was gone. However, I understood that to continue denying the disease would only put Mother in greater danger and wouldn't change the fact she had a debilitating and terminal illness. Even then, I had to fight the urge to run, hide, and pretend that everything was going to be OK. I'm sure I would have felt the same if she had been diagnosed with cancer or any other progressive disease like Parkinson's or multiple sclerosis. However, I think the stigma of Alzheimer's is greater because of the mental impairment the disease causes, the burden of caring for someone with a brain disease, the lack of information and support available, and society's inability to differentiate between mental illness and diseases of the brain.

Mother was seventy-six when she was finally diagnosed with "the disease that shall not be named," although her symptoms began when she was only seventy-one. She was already exhibiting the symptoms of the middle stages of Alzheimer's. What would become of her if I wasn't there to fill in the gaps that were opening up in her life? I made sure she wasn't taking too much or too little medication, I pushed for a diagnosis, and I tried to keep her stress level down by helping her manage her day-to-day tasks. My anger grew when I thought of the lack of information and support I had received from the medical professionals I had consulted. I had seen other people, famous people like Ronald Reagan, whose doctors called out Alzheimer's by name, and by doing so, seemed to get all the support possible for this devastating illness. Why could I not claim the same for my mother? I was not afraid to say "Alzheimer's." At least I knew what I was up against. In my heart, I do feel that my mother suffers from this terrible disease, and if it's something other than Alzheimer's, shame on those who refused to help me find what else it might be so that I could care for and support her appropriately.

The first thing I needed to do was to get a grip, take care of myself, allow myself to grieve, and talk to someone about my fears and concerns. This equally affected Marie, so we cried and talked to each other about our feelings and our fear of what was ahead. We decided that, together, we should visit the psychologist Mother had seen. She was familiar, we liked her, and we felt she would understand what we were facing. We made an appointment, but because she was Mother's psychologist, she was not able to accept our insurance. She scheduled the appointment with us anyway and offered to let us pay out-of-pocket because she felt it would be very helpful to discuss our feelings about Mother's illness. I told Marie, "I can't really afford to see the psychologist right now."

Marie said, "I'll pay for half, and if you can't afford your half, I'll just pay the whole bill. I think it's important that we go together."

The next task on my plate was to share the unhappy news with my eldest sister, Lee. I hadn't spoken to her in a very long time and was a bit nervous when I called her. I hoped that because she was a nurse, she would be able to give me some insight and good advice. Lee seemed pleased but a little suspicious when I called. We exchanged the prerequisite pleasantries briefly caught up on each other's lives, and then I launched into my real reason for calling. "Lee, I've been worried about Mother for a long time, and finally took her to a neurologist. He diagnosed her with dementia and thinks she has Alzheimer's disease." I let that sink in and waited silently for her reply.

"Are you sure? If it's Alzheimer's, this isn't going to be pretty. I've cared for Alzheimer's patients before; if that's what she has, she'd be better off dead."

Her unemotional and matter-of-fact tone surprised me more than her shocking statement. I tried to hold my anger in check. "I certainly hope that she won't die anytime soon. I plan to do everything I can to support her. She really is doing well right now – just a bit confused and hard to deal with sometimes. Nothing I haven't been able to handle. She is still very much present and aware and able to live on her own, at least for now. I'm just worried about what's to come."

Lee snorted. "Oh, it's going to get a lot worse if she has Alzheimer's! I find all of this hard to believe. When I call Mom, she seems perfectly fine." Lee took the news well, too well, I thought. Their estrangement meant that Lee didn't have as much contact with Mother and I did, so I wasn't terribly surprised that she didn't believe me. She changed the subject, and seemed unwilling to continue talking about our mother. We said our good byes, and after I hung up, I sat down and cried. Lee's cold reaction filled me with anger and disappointment. I don't know what I expected, but it wasn't this. She offered no help or guidance, only negative comments and disbelief. From that day forward, I knew that I couldn't expect any help or support from Lee. Knowing how much Mother loved her, I promised myself that no matter how I felt, I would never let my feelings get in the way of making sure Lee was informed about what was going on with our mother. That is what mother would want me to do.

Marie was disappointed but not surprised to hear about Lee's reaction. I told Marie how much I was looking forward to meeting with the psychologist. "I know she will have a lot of good suggestions on how we can work together to support Mother. I really liked her and am hopeful she can help us get a handle on this. What time and where do you want to meet..."

She interrupted, "I've been meaning to call you about that. I won't be able to go."

"Are you kidding? What could be more important than this?"

"I've been offered a fantastic opportunity, one I can't refuse. I've already committed to going and have bought my airline tickets. I can't wait to tell you all about it!"

Well, I thought, if you couldn't wait, then why the hell didn't you tell me sooner? I was stunned into silence.

Taking my silence as permission to continue, she said, "I'm going to London for a week with a group of businesswomen to attend a conference, and then we're going to Africa to help the indigenous population start their own sustainable businesses. I'll be out of the country for almost a month. This is a tremendous opportunity for me. I'm so excited! I've no idea when I'll be able to reschedule the appointment with the psychologist. There is so much to do!"

I was floored and didn't know what to say, listening silently as Marie went on and on about what a great opportunity it was and how many people she would be helping. It was as if the floor opened up under my feet, and a hand was pulling me farther down into the dark hole in which we had found ourselves. I didn't want to listen anymore so I cut her off. "You need to do what you need to do. I'm still going to see what the psychologist has to say." Just great, I thought, now I'm stuck paying for the whole visit, when Marie had offered to pay half. I was too proud to ask her for the money, but tersely said, "I'm going ahead with the appointment without you. I need this. I cry myself to sleep every night and I need the strength to face this head-on. I wish that you could go with me. I'm not happy about you leaving, but I'm sure I'll get over it."

She seemed relieved. "I think that's a good idea. I'll call you when I'm back and settled. I'll look forward to hearing all about what the psychologist has to say."

Fat chance, I thought angrily. If you want to know what the psychologist has to say, you can damn well see her yourself. Instead, I bit my tongue. "Be safe. I love you. Call me when you get back." Quickly ending the conversation before my anger got the better of me, I tried hard to understand that this was a great opportunity for her and had just happened to come up at a very bad time. Who was I to argue with helping struggling people in Africa? I was assaulted with anger and disappointment, but I also loved Marie and wanted what was best for her. I felt conflicted.

She had a history of running away from anything unpleasant or ugly, but I justified her actions by telling myself that she was just grieving in her own way. I'd get over my disappointment eventually, but a wedge had been driven between us and would be forced even deeper as we chose our own paths, following our mother into the darkness of her dementia.

7 *Taking Control*

Several days later, I sat down with the psychologist. She was as I remembered her: well-dressed, professional, pleasant, and soft-spoken. When I arrived for the appointment, she greeted me warmly and held out her hand to shake mine as she looked over my shoulder. She had expected to also meet with Marie, so as we sat down, she asked, "Where's your sister?"

I took a deep breath and expressed my disappointment with a sigh. "Well, that is a long story. Marie was supposed to be here, but something came up." I told her about Marie's opportunity and took another deep, conscious breath.

Looking thoughtfully at me, she asked, "And just how did that make you feel?"

I couldn't help but smile. "Angry, alone, and abandoned. But how do you argue with helping starving people in Africa? If you have a good argument, I'd love to hear it!" I laughed a little and she smiled back at me.

"I agree. That would be a difficult argument to make." With the ice successfully broken, we shifted the conversation to my mother. She talked about how important it would be to care for not only my mother, but myself as well. She echoed the neurologist's recommendation of *The 36-Hour Day*, and recommended that I learn as much as possible about the disease and how to handle problem behaviors. She pointed me toward the Alzheimer's Association, the organization I'd found on my own. Before we concluded our session, she emphasized that if I felt the need for counseling, I should seek it without shame or fear. Unfortunately, she was leaving her practice for a job opportunity out of state, so I would be unable to meet with her again.

In the weeks that followed, Mother was stable and little changed. I devoured as much information as I could about Alzheimer's disease. I started by ordering *The 36-Hour Day*, and since Marie was out of the country, I also ordered a copy for her so that both she and her husband could read about what we could expect. I called the Alzheimer's Association hot line and was pleased by the prompt, friendly, and expert advice I was given, as well as the free information they sent me regarding aspects of the disease that I wanted to learn more about. I also ordered a book called *Coach Broyles' Playbook for Alzheimer's Caregivers*.

I won't go into detail about what I learned about Alzheimer's disease, as that information is best shared by the professionals. I will say I discovered that there seems to be more that is unknown about the disease than is known. I decided to concentrate on steps I could take immediately. I understood I couldn't cure Mother or change her fate, so I focused my energy on learning how to communicate with her as her disease progressed, how I could avoid problem behaviors, and what I could do as a caregiver to keep my mother safe. As soon as they came in the mail, I anxiously started reading *The 36-Hour Day* and *Coach Broyles' Playbook*.

The 36 Hour-Day was a difficult read. It was long and technical, and graphically outlined the details of my mother's impending demise. Instead of trying to read and process the information all at once, I focused on the chapters that applied to Mother and kept the book handy to reference as the information became relevant. *Coach Broyles' Playbook* was much easier to follow and provided information about the different stages of the disease, including helpful strategies for each stage as Mother's condition changed.

I'm very glad I took the time to learn as much as possible, despite the unpleasant realities of the subject matter, because I felt more prepared to handle what was coming. My task would have been much more difficult if I hadn't done this early research.

The more I learned, the more apparent it became that I needed to take control. My mother's disease impaired her memory and caused her to do things she otherwise wouldn't, such as putting unpaid bills away in drawers, not eating right, not taking her pills, and not cleaning her house. I could no longer assume that she would be able to care for herself, and since Marie always seemed to have other business to attend to, I took it upon myself to take charge. There was no time to waste.

My mother was an adult, and making any decisions on her behalf was not going to be easy, even as she lost the ability to make them on her own. I was in tricky territory. She was still cognizant enough to have a say in what happened to her, and I didn't want her voice to be diminished. She was still my mother, after all, even though she would often accusingly say, "You think you are the Mother!" Although I had durable power of attorney and now had a doctor's diagnosis to back it up, I wasn't ready to treat her as if she were incompetent. I wanted her to have as much control over her life for as long as possible. There was a lot of my mother still in there – a strong and proud person with an iron will. She was just a bit more unpredictable and unpleasant to deal with. In the weeks and months that followed her diagnosis, we made many of the early decisions together. Although it wasn't easy for either of us, it helped her transition control of her finances and day-to-day affairs to me when she was no longer able to make decisions on her own.

Early in our journey, I decided not to label her disease or try to convince her something was wrong with her. I never wanted her to think that she was ill and not capable, so I worked hard to help her believe that she was making the decisions and was in complete control. I was merely her secretary. It wasn't always easy, but this strategy worked well for me.

Knowing that she would be soon unable to manage her finances, I identified all of her sources of income, including pensions and Social Security. Instead of having checks mailed to her, I helped her set up direct deposits to avoid lost or stolen money. Eventually, I had her bank statements mailed to me so that I could balance her checkbook and monitor the activity in her accounts.

Mother had multiple credit cards, and I felt that having so many made her vulnerable to theft. Together, we cut up all but one. I said, "You're a target for thieves! If your purse is snatched, how will you be able to get all those cards canceled before someone charges up a storm? It would be a lot safer if you don't have so much to steal. It would be smart to keep only one major credit card in your wallet." Luckily, she agreed. I would have cut up her credit cards even if she hadn't agreed to it, since she didn't use them or even know how many she had. She signed the letters I wrote to each of the credit card companies, closing the accounts and requesting written confirmation.

Marie and I bought her a closet safe to store her extra cash and valuables, including her Medicare card, Social Security card, and credit card. Not wanting her to have access to the safe, Marie and I kept the only keys. When she asked where her key to the safe was, we told her that she put it in a safe place where we would never find it, so we kept spare key for her as a precaution. If she wasn't satisfied with our explanation or demanded access, we told her that we would hold onto the key until another one could be made. Soon enough, she'd forget all about it.

When we went out, she liked to pay cash for her meals and wanted the freedom to purchase things she saw. Every week, Marie or I took her to the bank to withdraw two hundred dollars, which she felt was just the right amount of pocket money. After all, it was her money and I didn't want her to feel like we were giving her an allowance or treating her like a child. She preferred to go to the ATM, but she often forgot her PIN, so she liked Marie or me to go with her. I paid attention to the amounts she withdrew. Before we left the house, she always liked to count her money to make sure she had just the right amount. I was able to monitor her expenditures, making sure that no large amounts of cash were disappearing. This worked well for us and she was happy as long as she had money in her wallet and felt she was in total control.

Mother's disease made her increasingly forgetful and vulnerable. I stayed vigilant and looked for signs that someone may be taking advantage of her. I registered her phone number on the

National Do Not Call List and paid for it to be unlisted, even though it cost a little extra. I felt that a few more dollars a month was worth it to avoid giving a potential scammer easy access to her phone number.

Even when Marie finally returned from her travels, she never seemed interested in taking control. Fed up, I finally asked, "Why don't you do more to help? Why do you leave it up to me to do everything?"

She said, "I'm a leader, not a follower! You're doing such a good job. I don't see any reason why I should take over. If you need help, all you have to do is ask me." I thought that was absurd. We both were control freaks and I knew she would never take direction from me. Her life was busy and full, so I thought this must have been her way of saying, "I'm glad you are in charge, so I won't have to be." I kept her in the loop, asked for her opinion, and explained in great detail things that I had done. The chasm between us was growing as the burden of the day-to-day tasks, endless details, and paperwork fell squarely on my shoulders. I had the added work of reporting what I had done, answering her questions, and sometimes receiving her criticism. I started to drink heavily from the poison cocktail of anger, resentment, and jealously.

My resentment toward Marie grew deeper by the day as I realized that I couldn't do everything myself. I knew she was capable of doing a lot more than she was doing; she was intelligent, strong, and very talented, and I was sure of her love for our mother. When she did help, it made my life so much easier, but then she would disappear again, leaving a vacuum in her wake. If Marie made a dentist or a podiatrist appointment for Mother and something else came up, it was common for her miss the appointment without even bothering to cancel it. Since I was the primary contact, I often received calls about a missed appointment, and had to make apologies or try to talk them out of charging a penalty fee. Her thoughtlessness infuriated me. After all, I told myself, I had a life to live, a very demanding job, and was planning my wedding to Lyle. Who the hell did my sister think she was?

Things came to a head two weeks before my wedding. Marie, my maid of honor, called to say, "Tom has planned a vacation getaway to a remote island up the coast of Canada. We're flying his mother and her husband out to join us. We'll be gone for two weeks, but I'll be back the day before your wedding. I promise I'll take care of anything that needs to be done when I get back." Yet again, I was at a total loss for words. I let her go on. "This was Tom's idea and I have no say in the matter. He's already spent the money and made all the arrangements, so I have to go. It will be all right. I promise!" Why I was surprised at her announcement, I don't know, but I was. It was mid-July and was unusually hot. Selfishly, Marie asked, "While we are gone, can you please water our plants and check on our cat?"

I bit my tongue and agreed. Perhaps I did it because Marie was footing part of the bill for my reception as a wedding gift, and I was grateful. I also knew that once Tom got an idea in his head, he was going to do it regardless of what Marie wanted. I liked Marie's cat, as did Mother, so I thought that this task might not be such a chore after all.

I'd soon regret my decision. I already had the stress of finalizing my wedding plans, checking on Mother, playing hostess to Lyle's mother and brother, and working until the day before the wedding so we could afford it. Now, on top of it all, I had to go to Marie's home every day to water her plants and feed her cat. I could have tended to Marie's request less frequently, but the temperatures were soaring into the nineties; I was worried about the cat and the plants needed daily water to survive.

Before she left, Marie told me she'd arranged for one of her friends to help me, but when I called, her friend said, "I'm not sure when I'll be available to help. I may get a charter plane and fly out to stay with Marie and Tom. I'll let you know when my plans are firmed up." Whatever, I thought. I was not going to chase her down. I already had too much to manage without adding her to my list. She called me a week later in a minor panic. "Oh my God, was I supposed to be feeding the cat?" I don't think I was very understanding or kind, since the friend later commented to Marie about what a Bridezilla I was. Godzilla was closer to the truth. I felt like tearing down the whole damn city and breathing fire, I was that angry. Lyle came to my rescue several times and took care of the cat and plants for me, even taking an under-loved palm tree home to nurse back to health. I will never regret the choice I made to marry Lyle. He even called a few of my close friends and invited them over, feeling badly that Marie had not planned a wedding shower for me.

I spent many dark days wasting precious time and energy on anger and resentment. I told myself that I would seek counseling as soon as things settled down. Marie came home the day before my wedding and as promised, sprang into action. She was a hurricane of helpfulness, orchestrating my large wedding reception of over two hundred people without a hitch, but the damage was done. The poison had reached my heart and nothing would ever be the same between us again.

The stress was starting to affect my health. I wasn't eating right, had gained weight, and my blood pressure was high enough that I needed medication to get it under control. I needed to start taking care of myself or I would be unable to take care of Mother. Enjoying a nice glass of wine (or two or three or four) after a long and stressful day became a more frequent occurrence. I visited my doctor regularly to discuss my concerns and tried not to sink into the black hole of despair that always was just ahead of me, threatening to swallow me whole. I was bitter and angry almost all the time. Lyle was very supportive, but he was worried and began to insist that I take better care of myself and stand up to those who took advantage of me. I didn't know what to do. I was afraid that if I confronted Marie, she would no longer provide the support I was getting. I knew that she loved Mother and had good intentions, and I didn't want to hurt her feelings. She had her own demons to conquer.

Eventually, I got a referral from my doctor to a Christian counseling service. The day of my first session, I stepped into a comfortable and relaxed office and met my counselor, an elegant woman in her fifties, expensively dressed, with short blond hair and a kind face. I sat across from her in an overstuffed love seat, and I distinctly remember staring at her bright red shoes and thinking what alarmingly high heels she was wearing. With a pleasant but neutral expression on her face, she asked, "Now, what has brought you here today?"

I proceeded to rant about my plight, my fears, my poor mother and my awful sisters, and how disappointed I was in their lack of help and support. I discussed my feelings of resentment at having to do so much while my sisters lived their lives, unaffected by our mother's constant needs. "I am so full of anger that I can hardly function anymore, and my husband is worried about me," I whimpered.

When I'd let my pent-up anger and frustration out, this seemingly kind woman spoke frankly. "In order to get the help you need, you first must let go of any resentment and anger you're holding onto. It's important that you accept the help that others are willing and able to provide. You simply need to find the right way to approach them if you are serious about getting help. Not everyone is as capable as you seem to be. Remember: the only person you can control is yourself. It may be hard to hear this, but it is important that you realize everyone in your family has a right to their own feelings and actions, especially as it relates to your mother. Not everyone handles something as traumatic as a family member with Alzheimer's very well. It's human nature to avoid something so overwhelming, unpleasant, and frightening. You need to focus on yourself because you don't know what motivates others. If you want help, you need to communicate your needs and be willing to ask for help. You must also accept that your family may not be able to do what you ask of them. If you place expectations on others, you will continue to be disappointed."

This was not at all what I wanted or expected to hear. I had gotten up on my high horse, looking down upon those who I felt weren't doing their part, only to be thrown off and land flat on my face. It was a hard truth to swallow, but it was the honest truth. I felt deflated and started to cry. The counselor gave me a tissue and more good advice. I saw her six or seven more times, and eventually, I started to let go of my anger. I came to realize that I had to take responsibility for my own feelings and need to learn how to communicate more honestly and effectively. I learned to set boundaries and limits. If I couldn't turn to my family for help, I would have to use Mother's resources to hire help when I needed a break. When I drank from the poison cocktail, I was only harming myself, not the people with whom I was angry.

Once most of my anger had faded, I asked Marie and her husband, Tom, to join Lyle and me for dinner at our home. I planned to outline every task that needed to be done, and my goals for Mother's long-term care. I saw no point in calling Lee because she hadn't offered any help and hadn't reached out to me since I told her about Mother's diagnosis. As far as I knew, she still thought Mother was fine. I prepared a spreadsheet of Mother's income and expenses, and a list of tasks that needed completion on a routine basis. I asked everyone at the table what he or she was willing and able to do and got a verbal commitment from each. I felt that if Marie committed her help in front everyone, she would take her responsibilities more seriously and would be less likely to forget them.

The tone of the meeting was friendly, and now that I had better control of my emotions and kept my expectations low, it was very positive. Marie and I divided the tasks, such as taking Mother to the hairdresser, scheduling and keeping doctor's appointments, and managing her finances. I only gave Marie tasks that wouldn't compromise Mother's health if an appointment were missed, such as her hairdresser, podiatrist, and dentist. I also asked that if she couldn't keep an appointment, that she let me know ahead of time so it could be canceled without penalty. We agreed that I would continue to tend to her finances and taxes, clean her house, organize her medications, and take her to her doctor and neurologist. Lyle and Tom would play supporting roles, but in reality, Tom continued to do what was in his best interest. Other than helping with the small task of repairing Mother's easy chair, he went on with his life as normal, unaffected by Mother's disease.

I pulled Marie aside and asked, "Has Tom read *The 36-Hour Day* yet? The way he is acting, I get the impression he has no idea what we are up against."

With a defeated look, she sighed. "He didn't think it was worth his time." Seeing my shocked expression, she said, "He is a very busy man and has many demands on his time. This is just how he is going to handle it, and that is his business!" She had become so defensive and I realized there was no point in discussing Tom's involvement any further. This information about Tom made me wonder if part of my problem with Marie had to do with the lack of support she received at home. My feelings about Tom were neutral. He wasn't a bad person; he was a decent, upstanding man and a highly successful business owner. I tried to understand that he just had different priorities. Unfortunately for Marie and me, his priorities had nothing do with Mother's care. The meeting was productive and relieved some of my burden, but things were still not perfect. I had to accept the fact that others didn't think the same way I did, and sometimes, things would just not get done.

When I was as prepared I could be, I concentrated my efforts on three critical areas: Mother's safety, health, and happiness. My goal was to cast a safety net around her and allow her to do anything she could for as long as God was willing. I would draw the net tighter as her condition deteriorated. I planned to watch and monitor her carefully, taking action when appropriate as the disease slowly progressed and claimed my mother day by day, month by month, and year by year.

8 *Casting the Safety Net*

The first area I focused on was her safety, as she lived alone and was still driving. Her disease put her at a higher risk for accidents, falls, getting lost, and other dangers. We were lucky because before her diagnosis, Mother had been driving very little and only for short distances, and soon after her diagnosis, she gave up driving willingly. Although she was still in denial that she had any impairment, she never liked to drive and only got behind the wheel when necessary. When she started to have small accidents, Marie and I had already intervened, and for the most part, were taking her wherever she needed to go. Thankfully, Mother called me one day and said, "I want you to come and get my car. I'm too old and have no business driving. It's only sitting in the parking garage anyway, so you might as well come and get it." I was relieved but surprised. She had always been resistant to giving up her car, so I assumed that something happened that scared her; perhaps she had gotten lost or almost had an accident.

Her explanation was filled with drama. "I was coming home from the store and was on the boulevard. You know how narrow it is. There was a young man behind me in a sports car and he kept riding my bumper. I didn't have room to get over, so he almost ran me off the road to pass me! I barely managed to keep my car from going into the ditch. I was so mad that I almost crashed my car into him on purpose instead of getting over as far as I could. I really wanted to hit him and almost did. He had no idea how close I came to smashing into his pretty car. If I can't control myself, I have no business driving. If I had hit that little shit and caused an accident, I would have been the one arrested. I don't need to be driving."

This was the answer to my prayers. She would have to stop driving at some point, so it was lucky that she chose this for herself. Impaired driving is dangerous, whether it is because of dementia, alcohol, drugs, or lack of sleep. It was only a matter of time before she had an accident or got lost and was unable to find her way home. Had she not given up driving willingly, I was ready to intervene. I couldn't have forgiven myself if something bad had happened because I didn't stop her. Mother was able to confidently hand over her keys because Marie and I had already ensured that she had the freedom and ability to go wherever she wanted.

Mother loved living on the waterfront, and I wanted her to stay in her own home for as long as her disease would let her. She had always made it clear that she would never live with any of her daughters. It was important for her to maintain her independence. She didn't want to move and I couldn't have talked her into it even if I wanted to. However, worry was my constant companion while she lived alone. As her disease progressed, I called her daily and visited as often as I could to watch for clues indicating that living alone was too difficult. Marie and I coordinated our out-of-town trips with each other so that one of us was always in town and able to check on her. We called each other if we took Mother out, to avoid unnecessary worry if one of us tried to contact her while the other had her on an outing. Her annual visits to the neurologist also helped me determine whether she could safely continue living alone. Marie and I both had a key to her home and notified the managers of the condominium about Mother's condition.

Worried that she may wander or get lost, I signed Mother up for MedicAlert Safe Return, which I discovered through the Alzheimer's Association. They keep a file with emergency contact information, medical conditions, medications, allergies, and a physical description. If she got lost, emergency responders would have access to the information they'd need to get her home safely. The cost was minimal, less than seventy dollars per year. She had an ID bracelet, but refused to wear it until much later on. She also had a MedicAlert ID card, but I had to hide it in her wallet because it plainly stated that she had Alzheimer's. Periodically, she would find it and ask, "What the hell is this?" Furious at me, she would throw it away, so I kept it well hidden and took comfort that at least if she did wander away, a good Samaritan or police officer would be able to help her. There was a toll-free number I could call to report wandering and to get assistance locating her. Luckily, wandering didn't become an issue until later in her disease.

As time went on, I watched for ways that I could support her safety. Although she knew how to use her phone, she could no longer remember phone numbers or where she stored her phone book. I solved this problem by placing a list of emergency and important contact numbers next to her phone on the kitchen counter. To keep the list from getting wet and to prevent Mother from stuffing it in a drawer, I laminated and taped it to the countertop. This strategy worked well for her. She used the list often and felt confident because she could always find important phone numbers.

Because I visited often, I began to take responsibility for more household tasks as things became too difficult for her to manage. I continued cleaning her house, and Marie and I took turns doing her laundry. I watched for potential hazards, such as spoiled food and slippery rugs. As she became more forgetful, taking care of Mother became a full-time job. Marie and I decided to hire a caregiver to visit her, help clean her home, cook meals, watch for spoiled or hidden food, and take her to the store, to lunch, or on outings when Marie and I weren't available.

Marie located a company that specialized in home assistance and care. We used a reputable, licensed, and bonded company, ensured that all the employees had criminal background checks, and monitored their visits. We interviewed the caregivers before the service sent them over. As expected, Mother didn't feel that she needed help and was very resistant. I had to come up with a good reason for her to accept help that didn't make her feel incapable of taking care of herself. I said, "Mother, you've worked all of your life and have earned some time off and extra help. I know you feel badly that I clean house for you and that I won't take any money for doing it. I have a solution: you can hire a housekeeper."

"I don't want a stranger in my house. I can do my own housework."

Just as I had done with her pills, Marie volunteered to take on this task and proceeded to set it up without her blessing. We both became deaf to her tirades. It was something we just had to do. She needed a lot of convincing to accept the help of the caregivers, so it was no surprise when she refused to pay for the service. Marie and I paid for the service and told her that it was our gift. Then, I kept detailed records of the expense and used Mother's resources to reimburse us. Without the extra help, she would've had to give up living in her beloved home on Puget Sound.

We cycled through a few caregivers before we finally found a person with the right personality. Caregivers are paid very little and have minimal training, so it wasn't easy to find someone who could get along with our feisty mother. The first person was too aggressive. She felt that because Mother had dementia, she could be bossed around and forced to do things that were "good for her," such as taking a shower. That caregiver didn't last a day. We monitored each caregiver and Mother's response, and she clearly didn't like the first person the agency sent. "She thinks she's the boss and I'm a bit afraid of her!" The next person didn't speak English very well, and would sit and stare at Mother without saying a word. This made Mother uncomfortable. "The new housekeeper gives me the creeps," she said. "She just sits there, staring at me. I don't know what the hell to say to her!"

Eventually, we found the right person. She was levelheaded, spoke fluent English, and had a sweet and pleasant disposition. Mother warmed to her right away and told me, "My housekeeper is too smart to be just a housekeeper. I hope she finds a job that suits her better, even if that means I'll lose her." It was worth the effort and worked out well for us. Our hired caregiver became our extra eyes and ears and helped us decide when Mother was no longer safe living alone.

Maintaining my mother's health was equally important as her safety. Because she was memory-impaired, she could easily forget to take her medication, or conversely, take too much. Even before I understood the scope of her illness, I had already begun setting up and monitoring her medications. She was more likely to hide or forget to take her medication than she was to take too much. To avoid a preventable accident, I put all extra medications, including over-the-counter medication, in her safe. I also continued filling her weekly pill box. Mother had stopped protesting and jokingly called me her Pill Nazi. Being able to take her own medication made her feel in charge. Every morning, she took the day's pills out of her pill box and lined them up on the kitchen counter by size. This became one of her ingrained daily rituals. It would be many years before this task would finally prove too much for her.

Even mild side effects from medication, such as an upset stomach or diarrhea, could cause a catastrophic behavior, which is a behavior so out of proportion to the situation it becomes catastrophic. If a medication gave her diarrhea, she would become anxious and not know what to do. She would search for a cure, but if she couldn't find what she was looking for, she called me, day and night. If I couldn't help, she wanted to leave her home in search of what she needed. There were no stores nearby and she didn't have a car, so leaving the house without an escort was the last thing I wanted her to do. This became a pattern of behavior, playing out any time she experienced discomfort, including cramps, a headache, or nausea. I received many late-night phone calls and had to rush over with Tylenol or Pepto-Bismol. When she had an appointment, I always grilled the doctor about any new medications and carefully weighed the benefit of the medication against the risk of the side effects. Her doctor had to assure me that the benefit far outweighed the risk of side effects before I allowed her to start new medication. I was extra cautious because Mother was very sensitive to medication, and more often than not, would suffer adverse reactions. She never started a new medication unless I was available to monitor her and watch for side effects or allergic reactions.

I tried to identify all the areas in which I could support Mother's overall health. We visited the neurologist once a year, as her disease was slow to progress. He watched for side effects from the Aricept and monitored its effectiveness. He reviewed her living situation, level of care, and medication to confirm that they were appropriate for her condition, based upon the progression of her disease. Although Aricept didn't work for many of his patients, it worked beautifully for Mother and slowed the progress of the disease. We were very lucky.

Because she was diabetic, proper foot care was also important. Her toenails were thick and would curl in, and because she was unable to trim them herself, they became uncomfortable and would eventually break the skin. This was a potential source for infection, which could lead to a life-threatening complication due to the lack of circulation in her feet. It was imperative for her comfort and health to see a podiatrist regularly. Keeping her feet healthy avoided unnecessary discomfort and infection that could have resulted in dire health or behavioral problems. To this day, Mother sees her podiatrist frequently.

She also had regular dental cleanings and checkups to maintain healthy teeth and gums. However, because of her disease, I needed to be nearby to reassure her. I often made my appointment for a dental cleaning at the same time as hers in an adjoining exam room. Being close by not only helped Mother, but also aided the staff. I was there to help explain a procedure or reassure her if she became anxious. My presence made for a much more pleasant visit for all. Tooth decay and gum disease can cause health problems, discomfort, and increase problem behaviors if they are not addressed. Monitoring her oral health also helped me recognize if she stopped brushing and flossing her teeth.

In addition to needing regular checkups with her neurologist, podiatrist, and dentist, Alzheimer's put her at a higher risk for infection, dehydration, and malnutrition. It didn't help that she was diabetic, had hypertension, high cholesterol, kidney stones, anemia, and a history of minor strokes. With her long list of health problems and risk factors, preventative care was crucial. I scheduled appointments for her, got her there on time, and followed the instructions or course of treatment that the doctor prescribed.

She liked her primary care doctor and resisted change, but I finally began the search for a new one. When the neurologist sent his diagnosis that Mother had dementia and probably Alzheimer's disease, I attempted to schedule an appointment for a regular physical, but Dr. C just looked at me and said, "Why would you want to do that? Medicare doesn't pay for physicals." That was the last time we went to see that doctor. I felt it was important to have a doctor who was familiar with diseases of the elderly and the complications of Alzheimer's. I wanted and needed a doctor who would watch for the signs of dehydration, urinary tract infections, anemia, inadequate nutrition, or sores due to inadequate hygiene. Locating such a physician was no easy task; there were very few doctors in our area who specialized in geriatric care.

I was frustrated and disappointed by the limited options that were available. Local clinics and hospitals seemed to place very little importance on the special needs of the elderly. How odd, I thought, that society pays such little attention to a condition we all hope to achieve some day: old age.

Through a physician friend of Marie's, we eventually found a family doctor with her own private practice. She didn't accept Medicare or private insurance, but instead, charged an annual fee and would see Mother every two to three months, depending upon her condition. The new doctor had a small clinic located in a strip mall not far from Mother's home, and it was also convenient for me. I arranged for Mother's medical records to be transferred before her first appointment, so the doctor would have all the information she needed. I scheduled a morning appointment so we would have time for a leisurely lunch, knowing that if I felt rushed, Mother would be anxious. I picked her up on an overcast Northwest Washington morning and felt a little anxious myself as I pulled into the clinic parking lot. Would this new doctor be experienced enough with geriatric care? Would Mother like her? Would Mother fight me about the change?

Nothing seemed familiar to her, and Mother was lost. "Where

are we? I don't know anyone here."

"We're at your new doctor's office."

She wasn't happy with my answer. "I already have a doctor! What kind of a doctor am I seeing?"

I lied to move things along. "Just a regular doctor. Don't you remember? Your last doctor moved away." I crossed my fingers and hoped that her forgetfulness would work to my advantage.

She became anxious and refused to get out of the car. "I'll just wait here."

"Mom, this is your doctor's appointment, not mine."

"My doctor isn't here." The train was going off the tracks. I needed to get the situation back under control.

I tried to relax. If I were calm, she would be calm. With a peaceful smile, I said, "Mother, this is your new doctor. I promise we won't be long, and as soon as we're done, we can go to lunch. I'll even pay!"

She frowned, but hesitantly got out of the car. As soon as we stepped inside the small, orderly waiting area, a cheerful voice greeted us. "You must be Barbara!" Mother smiled when she heard her name. A short, slight, middle-aged woman with a pixie haircut and thick glasses stood up from behind the tall panels of the reception desk. She was expecting us. Her sunny tone and polite manner put Mother at ease right away. Maybe this transition will go well after all, I thought. We sat down in the waiting area and I filled out the paperwork while Mother looked around. It was a small room, well-appointed with the standard-issue waiting room chairs, a small bookcase full of interesting books and knickknacks, and a couple of potted African violets that looked lush and well cared for. We were the only ones there. Mother seemed at ease and made light conversation about the interesting photographs on the walls as we waited to meet the new doctor.

I hadn't yet finished filling out the paperwork when a nurse stepped into the waiting area. She smiled in our direction, looked at Mother said, "You must be Barbara?"

Mother was pleased with all the attention, and replied, "Why yes I am!"

"Well, come on back," said the nurse. We both followed her into a small exam room. It was as I'd expected, filled with the usual exam room items: an exam table, a sink and countertop, and jars filled with cotton balls and tongue depressors. There were a couple of chairs for the patient and family, and a small stool for the doctor. To give the room a homier feel, there was a small, wooden roll top desk in the corner, and the chairs looked more like dining room side chairs. The nurse gently instructed Mother to sit in the chair closest to the desk, where the doctor would sit. She took Mother's vital signs and then left the room.

We didn't have to wait long. With a knock on the door to announce her entrance, the doctor came in and introduced herself. Dr. R was in her late fifties or early sixties, and had short, gray hair, cut in a casual style. Her face seemed open and kind, with rosy cheeks and a caring smile. She wore stylish glasses and had a stethoscope hanging around her neck. She had an earthy and natural air about her. Her voice was soft and she looked Mother in the eye as she introduced herself, making her feel like the most important person in that room. I liked her immediately.

The doctor had already received Mother's complete medical

chart, was aware of her dementia, and had a copy of my power of attorney. The doctor asked Mother how she felt and if she had any concerns to discuss before the physical exam. Mother was pleased with the interest the doctor was showing, and said, "I feel just fine, and I have no problems. I know who, what, where, and how much! Not too many old people can say that. I'm a lucky old sweetheart, heavy on the sweet!" She frowned a bit and held up her hands. "I do have Arthur in my hands and they hurt all the time, but I guess that's part of getting old."

Dr. R gently took her hands. "I see how that could be painful. Perhaps we can do something to help." She gave me a look as if to say that she would discuss pain management options with me later. Thank God, I thought, a doctor that actually realizes that Mother isn't able to understand complicated instructions or provide complex details about her medical history. Mother began to tell the doctor about her difficult childhood, growing up in the South, my father's death, and her special cat, Honey, who had grass-green eyes. The doctor smiled and listened patiently to every detail of her stories. When it was time to do the physical exam, Mother seemed relaxed and wasn't the least bit concerned when I left the room to give them privacy.

I was so grateful we had found Dr. R. From that first visit, I felt confident in her ability and knew that Mother would get the very best medical care. Best of all, she made Mother feel like a real person and not just another insurance code to achieve reimbursement. Mother loved her conversations with her new doctor, who always seemed genuinely interested in hearing repeated stories about Honey or anything else on Mother's mind. The doctor respected me, always contacted me with test results, and provided instructions to both of us. She understood that it was in my , mother's best interest to keep me informed. Incredibly, she also made house calls, a priceless service for the elderly or someone with dementia. Her willingness to go the extra mile would be the difference between life and death for my mother. The individualized care Mother received was worth the expense, and in truth, we probably spent no more than we would have paid in annual deductibles. Mother had Medicare and private insurance, which still covered medical tests, specialists, skilled nursing, and hospitalization. Dr. R didn't limit her time with my mother, and was able to provide very focused and concentrated attention.

Whenever we needed to see an outside doctor for specialist care, tests, or X-rays, I always informed them about her dementia and problem behaviors in advance. For the most part, everyone was cooperative, but many times, the doctors and nurses didn't seem to have all the information and couldn't understand why Mother was unable to answer complicated questions or follow directions. I always brought a copy of the power of attorney and a letter from the neurologist explaining Mother's condition and my role in her care. This saved me from giving lengthy explanations in front of Mother, who, of course, had nothing wrong with her. This small step made for a more pleasant experience.

I learned that if I left her alone in an exam room for more than a few minutes, she would forget where she was and would be unable to remember directions just given to her. When instructed to undress from the waist down and put on a smock, she would either become distressed and do nothing or take off all her clothes and not know what to do next. Sometimes, however, she was able to follow simple instructions and didn't want me hovering over her. I always stayed close, asked if she wanted help, and let her do what she still could.

While she still lived alone, I couldn't rely on her to eat properly and drink enough to stay hydrated. I visited often, encouraged her to drink water, had her over to my house a couple of times a week, and took her out on Saturdays. Marie and the hired caregiver filled in when I couldn't be there, and we all stayed vigilant for signs that she wasn't eating or drinking enough. Regular doctor visits and blood work also helped me determine if intervention was necessary.

Hygiene was important for both her physical and mental health. Mother was always a very private person and I needed to respect her privacy, but I also needed to make sure she was taking care of herself. I checked to see if she was using her shower, looked for wet towels, and paid attention to how she looked and smelled. Eventually, when taking a shower became too complex a task, she stopped showering altogether. Although her skin was dry and she would have benefited from bathing or showering, she still washed up in the sink daily with soap and water. When I asked her why she didn't take a regular shower, she said, "I don't need a shower as long as wash up in the sink and take my PTA bath." (PTA stood for Puss, Tits, and Armpits.) Our regular visits to the doctor confirmed that her hygiene was adequate, so we didn't intervene.

Marie took her to get her hair done once a week and that worked well for a long time until I noticed that Mother's hair was no longer clean. It looked less tidy than before and started to smell funky, as if it hadn't been washed in some time. Marie hadn't mentioned any problems with Mother's trip to the hairdresser, so I was curious about what was going on. I called her and said, "Mother's hair looks dirty, and she smells weird. Are you still taking her to the salon?" I wanted to give Marie the benefit of the doubt. Perhaps this was a temporary glitch because of some special project she was working on.

I was disappointed in her response. "Mother doesn't want to go to the hairdresser any more. She was getting fussy when we went, and she flat-out refused to go last time. I didn't want to force her, so I didn't take her." It didn't take long for me to discover that Mother would go, but that someone needed to stay to reassure her, not just drop her off and come back later to pick her up. I knew Marie had a very busy calendar and taking Mother every week was a strain. I assumed that because she could no longer just drop her off, the errand had become more of a time commitment than she was willing to make.

I didn't confront Marie about it. Instead, I started taking Mother to the hairdresser during my normal Saturday visits and stayed until she was finished. We talked and laughed; I tried to make it a safe and fun experience. She was upset at first, concerned I was taking so much of my own time to help her, but I always made her feel like I was having a good time. (Really, I wanted to drive an ice pick into my eye. Spending a weekend afternoon with a salon full of octogenarians was tedious and boring.) I longed to be free to pursue other things. However, the familiar act of going to the hairdresser, being clean, and looking her best kept her from having problem behaviors and made a huge difference in her life. To me, the benefit was well worth the sacrifice of an additional hour or two on a Saturday afternoon. Adding this additional task to my already full Saturday pushed the resentment I felt toward Marie closer to the surface. Once again, it began to fester inside me.

Exercise was also important, and although she never liked to exercise, I encouraged her to walk and use the stairs as much as possible. She enjoyed doing crossword puzzles to exercise her mind, so I made sure she always had one on hand. Taking her out regularly and keeping her socially engaged also kept her mind active.

9 Unlocking the Secrets to Her Happiness

Mother's happiness was important to me, but she had little chance at happiness unless I addressed her safety and health first. Without safety, she would be fearful and face potential danger. Without maintaining her health, she would be uncomfortable, ill, or perhaps even die. Once I had safeguards in place to manage her safety and health issues, I wanted to do my best to help her live with a disease that was stealing her memory and cognitive function. I wanted her to be happy and to have the best life she could, given her circumstances. I was unwilling to stand by and watch her succumb to confusion, loneliness, and unhappiness. It was a long and complicated journey to unlock the secrets of my mother's happiness, and it proved to be more difficult to address her happiness than her safety and health.

Because she was incapable and unwilling to accept her Alzheimer's diagnosis, I decided not to try to convince her she had a devastating, terminal brain disease. As far as she knew, she was fine. I had no reason change her perception. She was more likely to be happy if she wasn't branded with a terminal illness she no longer had the ability to understand. I focused on what she could still do, and supported her by slowly taking over day-to-day tasks as she became more disabled by her disease. Perhaps she was resistant to a diagnosis because of her fear of becoming a burden to her family or because we didn't get an accurate diagnosis until her disease had robbed her of the ability to understand it. I will never know.

I learned to be flexible depending upon the situation or the behavior. Although her disease affected my life, it was not about me anymore. For most of my life, I had enjoyed a very close relationship with my mother and she had been my foundation and support for so many years. The mother I had known was already lost to me; this was one of the hardest things for me to accept. Alzheimer's had already caused a great deal of damage, and what was lost was lost forever. I couldn't expect her to be any more than her disease allowed her to be. If my actions or words caused her distress, I had to be willing to change what I was doing to accommodate her. In her mind, it was the world around her that was going crazy, not her. I always paid attention to what her behavior was trying to tell me. Our time together was all about her, what she wanted to do, when, and for how long. I let her lead me where she wanted to go, and we did what she wanted to do. Sometimes, what she wanted was for me to lead her and make all the decisions. I never pushed, never scolded, and I tried not to be sad or angry in front of her. I never expected too much of her, and I strived to make her feel loved and important.

It was not always easy to understand her behaviors. There were many days when my overwhelming grief and frustration got the better of me, and I laid my head in my hands and sobbed. I made so many mistakes and lost my patience so many times, but eventually, I got the hang of it. Once I learned how to cope with her behaviors, our time together and our outings were full of joy. Mother had a strange sense of acceptance, calm, and happiness that I don't think she would have had if we hadn't learned to inhabit her world and discard our own.

In order to inhabit Mother's world, I first needed to realize that her ability to understand logic and reason was severely impaired. I had to determine what she was trying to communicate and learn how to respond appropriately and in a way that she could understand. Any time I tried to employ logic and reason, I was disappointed with the results. I couldn't expect that she would remember someone she just met or a conversation she just had. Instead, I assumed she would forget and was pleasantly surprised if she remembered. If I tried to force her to remember something she couldn't, she became anxious, frustrated, and unhappy.

As her disease progressed, she had difficulty finding the right words and following conversations. Because of these struggles, she stopped socializing or calling her friends. She isolated herself. This was particularly sad because she pushed away her close friend, Nancy. Mother and Nancy had been best friends since high school. I cannot remember a time when Nancy wasn't a part of Mother's life, or mine, for that matter. When she was no longer a topic of conversation, I asked Mother, "Why don't you call Nancy anymore? I'm sure she would love to hear from you."

"Nancy stopped calling me because she is busy with her other friends. She doesn't have any time for me."

Of course, that wasn't true. I called Nancy and explained that Mother had Alzheimer's. She was sad for Mother and for me, but thanked me. She had been worried that she had said or done something wrong, but I assured her that Mother had always been grateful for their friendship. Little did I know that dementia was slowly eroding the mind of my mother's best friend, as well. Because of Mother's self-imposed isolation, I realized that I needed to visit and take Mother out more frequently to prevent her from becoming lonely, isolated, and depressed. This wasn't always convenient, but it was necessary to her well-being.

As she lost the ability to remember what she'd just heard, she started to repeat the same questions over and over and conversation became very one-sided. If I had a dollar for every time she asked me, "Who is today?" I would be a very rich woman. I knew that it wasn't her fault that she couldn't remember what day it was, but that didn't make it any easier for me to tolerate. For whatever reason, it was very important to her to know what day of the week it was. Like a broken record, she asked, "Who is today?" over and over again. I sometimes wanted to scream with frustration. It was mind numbing to give the same answer to the same question countless times. If I ignored her question or reacted negatively, she became very angry and yelled, "Pay attention! Why won't you answer me, damn it?" Sometimes, she would hit me in the back or push me to get my attention.

Unfortunately, I lost my patience many times over the years. I would pretend I didn't hear the question or would snap at her. "I told you what day it is a hundred times already! Would you please stop asking me?" Losing my temper was never a good solution. I always suffered the consequences and had to forgive myself for the havoc my insensitive response caused. Years later, the question, "Who is today?" would bring tears of joy to my eyes and fill my heart with love and admiration for my resilient mother.

When she lost the ability to follow a conversation, body language became very important. I learned to stay relaxed and keep a smile on my face, even if I felt far from calm and happy. It was hard for me not to become irritated when faced with constant repetition and childish behaviors, but she could read my tone, my body language, and my facial expression better than she could understand or remember my words.

One day, when Mother and I were shopping at the drug store, I learned just how important the tone of my voice and my body language were. No matter where she went, she always had to have a shopping list with her. It made her feel less confused and gave her a purpose and a goal. This day was no different, and she had brought a list of items she wanted from the drug store. She kept misplacing her list by putting it in her purse or tucking it away in her coat pocket, and then forgetting where she'd put it. She happily followed me around the store, repeatedly asking me where her list was. I would find it for her, put it in her hand, and then a short while later, she would ask me for her list again. I was getting annoyed. When I'd had enough, I clenched my teeth and said, "For the last time, it's in your purse or your pocket! How many times do I have to find it for you?"

Mother froze in place. With a very angry expression, she began to make a loud growling sound from deep within her throat. This was a completely new level of crazy. I was shocked and mortified that she would do such a thing in a public place. I turned and walked quickly away from her, but she just followed close behind, growling louder and louder as I ignored her. People were starting to stare at us. I wished that the floor would open up and swallow me. I was upset and couldn't understand what I had done to deserve such public humiliation. Then it hit me: I had done this and her reaction was my fault. I started to laugh as I realized how ridiculous we must look. Still laughing, I turned around, gave my growling mother a heartfelt hug, and said, "I love you so very much!"

She calmed down immediately, stopped growling, and smiled back at me. "I love you, too, silly. What's the matter with you?"

Mother mirrored any emotion I projected. If I were anxious, she was anxious. If I were angry, she became angry. If I were afraid, she would fret and become nervous. If I were relaxed and happy, more often than not, she would soon be relaxed and happy. She could also sense when I was trying to project an emotion that I just did not feel. Sometimes, when I was trying to be nice and pretend that I wasn't annoyed, she would look at me slyly and say, "You don't have to fake being nice to me. I'm not stupid, you know." She always reacted badly to negative emotions. If I had a particularly bad day at work or felt depressed and anxious about something in my personal life, I made the decision not to be with Mother. Being with her when I was in a bad mood was a recipe for disaster.

I only talked about things she wanted to talk about, and I tried not to overload her with too much information. Our relationship was not about me anymore. Although she was becoming more childlike every day, she was still my mother. I treated her like an adult and with respect, no matter how childlike she became. I avoided talking down to her and always addressed her as an equal. If I slipped and spoke to her like a child or tried to scold or correct her, her reaction was always swift and angry, similar to the response she gave if I ignored her or lost my patience with her. She loved to say, "I'm still the mother, and don't you ever forget it!"

It was imperative that I agree with her and validate her complaints and perceived transgressions. Alzheimer's disease was not only taking away her ability to remember what she just heard but also what she had just done. Mother would place her newspaper in a drawer and then forget where she put it as soon as she left the room. With no memory of where she had left her paper, in her mind, the paper was gone and she assumed that it had been stolen. In a way, she was right: things were being stolen from her, but it wasn't her paper; it was her memory. Anytime she complained about a stolen item, I always agreed that something must have happened to it. Instead of arguing with her, I gently assured her that we would get to the bottom of it. If I found or replaced the missing item, she would soon forget it was ever gone.

Mother complained constantly about her food. Instead of telling her to stop complaining or asking if she wanted something else, I validated her complaint, even if it was unjustified. Whenever possible, I encouraged her to order food I knew she would like and would be less likely to be under or overdone. Sometimes, I could tell that she just wanted to complain, and it was often about more than just her food. In these instances, I asked if she felt all right or if something was troubling her. More often than not, she was trying to verbalize her unhappiness because she didn't feel well, was worried or anxious, couldn't remember something, or just wanted some attention. She didn't complain because she wanted to be difficult. She didn't act out of spite or have some hidden agenda. She simply tried to meet her needs in the only way she knew how. I became a very good listener. When all else failed, I gave her a hug.

I began to see a very clear pattern in her behavior. If I didn't listen, spoke to her in a demeaning manner, or reacted negatively, I triggered a catastrophic reaction, such as slapping my back or growling at me in public. In Mother's world, the smallest of problems had the potential to become a catastrophe. Her damaged brain was the cause of her abnormal behaviors, and it didn't matter if I felt her disease was at fault or that she was just being willfully difficult. Trying to reason with her or expecting her to react normally only made the situation worse for both of us. Identifying as many obvious triggers as possible helped to prevent catastrophic behaviors before they happened. Once I discovered what triggered a catastrophic reaction, I was able to put safeguards in place to avoid them.

One of Mother's triggers was the newspaper. She oriented herself to the date by looking at the newspaper. She also used it as her TV guide for the day. If she didn't get her paper at exactly the same time each morning, she became uncontrollably angry and she would swear, yell, and pound her hands on the wall. She would call me in a state of panic and say, "Someone has stolen my paper again! I'm getting so goddamn tired of someone stealing my paper. I think it's that damn neighbor next door. He probably thinks it's OK to take it and read it, as long as he brings it back."

Sometimes, she tore her house apart looking for the paper.

She wouldn't calm down until she found it or I brought over a replacement. Frequently, she had put the paper in a safe place because it was important to her. I knew that it probably was in a cupboard or somewhere inappropriate, like a dresser drawer. First, I calmly and without a hint of accusation said, "You know, I think you keep it in your side kitchen cupboard, the one with the Tupperware." If it wasn't there, I'd say, "Have you checked the top drawer of your dresser? I think I saw it there." Often, she would find her paper and all would be well. If she couldn't find it, I went to her house to help her look. Just in case, I always brought a spare paper and a good story about an ill paperboy or a mix-up at the subscription office.

Every time I identified a trigger, another one popped up to replace it. One of her most persistent triggers was running out of important items. For example, she loved to spoil her cat, Honey, but because she was memory-impaired, she couldn't remember if she'd fed her already and began to overfeed that poor cat. Mother constantly ran out of cat food, and that would cause her to panic. In a frenzy, she'd call me and say, "Honey is out of food. I need to go to the store right now! Can you come over?"

If she called late at night, I said, "I'll come over first thing in the morning. It's late and I want to go to bed. I'm sure your fat cat will be OK until I can get there in the morning."

It didn't matter what time it was or that there was no store nearby; if I was unable to run right over to help, she was determined to go to the imaginary store across the street. "Honey can't wait. I'll just go to the store across the street on my own. I don't need your help anyway." If I tried to talk her out of it, she became angry. "You don't know what the hell you're talking about. I'm going to the store. My cat needs food and you can't stop me." Afraid that she'd leave her home and get lost, I had to give in and bring some over. Satisfied, she said, "Make sure you get the right kind!"

If I hadn't already done my homework and knew that she wasn't doing this on purpose, I would have been angry and even more frustrated than I already was. The inconvenience of dropping everything to help her was better than the alternative of her wandering away. To solve this trigger, I made sure that there was always plenty of cat food on hand, and even kept some hidden. When she called me (and she would always call), I could tell her where she could find more.

Some triggers caused her to act out with unreasonable anger and aggression. Fortunately, she directed her fury at inanimate objects or herself, and never attempted to physically harm Honey or innocent bystanders. I was very concerned and troubled when I started to notice bruises and other injuries. Small pinprick wounds often appeared on her face, and when she lifted her pant legs, she sometimes had deep, bloody gouges on her shins. Both injuries made me very curious and concerned, but Mother could never remember how they had happened and made up stories to explain them away. When I asked the doctor to examine her curious wounds during a routine visit, Mother said, "I was over at Anita's house, and when we were walking up the driveway, she pushed me into some barbed wire in the garden!" Pleased with her story, she smiled at the doctor. Thankfully, Dr. R knew me well and was familiar with Alzheimer's disease.

I discovered the cause of the wounds on her face one day when Mother and I were getting ready to go out for a day of shopping. She had gone to her bedroom to change her clothes and brush her hair, and I caught her looking in the mirror and swearing at herself. "You stupid bitch, how could you forget that?" As she hurled insults at herself, she slapped her face with a metal spiked brush. I couldn't prevent this behavior, as heartbreaking as it was, and could only get her a softer brush. I always intervened by hugging her and reassuring her when she became frustrated. I never did find out what caused the wounds on her shins. That will remain a mystery, the answer locked away forever in Mother's brain. If she felt that she was being ignored, was not being taken seriously, or if someone suggested that she was not behaving normally, she got very angry and pounded her hands against anything she could find until they were bruised. Once, she even sprained her little finger in a fit of rage.

As I spent more time with Mother, I learned her daily routines and rituals. She awoke at the same time every morning and followed the same routine. She washed her face, brushed her teeth, and got dressed. Then, she made herself a cup of instant coffee with dry creamer, and drank it while she read her newspaper. Often, she turned on the local news for company. She couldn't retain anything from the paper or the TV, but the process was important and familiar. She made a toaster waffle with butter for breakfast every day, as it easy for her to do and something she could remember. I called her every morning at nine o'clock to remind her to take her morning pills. As soon as we hung up, she lined up her pills according to size and swallowed them. I made sure she had what she needed in order to follow her routine, and always called her at the same time every day.

When she was alone, she worked crossword puzzles, watched TV, and looked out at the waterfront. Although she lived alone, she always said, "I never feel lonely here." She watched TV until eleven thirty, and when the news was over, she changed into her nightgown, washed her face, took her PTA bath, brushed her teeth and hair, wound up her alarm clock, and went to bed.

Mother had a closet full of new clothes, but insisted on wearing the same shirt and pants every day. She had one outfit that she called her "inside clothes," and another set that she called her "outside clothes." She wore clean underwear and socks, but always the same old bra, the same old blouse, and the same old pair of pants. Curious, I asked, "Why won't you wear any of your new clothes? You have a closet full of them, just waiting to be worn."

Patiently, as if I were a dim bulb, she explained, "I don't want to stink up my good outside clothes by sitting around the house in them. I know what I should wear when I go out, and I certainly don't want to wear something new. My new clothes need to be saved for special occasions."

This was hard for me to understand, as most of her clothes had never been worn, and some still had the original tags attached. No matter how old or tattered her clothes became, she refused to wear anything else. Marie is a very good seamstress and was able to keep both sets of clothes in reasonable repair. She and I did Mother's laundry to make sure the clothes she did wear were always clean. The fact that she only wore two sets of clothes made our job a bit easier. For whatever reason, her familiar clothes gave her a sense of calm. This was something that was easy to allow.

The veterinarian instructed Mother to feed Honey twice a day, but she often got extra meals by standing near her dish and pleading loudly. Mother had a very specific ritual she followed when feeding her cat. It was amazing and unbelievable, but always the same. She put a small amount of wet cat food in a dish and stirred it up with a knife. She then put the dish in the microwave for three seconds before she took it back out and put her finger in the food to test the temperature. Of course, it was never hot enough after three seconds, which always made her angry. "This goddamn microwave doesn't work right. I need to get a new one!" She would put the food back in and forcefully slam the door closed. She would heat it up for another three seconds, repeating the same process until the food was hot enough or too hot, all the while cursing and slamming the microwave door. Once the correct temperature had been reached, she stirred the food again. She finished by using her fingers to sculpt the food into a mountain with a pointy top. Only when the food was the right temperature and the mountain was exactly right, would she put it down for Honey. Honey was obese because she ate multiple times a day, and would often only eat a bite or two before she sauntered off to lick her chops. If Honey didn't eat all the food she had so painstakingly prepared, she would get very angry. "You fucking cat, I'm going to tear your fucking head off!" At this point, Honey usually decided it was a good time to hide because Mother chased her around the room with the dish of uneaten food.

It seemed ridiculous that she heated the food in three-second increments and yelled at her already-obese cat for not eating, but

I couldn't tell her that she was being unreasonable. When I did, it would cause a catastrophic reaction. She would immediately direct all her anger toward me. "You need to mind your own fucking business! I know how to take care of my own fucking cat! What do you know about it, anyway?" At first, I was shocked by her routine, but for whatever reason, she needed to follow this process to feel normal. It was a crazy ritual, but it was her ritual. It did no good to disrupt it in anyway. No matter how offensive or aggravating, I had to walk away and just let her be.

On days I took Mother out, I always left enough time to allow for her ritual behaviors. I became an expert in not reacting to her rituals, no matter how ridiculous or shocking they became or how late they made us. If a behavior gave her a sense of purpose and caused no harm, I supported the behavior because it supported her sense of normalcy. To try to change the behavior, rush her, or tell her that she was acting crazy did more harm than good. Of course, I intervened if a behavior became dangerous. I redirected her when I felt she was too aggressive with Honey. I was concerned that if she started to harm Honey, I would need to take the cat away. Thankfully, that never happened and Mother and Honey continued their odd but mutually supportive relationship for many years.

I thought it was odd that someone who can't remember the day, date, or time was so dependent on routine. Any disruption to her schedule caused confusion, and more often than not, she became anxious, agitated, and couldn't understand why things weren't right. I decided not to waste what little time I had looking for reasons for her abnormal behaviors. Instead, I tried to call

Mother at the same time each day to check on her and remind her to take her medications. Before visiting, I made a plan I could commit to and tried not to disrupt her daily routine. I visited her after work on Mondays and Wednesdays, and we spent all day together on Saturdays. We always went to the same restaurants, ordered the same food, went to the same stores, and then I took her back home. She made a note in her calendar about when I would be back. We kept this familiar routine for many years. There were occasions when I couldn't keep to the routine, due to illness, vacations, or circumstances beyond my control, and the results were always the same: she would sense that something wasn't right and was more prone to problem behaviors and fits of anger.

Supporting Mother's important routines and rituals made both of our lives better, as it decreased our stress levels and helped avoid catastrophic reactions and problem behaviors. Learning to communicate with her, supporting her crazy routines and rituals, and identifying her triggers was not easy. It took a tremendous amount of education, thought, and effort. Marie and I were surprised when we encountered trained professionals who didn't seem to put much thought or effort into communicating with a memory-impaired person. We cringed when we heard someone say to Mother, "I told you that already, don't you remember?" "You know where your room is." "What did I just say to you?" Or, "I was here yesterday. Remember me?" These statements were even more shocking when they came from a caregiver who knew about her condition. I was surprised when people tried to use logic and reason or argued with her if they felt her complaint was unjustified. I understood this thoughtlessness if the person was unfamiliar with dementia, but I had a hard time understanding when the comments came from doctors, nurses, caregivers, or employees of facilities that specialized in memory care. I expected those people to have the training and experience with the memory-impaired to avoid these obvious pitfalls.

Marie and I did our best to understand, and patiently explained our mother's limitations when necessary. Once again, we had to accept that our expectations were far from reality. When Mother was asked a question she obviously couldn't answer, she looked over at me and gave me a look as if to say, "Who is this person and what the hell are they talking about?" I would just shrug my shoulders and roll my eyes, which usually made her smile or laugh out loud.

10 *When Living Alone Was No Longer an Option*

Our efforts were well rewarded; she was able to continue living alone with her beloved cat for several years. Marie and I adjusted to her odd behaviors, and although she seemed content, her life was far from perfect. I think she knew she was failing and was fighting hard to keep up appearances in order to maintain her independence. She clung desperately to her routines and rituals, trying to hold onto anything that made her feel valid and normal. I sometimes saw the fear and uncertainty in her eyes when she became confused and couldn't understand why she didn't know what day it was, why so many items were going missing, or how she'd wounded herself. My heart ached for her. I continued to put new safeguards in place as her needs changed, and life returned to a new and bizarre kind of normal.

Lee still maintained some phone contact with Mother, but only called me when she was in town and had stopped by at Mother's only to find her out. I explained our Saturday routine and asked her to let me know ahead of time if she wanted to see Mother. It was important for Mother to be able to spend time with Lee whenever possible, so I was willing to make her available on our Saturdays. I knew that one day she would forget us all. Mother asked about Lee all the time, and even though Lee called her periodically, she forgot their conversation as soon she hung up. Usually, when Lee called me, Mother was within earshot so I could never explain how forgetful she was getting. When I tried to call her, my call typically went directly to voice mail. Lee had very little contact with Mother, and dismissed everything I said about her memory loss. She still didn't accept Mother's diagnosis, or even that she was forgetful. I couldn't understand. Lee was a nurse, after all. Did she really think so little of me that she thought I was trying to deceive her or that I was trying to keep her away our mother? Lee had no idea what a nightmare our lives had become, and frankly, I had too much on my plate to chase her down and convince her.

I was always looking for signs of wandering or dangerous behaviors, such as forgetting that the stove was on or leaving the door unlocked. These behaviors had to be acted upon immediately. Marie and I wanted her to be able to stay in her condo and live independently, but we didn't want to wait for a tragedy to occur.

Those who knew our story constantly said things like, "What a good daughter you are. Your mother is so lucky to have you. I don't think I could do what you're doing." Their praise often made me feel guilty because I didn't think I was doing anything special. I often brushed their praise aside, wondering why my actions seemed out of the ordinary. Would they behave any differently? I took care of my mother because she was ill, not because it was something I wanted to do or enjoyed doing. Watching over Mother while she lived alone was a constant strain. I longed for the day that I would be able to give up some of my responsibilities. I was in my late forties and felt that life was swiftly passing me by. I desperately wanted to be just her daughter again, instead of the watchful, careful, nurturing parent that I had become. I hadn't been prepared for the major detour my life had taken due to my mother's illness. Many days, I daydreamed about how much easier it would be if she lived somewhere that assisted her. That would mean fewer trips to her house to find a lost item, less time spent repairing broken things, and less time spent worrying about her welfare.

Lee's words haunted me: "She'd be better off dead." I even started to think that her death would be preferable to watching her life slowly unravel before my eyes. I was worried about how I would handle the later stages of the disease, when she was completely dependent and lost. I knew it was only a matter of time. The prospect of what lurked in the future was more frightening than my present nightmare. Even though we had a hired caregiver, I was still in charge and seemed to be the one that was always in town. Marie frequently traveled for business and was fortunate enough to take many exotic vacations, leaving me holding the bulk of the responsibility. My burden was heavy. I felt trapped and tired, and this was only the beginning.

I chased away the awful and fleeting thought of wishing my mother dead. Instead, I prayed to God for the strength I needed and asked for his forgiveness and guidance. When I felt weak, I heard my mother's voice inside my head: "What doesn't break you will make you stronger. Thank God even if you have the plague, and you will find comfort." The words of wisdom she'd given me when I was nursing a broken heart or facing adversity kept me strong as I learned how to care for her.

Even with our safeguards and interventions, there was nothing we could do to stop Alzheimer's from slowing taking away our mother's ability to live alone safely. During my routine visits, I began to notice that she kept her blinds closed during the day, shutting out her beautiful view. Her home felt dark and stale. When I tried to open the blinds, she said, "Why the hell did you do that?" She followed behind me and closed the blinds again, as if my behavior was abnormal. Practiced in keeping my voice level and my demeanor calm, I gently asked, "Why do you want the blinds closed on such a beautiful day? Is something bothering you?"

She seemed glad that I asked. "The people on the ferry have been watching me. I'm in a fish bowl, on display for all to see. I prefer to keep my blinds closed, so I won't be watched." I tried to convince her otherwise, but she was adamant. I wouldn't force her to open the blinds if it made her feel uncomfortable. I was sad that she could no longer enjoy her room with a view, and although I was concerned, it wasn't a safety issue. I just made a note of the change and watched for other troubling signs.

The next drastic departure from our new normal happened one Saturday when we returned from shopping. As we stepped out of the elevator on our way to Mother's condo, we ran into one of her neighbors, a lovely woman in her late sixties, fashionably dressed with straight, shoulder-length gray hair. We had passed this neighbor on many occasions and had even met her at one of the community functions, but her name always escaped me. The neighbor smiled and approached us. "Barbara, I was just at your condo, hoping to invite you up for a cup of coffee sometime."

Mother looked pleased. "I'd love to come over for coffee, as long as I can bring my gun!" The neighbor and I were stunned and just stared at her, wide-eyed. Mother was smiling. "Don't you believe me? I have lots of guns and if I come up, I promise I'll bring one!"

I gave the neighbor a pleading look, as if to say, "Please forgive us. I'll explain later." I was mortified, so before she had the opportunity to say anything else, I said, "Thank you for the invitation. We'll get back to you on that."

The neighbor looked uncomfortably at Mother and then at me, gave a terse nod, and quickly made her getaway. Of course, Mother didn't have a gun. She was likely afraid of having a conversation she couldn't follow, so she said something to scare the neighbor away. It worked; Mother wasn't invited over for coffee again. I eventually explained my mother's condition to the poor woman and asked for her patience and understanding. When I told Marie about what had happened, we laughed about how crazy her disease was. If someone had ever told us that our polite, socially skilled mother would say such a thing to anyone, let alone a neighbor, we would never have believed it.

The late-night phone calls became more frequent as she grew to be more forgetful. I could tell that she no longer felt safe being alone at night. She called Marie and me multiple times each evening to ask where things were or when we were coming over. Her memory had gotten so bad that I was concerned she might leave the oven on or wander away from her home. Although Marie and I checked on her frequently and hired a caregiver to fill in the gaps, it was not enough, as we were unable to cover the overnight hours. I worked days and was unable to spend the night with her, and hiring someone to stay the night was a very expensive option. It was difficult enough to find the right person for a few hours a week during the day. The thought of hiring someone to stay with her every night was overwhelming.

Fearful that she may leave her condo, Marie and I began the search for a different living situation. Convincing her that she was unable to manage living alone was going to be a monumental task, but was deeply necessary. I wasn't looking forward to the conversation, but I knew it was in her best interest and I would finally have some relief.

In preparation for the inevitable, Marie and I started to slip the virtues of assisted living into everyday conversation. "Today's facilities are more like fancy hotels or resorts than nursing homes! Retirees want to enjoy life and have someone else do all the work so they're free to play." We mentioned this whenever we heard of an old neighbor or acquaintance who had recently moved to assisted living and loved it.

She always shrugged off our suggestions. "I'm fine where I am. I don't need any assistance. I already have a housekeeper, and you girls take me where I need to go"

It was important that she get the support she needed before something bad happened, so I started to play upon her fears a bit. "If you fell, it could be hours before someone found you," I told her. I learned from a maintenance worker that the elderly woman who previously owned Mother's condo had fallen and broken her hip and wasn't found for over three days. She survived but was unable to return home and ended up in a nursing home, where she died shortly after. Her condo was held in litigation for years after her death as her children fought over their inheritance. The story was sad and I didn't want the same thing to happen to Mother.

I told her a watered-down version, hoping to open her eyes. "Mother, you may not feel alone here because of all the activity around, but if you fell, it might take a little time for someone to find you. The lady who lived here before should have moved to assisted living when she got older, but she was too proud. Unfortunately, she fell and her family was forced to decide where she should live. She didn't get to choose for herself. Wouldn't you prefer to pick your own place instead of having me pick it for you?" I told her this story many times. I just kept throwing suggestions and scenarios at her, hoping something would eventually stick. I tried not to be overly negative because I didn't want to cause a catastrophic reaction. Instead, I kept my stories and suggestions calm and conversational, and gently focused on what could happen if she didn't take action. I told her I would rather let her make the decision about where she would live next, rather than be forced to make that decision myself if something bad happened.

About the time we starting looking at alternative living arrangements, our regular caregiver took another position and we had to replace her. We cycled through a series of caregivers, but none were the right fit. Losing our caregiver coupled with Mother's fear of being alone at night actually worked in our favor; she finally decided she was ready to move somewhere with more assistance.

One day, as Marie and I met to discuss potential facilities, Mother's caregiver called me. "Your mom wants me to take her to see an assisted living facility so she can look around. What would you like me to do?"

I was thrilled to hear this, although I was surprised that Mother had actually remembered what we had been telling her. I told the caregiver, "Tell Mom that she has to make an appointment first. I'll line up a couple of places for her to look at and will take her to visit them soon." Mother never ceased to amaze me, and the complexity of her disease was astounding.

11 *Finding the Right Home*

It was important to thoroughly examine each facility before I allowed my mother to take a tour. I considered her finances, memory impairment, medical condition, personality, and habits. The facility would also need to meet her changing needs as her condition became progressively worse. I was lucky that I didn't have to worry about how we were going to pay for her care. She had a very good income from Joe's pension and Social Security, as well as her own modest savings.

I began by searching the internet for assisted living, Alzheimer's, and memory care facilities in our area. I only considered facilities that were close to my office or home, since I would be Mother's primary caregiver and emergency contact. I called several facilities, and with Marie's assistance, scheduled appointments to view the ones that made our short list. I was honest with each facility about Mother's current level of impairment and her Alzheimer's diagnosis, and I wasn't afraid to ask hard questions. I didn't want to place her in a facility that wouldn't be able to keep her safe or would cause her to be unhappy. Honey was an important part of her life, so I only viewed facilities that allowed pets. Losing Honey would cause her unimaginable grief and stress that would only exacerbate her condition. Mother's cat gave her unconditional love and companionship, made her feel important, and helped her keep a grasp on reality. I put as much effort into finding the right home as Marie and I had done for everything else. Even though she could no longer live by herself, she was doing phenomenally well. We would make every effort to help her keep her tenacious hold on life.

The first facility Marie and I visited was an assisted living facility in the neighborhood that we grew up in. It was located in a renovated elementary school, the very school that Marie and I had attended as children. It was a beautiful facility in a stately brick building, with a couple of new wings for resident apartments built on what used to be the playground. The entryway felt like an old-fashioned hotel, with elegant, overstuffed sofas and side chairs. Brass, wood, and marble accents gave it a high-class appeal. We were greeted by the marketing director, a young man who seemed more like a high-powered insurance salesman than a marketing director for a retirement home. As we toured the facility, I asked about the cost and type of apartments available. The cost was very high for a studio apartment, at over $2,500 a month. That amount included two meals a day, but did not include any assistance, such as monitoring or help with day-to-day tasks. While touring the resident wings, the long, narrow hallways and many turns soon had me confused and I had no idea how to get back. There were many street-level exit doors, and I visualized Mother getting confused, taking an exit door, and wandering off. It was an unsettling thought. I voiced my concern. "I am so turned around and there are so many exit doors. If I'm confused, I'm afraid that my memory-impaired mother won't be able to find her way around without leaving the building."

The marketing director smiled. "It's easy to find your way. Just use the dining room entrance as a reference. All halls will lead you back!"

Or lead you right out the side door, I thought. Even using the dining room as our starting point, I promptly forgot how to get back and was glad we had someone to follow.

The resident apartments were sparse, small, and had very little to recommend them. The windows looked at the building next door, leaving the rooms feeling dark and gloomy. The appliances, a very small refrigerator and a four-burner range, were cheap and looked more like an afterthought. So far, I was not impressed.

When our tour of the facility was complete, he took us to the main dining room, a large, airy room that was bathed in natural light, thanks to the high ceilings and skylights. We had a very good lunch while the marketing director listed all the amenities of the facility. Then, the hard sell began. "You'd better act fast! We have limited rooms available, and there is a long wait for rooms close to the main dining and reception area." I understood why.

Marie said, "We'll think about it, and we still need to have our mother take a look. We are only interested in a room near the dining room or main entrance. If one of those rooms becomes available, would you please give us a call?"

"I would only be able to contact you if you are on the waiting list. There is a refundable $1,500 deposit." Marie put down the deposit, just in case Mother decided that she wanted to move in. To ensure that the facility was the right fit, a staff nurse would assess Mother's needs. The director promised that he'd call us soon.

Marie liked the place, but I was less certain and hoped we would find something better as our search continued.

Several days later, I received a call from the nurse and met with her the same day. She showed me an activity room. "We offer memory games twice a week for those who want a little extra mental stimulation. We also have a well-equipped exercise room available. Your mother will have access to all our exercise equipment, and she can sign up for guided exercise classes."

Fat chance, I thought.

The nurse also tried to ease my concern about Mother getting lost in the labyrinth of hallways. "Each resident has a shelf or space outside their apartment door to put something personal. This helps them know that they have arrived at the correct apartment."

"It's a nice idea, but I don't see how identifying her room door will keep her from getting turned around when she tries to get to the dining room. Frankly, I'm more worried about her getting lost and exiting one of the many doors."

"This is not a locked facility, and we have no way of preventing your mother from leaving if that's what she wanted to do." She handed me an application and medical form for Mother's doctor to fill out. "We can determine if she would be safe here and the level of assistance she needs as soon her doctor returns these forms." I knew that they didn't have a room available, and my fears still hadn't been alleviated. I called Marie and told her that I wanted to keep looking.

The next facility I toured was an Alzheimer's care facility. It was a locked facility that specialized in all stages of dementia care, from onset to end-of-life care. Prices started around four thousand dollars and went up to more than eight thousand dollars, depending upon the level of care needed, but there were no private rooms available at these rates. Like the first facility I visited, it was private pay only and they didn't take Medicaid. I had passed by this facility many times, as it was close to my home and located on a major highway. It was a large, single-story building painted a bright, sunny yellow. It had a welcoming feel. A high wooden fence surrounded it, but the grounds that I could see were well maintained. I made an appointment to tour the facility, and Marie agreed to meet me there.

I took an extended lunch break on the day of the appointment, and waited in the parking lot for Marie. After about fifteen minutes, my patience was wearing thin. I called Marie, hoping she was just running late. She said, "Oh my God, I'm so sorry. I forgot all about the appointment. I never should have said I would be there. Today is my son's birthday, and we're having a party at my house. I still have to pick up his birthday cake. There's no way I can make it."

Disappointed but not surprised, I prepared myself to go on the tour alone. The heavy, steel-framed glass doors at the front of the facility were locked, so I pushed the red call button to buzz the office staff. I peered through the doors and saw a second set of locked doors leading into the entryway. Although I understood the reason for the tight security, I still had the unsettling feeling that I was entering a prison instead of a potential home for my mother. There had been no response to my buzz, so I pressed the button again. A few moments later, an apologetic voice came over the intercom speaker. "Sorry to keep you waiting. Can you please state your name and business?" I answered her questions and apologized for being late. I heard a loud buzz and the heavy door lock disengaged. "The front door is now open. Please make sure that the doors are securely closed behind you before I buzz you through the second set of doors. Thank you!"

Once inside, I felt as if I had entered the Land of Oz. The large, open courtyard was connected to several hallways that fanned out in all directions. The halls looked more like streets; brightly colored street signs pointed the way to the beauty shop, dining room, and other important destinations. It was open and airy, but everything seemed overdone. I was assaulted by garish colors and an oddly cartoonish atmosphere. The facility was quiet and empty, giving me the feeling that I was in a large-scale doll house. I felt uncomfortable standing alone, as if I had left the real world behind me.

Soon, a tall, thin woman came down the hall to greet me. She introduced herself as the director, and ushered me down the hall into her office. We made ourselves comfortable and wasted no time getting down to business. I asked, "Why are there were no private rooms available? I'm concerned Mother will not understand or be willing to share her private space. She is completely unused to this type of living arrangement. She's always had her own space, and is doing so well. I don't want to upset her."

The director gave me a patient smile. "Your mother will be able to bring her own furniture, which will help her room feel more familiar to her. Our residents share rooms because it benefits them socially and is easier for our caregivers." I already didn't think this was the right environment for Mother, but I patiently allowed her to continue. "We have one caregiver for every two residents."

Perhaps Mother would need this level of care one day, but she wasn't there yet. Mother was clever, insightful, and clinging desperately to her carefully crafted routines, holding tightly onto reality. I could imagine her scoffing at this odd place and saying, "Like hell you'll leave me here!"

We started on our tour in a series of common rooms that all looked exactly the same. It was as if we were on a treadmill, always walking but getting nowhere. Each room had a kitchen with an attached sitting area and dining room. The building was a square, and in the center was an outdoor courtyard. Each door had an alarm, so if a resident wandered outside, a caregiver was alerted to ensure they didn't stay out too long. As we walked through the building, I noticed that each common area had a doll cradle just inside the door. I asked the director about this oddity, and she smiled. "One of the residents has a doll she thinks is her child. We have the cradles in each room so she has somewhere to place her baby." Poor thing, I thought. How can she remember where she left her baby when all the rooms look alike? Remembering Mother's perpetually misplaced newspaper, I wondered if the poor woman thought someone had stolen her baby.

We passed by the dining area, which was stark and institutional in comparison to the rest of the facility. It had harsh, unnatural lighting, plain white walls, and linoleum flooring. It was lunchtime and I finally got a glimpse of the people living there. It wasn't a happy sight. Most were in wheelchairs next to caregivers, who spooned food into their mouths. Some of the residents had their heads down, drool running out of their slack mouths that were pulled into gaping frowns. I saw no smiles and heard no laughter, just silence and profound unhappiness. Eyes were wild with fear or vacant and empty. It was like a bizarre episode of the Twilight Zone, and I was looking into the future, forced to see the cruel reality of Alzheimer's. I had to resist the overwhelming impulse to run for the door. The director was used to the appalling sight and didn't even notice my discomfort. She continued our tour, unaffected. "We offer our residents a variety of things to eat and never force them to eat what they don't like." Whether Mother liked the food was the last thing on my mind.

After the dining room, she showed me one of the shared resident rooms. It was wide-open and cheerful, with two beds and one TV. Each room had a small bathroom attached, with a toilet and sink. Thinking about Mother's PTA baths, I asked, "Where do the residents wash up?"

"All of our residents are given a shower once a week. We have one shower room per residential wing. Showers are given on a scheduled rotation. Our residents are not allowed to bathe themselves."

I was unprepared for that. "My mother will not take a shower. She hasn't had a shower in years because she doesn't like the sensation of water striking the top of her head. I'm not sure how she'll handle someone giving her a shower."

She looked at me in a superior way, and her voice left no room for interpretation. "We give all of our residents a shower."

One more strike against this place, I thought.

Seeing no phone in the room, I asked, "Do the residents have their own telephones?"

She smiled and walked me down the hall. At the end of the hallway, she showed me a phone mounted on the wall. "Our residents have access to this phone. None of the resident rooms are wired for telephone. If you insist, you can have a private line installed at your cost, but I wouldn't recommend it." She winked at me as if to say, "You won't need to worry about multiple calls at all hours anymore if your mother lived here."

I had seen and heard enough. In her present condition, Mother would not do well here. If I placed her in such a facility, I might as well kill her because this place would destroy her spirit and will to live. I couldn't imagine Mother being able to hold onto what little of her mind she had left in this type of institution. Perhaps a place like this would be appropriate when she was too far-gone to know or care what happened to her, but that time was not now.

I pointedly looked at my watch and thanked the director. "I appreciate your time. It's a lovely facility, but I don't think my mother is ready for this type of institution just yet. I really must be getting back to work now."

As she walked me back to the main entry, she said, "We pride ourselves in caring for those with all levels of dementia. I'm sure your mother would benefit from the care we can provide here, even if she's just in the early stages of Alzheimer's. If I can answer any more questions, please don't hesitate to call me."

When we reached the door, I turned and offered my hand. "Thank you again, I'll keep that in mind. I know my mother very well and I just don't think she would do well here at all. I doubt she'll be ready for this level of care for some time, that is, if I have anything to do with it. I do appreciate your time, but I doubt I will be calling you any time soon."

I anxiously waited to be buzzed out of the two sets of locked doors. I was once again cautioned to make sure the doors were shut behind me before opening the next set. As soon as I escaped into the parking lot, I was out of breath. I couldn't inhale enough fresh air to breathe normally. The placed hadn't smelled bad; it was clean and well kept, but I had felt so trapped inside that building and was deeply moved by what I had seen. I was shaken to my core. I sat in my car for a while before I felt able to drive. I started to cry when I realized that Mother might be one of those sad and desperate people one day. I was mad at Marie for not being there, and I told myself that I would not visit this type of facility alone again.

I couldn't imagine Mother living in either of the facilities I'd toured, so I widened my search. When I told Marie about my experience and my unwillingness to see another Alzheimer's facility alone, she understood. I arranged two more tours, and she promised to be there. Both facilities were a little farther away than I would have liked, but I was running out of options. When we reached the first facility, we just kept driving. It was old, outdated, and neglected, with a dead lawn, gardens full of weeds, and peeling paint. If they neglected the outside so badly, how did care for what was within?

The next facility on our list was another locked Alzheimer's facility. It was located near a large shopping mall and close to a busy highway. Just like the other locked facility, a tall fence also surrounded this one. The entry wasn't locked and was much more welcoming, resembling a motel lobby instead of a fairy tale prison. A receptionist worked near a small waiting area with comfortable chairs and lovely paintings of pastel landscapes.

After a short wait, a plain woman with long, dark hair came from a locked side door and invited us in. As soon as we crossed the threshold, I was stuck by the smell of the place. It smelled like I expected a nursing home would: urine, decay, and other unmentionable scents invaded my nostrils. The halls were narrow and the carpet was drab. An elderly gentleman shuffled down the hall, looking completely lost. A caregiver hurried past him, but when she spotted us, she immediately turned and went to help the gentleman. Would she have stopped if we hadn't been there? The rooms we saw looked remarkably similar to the ones at the other Alzheimer's facility. I quickly decided that this wasn't the place for Mother and stopped paying attention. When the tour was finally complete, Marie and I agreed that we would not place Mother in this type of facility, at least not yet. Years later, I heard accusations of terrible neglect at the facility we had just toured. I'm so thankful we didn't consider placing Mother there.

I worked during the day and had limited time, so Marie toured a couple of facilities on her own, all of which were like what we had already seen. I was getting discouraged. We were beginning to wonder if we were ever going to find the right home for our mother. Several weeks into our search, Marie called with hope in her voice. "There's a fairly new assisted living facility just a few miles from Mother's condo. One of my friends has a relative living there and told me all about it. I've already toured it and was impressed. This place has potential, Anita. You need to give them a call and see what you think."

On paper, it did seem to meet all of our criteria. They had private rooms with studio, one, and two bedroom apartments available, and they offered memory care assistance. A nurse would interview Mother and review her medical records to determine what type of assistance she needed. It was not a locked facility, so they accepted dementia patients as long as they didn't wander or pose a threat to themselves or other residents. The price was in-line with the other assisted living facilities in the area, starting around two thousand dollars and ranging up to four thousand dollars. The price included a private room and three meals a day.

The building was new and in an upscale area near my office. It looked like a hotel, with a covered entry and automatic sliding glass doors. The doors were unlocked during the day, but at night, one had to use a code to get in and out. Mother would be unable to remember a code, so at least she'd be deterred from trying to leave at night. The exterior and landscaping were well maintained, and a waterfall and sitting area added to the peaceful ambiance. I entered the facility with high hopes. Just inside was a large common area with a huge fireplace surrounded by two-story tall bookcases that were filled with books, pottery, and artwork. A rosy-cheeked young woman smiled at me from the reception desk. Intimate sitting areas with sofas and chairs looked inviting. Several residents sat in the comfortable chairs, and everyone seemed happy, reading the newspaper, talking and laughing, and thank God, looking quite normal. Everyone was older, of course, and some (but not all) were in physical decline. Some used walkers, wheelchairs, or canes, but I noticed no offensive odors and all the residents that I could see looked clean and well dressed. Now this, I thought, looks promising.

Unlike the other facilities I had visited, this one was privately owned and was not part of a large national corporation. It was smaller and had fewer rooms, but had a much friendlier atmosphere. It felt more like an apartment building than an institution. Like the others, this facility did not accept Medicaid. I was always told this up front, even though Mother would never qualify for Medicaid because of her income. I'm sure they didn't want to waste their time if we couldn't afford the price of admittance. I began to wonder about the options that were available to dementia patients without an income as stable as Mother's. I felt blessed but was deeply troubled at the same time.

I met with the executive director, and we discussed rent and amenities over a very good lunch of grilled salmon, fresh clam chowder, and a trip to a well-appointed salad bar. The dining room felt like a local restaurant and was in a beautiful room with a high ceiling and tall, sunlit windows. The tables were elegantly set, and the room was buzzing with conversation and the clinking of silverware against china plates. Impressive, I thought.

After lunch, she showed me the resident apartments. The building had four stories, and each floor had a north and south corridor that ran the length of the building. All hallways led to the main entrance and dining area. It was easy to navigate, even for someone like Mother. The residents that needed the most assistance lived on the ground floor, where all the medication and medical documentation were kept. The centrally located nurses' station looked organized. There weren't many windows on this floor, and of all the floors, it seemed the most institutional. The second and third floors had studio apartments, and one and two bedroom units available with different bathroom configurations. Some apartments had a washer and dryer, and some did not. The fourth floor was called the Penthouse and had the nicest apartments. Of course, the cost was the highest up there.

The common rooms were nicer than the resident rooms. I had come to expect cheap appliances and fixtures in facilities like this. More concerned about the staff than the appliances, I asked, "What is the caregiver to resident ratio?"

"That's a difficult question to answer. Not all of our rooms are licensed for assisted living, as not all of our residents need assistance. I can tell you that we have the required number of caregivers per licensed room as mandated by the state. All of our staff is well educated on the special needs of dementia patients. Communicating with a memory-impaired person requires a lot of education, skill, and effort. We have quite a few memory-impaired residents, and they are all doing quite well here." I was sold.

After learning about the cost of each apartment and a brief discussion on the level of assistance Mother would need, the director said, "If you'd like us to hold a room for you, we require a $1,500 non-refundable deposit."

"Why non-refundable?" I asked. "None of the other facilities require a non-refundable deposit to hold a room."

Her gentle expression became hard and intense in an instant. Her voice was firm. "We will not hold a room unless the prospective resident is serious about moving here. In our experience, most people struggle to make the important decision to transition from independent living to assisted living. We feel that making the deposit non-refundable helps them make up their minds." The director was soft spoken and pleasant unless I brought up costs or questioned the policies. After I left, I called Marie and she agreed that Mother should tour the facility. If she liked it, I would make the deposit and start the ball rolling.

Mother's tour of the facility went very well. As soon as we arrived, we recognized a former neighbor that used to live in Mother's condominium building. He recognized us and made his way over to Mother. "I'm so glad to see you here, Barbara! This is a very nice place to be!" When I asked him if he liked the facility, he replied, "It's fine for what it is. If I had my choice, I'd rather be traveling. I miss my condo on the water, but as far as places go, this is about as good as it gets." He looked sad and slightly confused, and he soon seemed to forget who we were and kept to himself. Seeing someone who Marie and I recognized really helped sell the place to Mother. After showing her the apartments and common areas and enjoying a delicious lunch in the main dining room, she agreed that this did seem to be the place for her. I made the deposit, filled out the paperwork, and scheduled an appointment with the nurse for a needs assessment.

With Mother's input, Marie and I selected a two-bedroom apartment. It was costly, but Mother had adequate resources and we knew that it would make the transition easier. We planned to eventually move her into a smaller, less expensive apartment, always keeping her income in mind and projecting how long her resources would last. Her care would become increasingly more expensive as her disease progressed, so we had to be smart with how we spent her income. Soon, I would be spending more money on her care than her income was bringing in. Her savings were limited, so there would probably be no inheritance. All of her resources would need to be used for her direct care, and once her savings were depleted, Marie and I may someday need to contribute to the cost of her care.

Mother was having one of her clear days when we met with the nurse. She seemed very aware, and if you didn't know otherwise, you wouldn't have imagined that she had Alzheimer's at all. I had already given the information from Mother's neurologist and a list of her medications and health issues to the head nurse. Together, we decided that I would continue to set up her medications and allow her to take them independently. It was something that made her feel in control of her own life, and I felt that it was important for her to continue doing the things she could still do. I liked that I could still control and monitor her medications. The nurse asked that I keep two clearly marked sets of medications on the premises at all times, in case I was unavailable. I kept one on her counter with a note not to remove it, and the other was kept in her safe. The nurse and I decided that Mother would be on their mandatory licensed room care level, which was about eighty dollars per month and included twice-a-day checks. Additionally, they would weigh her once a month and check her temperature and blood pressure. All additional assistance was charged on a per point basis. Points were assessed upon the assistance rendered. I decided to add an escort service to each meal, at least in the beginning, so that she would be able to find her way to the dining room and back without feeling overwhelmed. This service cost over seven hundred dollars a month, but it was an important step to ease her transition into her new life. I planned to stay with her for the first couple of nights to help her establish a routine and assure myself that things were set up properly.

12 *A Life in Transition*

On moving day, Marie arranged for a friend to stay with Mother at the condo and distracted her by packing and giving instructions to the movers. When Marie and I left with the movers, our friend stayed behind to visit with her, answer her questions, and make her feel in charge of the move. Mother seemed to enjoy the process and liked being the center of attention, but seemed a little nervous. She kept asking, "Have I made the right decision? Why am I moving? I don't understand. I like it here just fine, don't I?"

We tried to reassure her. "You've made a very wise decision to move before something bad happened to you. You're one of the lucky ones. You have enough common sense to do what is good for you, and you did it before someone else had to make the decision for you." Mother liked to hear this, so we repeated our same answer, hoping that the idea would sink in.

Marie and I had already packed and labeled most of the boxes, and with the help of an army of volunteers from the local Rotary Club, we moved essential items over to her new apartment. We packed her favorite clothes, medications, toiletries, and all trigger items separately, and made sure they were clearly marked. Marie and I took great care to arrange her furniture in a familiar configuration. We unpacked her essential items and made sure that her TV and phone were working before we brought her to her new apartment.

I stayed for the first couple of nights to reassure her and help her settle into her new living arrangements. The two-bedroom apartment we selected was well laid out, and the floor plan made sense to her. Her patio overlooked the parking lot and a large wooded area, and because her unit was on the second floor, I wasn't worried about her exiting through the patio door. Mother's bedroom and attached bathroom had a floor plan that was similar to her condo. I was relieved because she shouldn't have difficulty finding the bathroom if she was tired and disoriented after getting out of bed. The second bedroom made it much easier for me to spend the night.

We ate dinner together at the facility the first night, and then settled into Mother's familiar routine of snacking, watching TV, and going to bed after the eleven thirty news. Shortly after we went to bed, she came into my room holding her alarm clock. She stood over me silently until I asked, "Can I help you? Is there something you need?"

"I just want to set my alarm clock for when you need to get up."

I smiled to myself and let her set the clock for me. Satisfied, she shuffled back to her room and went to sleep. A behavior that I once found so annoying and strange gave me comfort and made me feel that everything was going to be all right.

For the next couple of days, I went to meals with her and followed her normal daily routine. We were given the red carpet treatment; there was always a space reserved for us in the dining room. When I had to go home and back to work, it was difficult to leave her, but I felt confident that she was safe, would have help if she needed it, and was no longer living on her own in a dangerous situation.

I called her every day at nine o'clock and four o'clock to check on her and remind her to take her medications. Knowing how important her routine was, I continued to visit on the same days, at the same time, and we did the same things. I slowly worked on getting her into a routine at her new home by encouraging her to eat at the facility and participate in the social functions and activities the facility offered.

I was relieved that we had finally completed this important transition and the move was behind us. I looked forward to not having to worry so much or be called upon to reassure her at all hours. She was in a care facility, after all, and I expected that they would know how to handle my memory-impaired mother. I was wrong. It wasn't long before I realized that the staff was not as well trained in caring for those with dementia as I had been led to believe. Mother started to complain almost constantly, and at every opportunity, said, "I hate it here. I want to move back home, and you can't stop me!" She was uncomfortable because she had to interact with her peers, and it seemed everyone who lived there had the same aversion to living with old people. She was fond of saying, "I hate being around all these old sweethearts. Would you just look at them? They're so old!"

She especially hated going to the dining room. "It's just like high school here. Everyone has their own clique. I never know where the hell I should sit." She was right. The residents were very territorial over their space, and woe be unto those who sat in the wrong chair or unknowingly took someone's spot on the bus. Unfortunately, because the facility didn't have assigned seating in the dining room or the bus, once a memory-impaired resident claimed and could remember a seat, they defended their place to the death.

One day, when I was having dinner with her, we sat at an empty table toward the back of the dining room. A sweet looking, tiny woman with white hair and thick glasses sidled up to our table. After taking one look at me, she threw her walker in my direction. I had made the mistake of sitting in her seat. I didn't want to cause her distress, so I quickly got out of the chair, apologized, and begged for forgiveness. I moved to a different chair at the table, and she immediately calmed down and took her seat. I retrieved her fallen walker and placed it by her. I could see the relief on her face as she gave me a shy and uncertain smile. A staff member looked suspiciously in our direction and came over to admonish the lady for her outburst. I just smiled at him and indicated that all was well. Mother was annoyed and gave me a look as if to say, "I told you so!"

When I saw the director later, I said, "I don't understand why the facility doesn't have an assigned seating policy. How does that work for your memory-impaired residents? Mother can't remember where to sit and it causes her a lot of anxiety because she's afraid she will sit in the wrong chair."

The director's eyes narrowed and her voice was firm. "We don't have assigned seating. No one can claim a seat, and all seating has been and will continue to be on a first-come, first-served basis. We know what we're doing. Reserved seating is for potential and new residents only." Arguing with her would do no good, so I let it go. I still wondered how a memory-impaired person was supposed to remember and understand her policies.

A staff member escorted her to meals three times a day, but I learned that they only took her to the dining room entrance and left her there. Not knowing where to go and unwilling to upset someone by taking their place, she would turn on her heel and go back to her room. Again, I consulted with the director. "Can you please have the aide just show her to a seat that is less likely to be claimed? I would greatly appreciate it."

Again, I was rebuffed. "You know our policy. No one can claim a seat, so there is no problem." Since it was up to Mother to find her own seat, I canceled the escort service. Frustrated, I joined Mother for many meals to help her find her way and to ensure she got the hang of things. Eventually, she found a place with a group of nice ladies who didn't suffer from dementia. They took pity on us and assured me that they would make sure Mother always sat with them. Once she was able to remember where her place was, a place she worked so hard to claim and remember, she wouldn't give it up to anyone. The shoe was on the other foot, and she became very territorial over her space. It was a good thing she didn't have a walker to throw!

Mother tried hard to fit in, but spent most of her time in her apartment, watching TV, working her crossword puzzles, and tending to her cat. She changed into her outside clothes before going to each meal, and upon returning to her apartment, changed back into her inside clothes. She complained, "It's exhausting to have to change my clothes every time I go to a goddamn meal!"

I just shook my head and sighed because no matter how hard I tried, I couldn't convince her that she didn't need to change her clothes three times a day. It became a routine and a ritual and couldn't be circumvented.

When I visited, I listened patiently to a litany of complaints, from the diarrhea-brown walls to the presence of too many old sweethearts. "I think they paint the walls this color to hide all the shit!" she said.

She was still able to make me laugh. I replied, "I can't imagine how an older person would be able to shit on the wall." She gave me a sly smile as she bent over, lifted a leg, and pantomimed how it could be done. We both dissolved into a fit of laughter, her complaint long forgotten.

She missed her condo and complained that she had no view and nothing to see. Her windows and balcony overlooked a large wooded area and parking lot, and although it wasn't as breathtaking as Puget Sound, it was green and lovely. I wanted to tell her that it didn't matter because she kept her blinds shut anyway. I had learned that it was best to validate her complaints, so I said, "I can understand why you feel that way. Anyone who had to leave such a spectacular view would have difficulty adjusting." Again, I praised her judgment for moving before something bad happened and then redirected her attention.

Despite her complaints, Mother was always friendly to everyone at the facility. She had to put a lot of effort into interacting with her peers, and to the best of my knowledge, Marie and I were the only ones who were treated to her more unpleasant side. One day, however, a member of the morning staff pulled me aside.

"Your mother gets very angry and is mean to me every morning. I don't appreciate it."

I was surprised, but tempered my response in an attempt to open the conversation. "I'm sorry to hear that. What do you think the trouble is?"

Relieved by my calm demeanor, she said, "Every morning, she asks for her bacon well done. If it's not crispy enough, she waves it in my face and tells me that I did it on purpose. If it's overdone, she accuses me of trying to teach her a lesson for complaining. It's not my fault. I have no control over how they cook the bacon in the kitchen. I tell her that it's not my fault, but that only makes her angrier, and she stomps out of the dining room and makes a big scene."

I was frustrated. Did she not realize that she worked in a facility full of dementia patients? I tried to keep my cool and said, "Mother has dementia, which affects her ability to react in a normal or logical fashion. If she complains about something, anything, just listen and validate her complaint. Tell her you understand why she is angry and let her know that you'll do all within your power to make it right. If it's not possible to bring bacon that is cooked how she likes it, just remove the offending bacon from her sight. Tell her you will personally let the cook know about her complaint and that he'll try to do better tomorrow. I'm sure that Mother will forget all about it until the next time."

Unfortunately, she didn't seem to understand Mother's illness, and the bacon became a trigger that caused many catastrophic reactions, such as leaving the dining room without eating, tearing her room apart in a fit of anger, or taking the bacon to her room so that she could show the manager later. Of course, as soon as the bacon was stashed in a cupboard, it was gone forever. I frequently smelled that something was amiss in Mother's apartment, and with a quick search, found rotting bacon. Once again, I had to remain vigilant for spoiled food in her cupboard. I notified the head nurse of this behavior, and although she said she understood, nothing changed. I continued to find rotten bacon in her cupboards.

Despite the fact that they knew she had Alzheimer's, most of the staff seemed unable comprehend that Mother was forgetful. They expected her to remember notices left on her door or instructions given over the intercom. One evening, she called me in a panic. "Anita, I just don't understand it. I can't get water to come out of my faucet and my toilet won't flush. I complained about it, but no one will do anything. I hate this goddamn place. You need to get me out of here!"

I promised I would find out what was wrong, and after I hung up, I immediately called the facility. The receptionist told me that a water main broke and water to building had been temporarily shut off. She seemed genuinely surprised Mother had called me. "I don't know why she would have called you. All of our residents have been given adequate notice. We announced the problem over the intercom, and placed a notice on everyone's door explaining the situation. We are supplying bottled water to all of our residents."

I literally banged my head against my kitchen cupboard, dumbfounded by the absurdity. I explained my Mother's dementia, yet again. "Unless someone tapes a note to her toilet and all of her sinks, she will continue to try to flush her toilet and turn on her sinks. The notice on her door has probably been put away in a drawer and forgotten!" The receptionist seemed inconvenienced. "Well, this is an emergency. We can't be running around putting signs on all the sinks!" I dropped what I was doing to go tape notes in Mother's apartment. This calmed her down, and before I left, I made sure that someone would remove the signs when the water had been restored.

After that incident, I instructed the director and the head nurse to contact me for all emergencies, maintenance, or changes at the facility so that I could help Mother understand and adapt to what was happening. This was the price I was going to have to pay to keep her out of the more specialized, depressing facilities. I felt badly for all the other memory-impaired residents who were left to figure out these changes for themselves. If I hadn't supported Mother in this way, she would have had tremendous anxiety and stress, both of which could accelerate the progression of her disease.

I stayed involved and tried not to worry. This was certainly not how I expected things to be handled, but after weighing all of our options, there was no better place for her to live. I continued to communicate my concerns and worked closely with the staff. She became well-liked by the residents and staff. She learned her way around and established a comfortable routine. Eventually, she found a group of friends and became part of one of the territorial cliques she once complained so bitterly about. It took the better part of a year for us to adjust and almost two years for her to truly settle in.

13 *Delusions and Other Bizarre Behaviors*

It was 2009, and Mother was almost eighty. She had adjusted to her new living arrangements and life once again settled into a new normal. I was still baffled when her assisted living facility expected an Alzheimer's patient like my mother to remember everything, but she was happy most of the time, so I tried not to complain.

Mother and I once again returned to our comfortable routine of daily phone contact and going out every Monday, Wednesday, and Saturday to get a bite to eat or go to the grocery store. Day-to-day life was a balancing act. I never knew how much I could expect from her on any given day, and often would either overestimate or underestimate her. Some days she struggled more than others, and I had to pay very close attention. She always did better and maintained her balance when she was healthy. Little things like a common cold were monumental problems. Mother was unable to cope with her discomfort and became angry and frustrated if her nose was congested or she didn't get enough sleep. I tried to utilize the resources and staff to help her. If I needed the nursing staff to provide her with any over-the-counter medications, such as nasal spray or even Tylenol or Pepto-Bismol, I had to get specific orders from her doctor. Even if I thought she was capable, I never left additional medications with her that would harm her if she took too much. I tried to leave Pepto-Bismol with her, but she would hide it, lose it, or be unable to remember if she had taken any or worry that she had taken too much. The Pepto-Bismol caused anxiety, and the phone calls would start pouring in. Finally, I had her doctor fax orders to the nursing staff and gave them a stash of Pepto-Bismol.

I focused on enjoying our time together because I knew that our lives would only get more difficult as her disease progressed. It was likely that Alzheimer's disease would eventually cause delusions and other inappropriate and strange behaviors. These behaviors could be the result of medications, dehydration, urinary tract infections, or malnourishment. Early on, I put safeguards in place because I knew that my memory-impaired mother may not be eating or drinking enough and would be unable to communicate urinary discomfort. I monitored her medication and watched for side effects. I was confident she was eating and drinking enough, and I always notified her doctor of any drastic changes in behavior so she could run blood and urine tests to rule out a treatable cause. I never assumed that Alzheimer's was the sole cause of her symptoms and tried to rule out any treatable problems that would exacerbate her disease if left undiagnosed.

Things remained relatively even and calm for a long time, until one Saturday afternoon, Mother crossed two fingers and proudly said, "You know that Bill and I are like this."

"Who's Bill?"

"Why, Bill Gates of course!"

I nearly choked on my food. I had so much experience with

keeping my reactions neutral, so I calmly said, "Really? When did this happen?"

She became very animated and excited. "I was a CPA for Bill Gates, don't you remember? I helped him found Microsoft. After I retired from my first job, Bill sought me out because he was starting a similar business of his own."

It was a familiar story with threads of truth, but on a much grander scale. My mother had been a bookkeeper, not a CPA, and had worked for a furniture dealer that furnished the original Microsoft campuses when they were just getting started. She indeed had retired from one company only to be immediately hired by another. I was absolutely certain that she'd never met Bill Gates.

I didn't know how to handle this delusion, so I just listened and didn't encourage her in any way. I smiled and nodded my head, and then changed the subject at the first opportunity. Apparently, she told the story so convincingly that everyone believed her, from the administrator of her assisted living facility to her own doctor. She had become very popular with her peers, probably thanks to her association with Bill, and demanded a new respect in her community. I never contradicted her in front of anyone, and only corrected her story when it was important.

Her cat, Honey, also gained exaggerated importance. Mother bragged about what a special cat she was to anyone who would listen. I often heard her tell her doctor or a caregiver, "I have an old cat named Honey. I've had her for a long time and she is so in tune with me. If I have a fit, she'll come over and rub me as if to say, 'Hey lady. Stop acting crazy!'"

I would smile to myself. She runs from you because you threaten to tear her fucking head off, I thought.

Mother had many Honey stories. "Honey's eyes are as green as grass and she's such a clean kitty. If she has an accident and throws up on the floor, she'll find some newspaper, shred it, and cover her own mess." I had to stifle a chuckle when I heard that, because Honey wouldn't even cover her own poop in the litter box. I constantly had to clean Honey's dried-up hairballs.

Mother's favorite story became a particularly helpful delusion. "Honey is such a special kitty. When she has to stay at the vet's, she cries. The vet feels so sorry for her that he takes her home with him. Not every kitty gets to go home with the vet!" When Mother and Honey were finally separated years later, this delusion gave her comfort. Without knowing it at the time, she had given us the only explanation that allowed us to separate her from her beloved pet.

She enveloped herself in her own reality, one that made her feel important, safe, and worthy. One day, she called me at work to say, "They just called to tell me they have raised my pension!"

I was immediately suspicious. "Who are they?"

"It doesn't matter who they are, I don't know, but I just found out they are going to increase my pension to $498,000 a month! Can you believe it?"

I went along. "Wow! That's great news, Mother. Congratulations. You know that's a lot of money, so it would be smart to keep your good news to yourself. You never know who could be listening."

Breathless from excitement, she said, "Good idea! I don't want someone knocking me on the head, thinking they're going to steal my money." After work, I went to her apartment to make sure there was nothing with a driver's license number or Social Security number on it.

To hear Mother tell it, she had a stellar career, an extraordinary cat, and was wealthy beyond imagination. Bill became a regular and familiar topic of conversation. I never understood how she could remember her stories about Bill so clearly, but not be able to tell you what day it was. What the hell, I thought. At least Mother's delusions make her happy. I decided to embrace and support them.

Alzheimer's eventually stole our time together from her mind. No matter how regular my visits or how much time we spent together, she always thought that she hadn't seen me in weeks. She complained to everyone at the facility about how much she missed me, how she hadn't seen me in over a month, and what a terrible daughter I was for not visiting more often. The first time a staff member told me about her bitter complaints, I was deeply hurt. If I thought I was going to get any extra credit for my efforts, I was sadly mistaken. I had to remind myself that her disease had robbed her of our time together; she wasn't willfully trying to hurt my feelings. I could never visit often enough to fill the great expanse of time she would experience when I wasn't with her, but I continued to visit as often as I could. Keeping to a schedule gave her comfort and a sense that all was well, even if she thought it had been a long time between visits. I did what I could to fill her life with a sense of purpose, love, and comfort.

Once her mind was no longer crowded with her short-term memory, the past was all she had. She constantly talked about where she was born, her experiences as a child, and when my father died. She told the same stories over and over as if they had just happened and it was the first time she had told the story. Her memories of the distant past were crystal clear, until Alzheimer's took even that away and turned all of her memories into a confused jumble, like a puzzle with too many pieces missing. I listened to her stories as if it were the first time I had heard them and let her tell whatever version of the story she needed to tell without interruption or correction. I kept old photo albums handy when she wanted to dwell on the past, and put them away when they caused her grief or confusion.

Losing her memory and sense of time was bad enough, but her disease also robbed her of her inhibitions and social filters. Mother had a very strict upbringing, and from an early age, learned good manners and how to behave in public. As children, my sisters and I had been held to a high standard for our public behavior. Punishment was swift and certain if we violated the expected rules of conduct when we were out with her. As her disease progressed, my once-strict mother acted out without the least bit of concern for what others thought of her. I never knew what she was going to do next. If we were out at a restaurant, she displayed all manner of embarrassing behaviors. She ate with her fingers, shot water at me with her straw, licked spills off her blouse, and swore loudly. If a child was crying or throwing a tantrum nearby, she would loudly say, "Somebody should knock that little shit down and make him shut up!" If she spotted a particularly large person, she yelled, "Not on my lap!"

When we went to the grocery store, she thought it was funny

to hide from me. She waited until my back was turned, and then would hide behind a display or dart down a different aisle. When I noticed that she was gone, I felt pure panic and dread, and began a frantic search for her. If she was hiding in a place where she could see my reaction, she laughed and giggled until I found her. However, if she lost sight of me, she would forget what she was doing and panic because she was alone. She tried to look for me, which only made her harder to find. Once I did find her, we both would be relieved but shaken by the experience. I learned to keep an eye on my mother and couldn't let her out of my sight for one second.

One day after grocery shopping, she pushed the cart to the car and held onto it while I loaded the groceries. As soon as the cart was empty, she said that she wanted to push it down the steep driveway. "If I push the cart downhill to the last cart return, it'll pick up a lot of speed. That would be a lot of fun to watch!" It was a large parking lot with a lot of traffic.

"I don't think that would be such a great idea. The cart might run into a car and cause an accident." I took the cart from her and returned it.

She wasn't happy that I had spoiled her fun, and defiantly stamped her foot. "I want to push the cart down the hill!" I ignored her, and as soon as my back was turned, she pointed her rear end in my direction, placed her thumb on her butt, wiggled her fingers, and made loud fart noises. I was tired and had to take a very deep breath to calm down before I turned to confront her. When I did turn around, I saw a man in the car parked next to ours looking at Mother and laughing so hard he was crying. I knew better than to scold her or treat her like a child. Instead, I gave my misbehaving mother a hug and said, "If I'd behaved this way when I was a child, you would've knocked me flat!"

"I guess it's payback, then!"

No matter what her behavior, when I look at my mother I see the woman who raised me with love, taught me to treat others as I would want to be treated, and always said that I am no better or worse than anyone else. I am proud of my wonderful, strong, and resilient mother who lived through the Great Depression, World War II, suffered the loss of two beloved husbands, went back to school late in life so that she could get a good job, and worked hard to achieve financial independence. I credit my successes and achievements to her. My love and admiration for my mother allows me to look past these bizarre and difficult behaviors and see the amazing woman underneath.

Alzheimer's disease slowly stole everything my Mother was and everything she had achieved. Her lifetime of living, loving, and learning was taken from her, and she became a vulnerable child again, with a child's need for support, love, and attention. She became a child trapped in an old body, wrinkled, diminished, ill, and difficult. Society sees my mother and others like her as a burden, someone to be avoided at all costs unless there is a financial incentive involved. While Alzheimer's was busy parting my mother from her mind, there was always someone else trying to part her from her money.

14 *The Strength of a Mother's Love*

After Mother moved out of her condo, I updated Lee on her living arrangements. Lee and her husband, Allen, came to see her new apartment shortly after she moved, but their visits were even less frequent than when she had lived in her condo. I rarely talked with Lee, but when I did, she never mentioned Mother's memory problems and seemed uninterested in talking about it if I raised the subject. Marie didn't visit as frequently as she did when Mother lived alone, but she did call regularly. She helped Mother settle into her new home, using her talents as a designer to make it warm and welcoming, with brightly colored shower curtains and beautiful pictures on the walls. I spent about the same amount of time with her as I ever had. I still set up her medications, managed her finances, and was the primary contact for the facility. There was always something going on that needed my attention, such as cable outages, power outages, quarantines, heating issues, and special functions. I received a lot of phone calls and had a lot of demands on my time. If it wasn't one thing, it was another.

The sale of Mother's condo had also fallen to me. Lyle and I moved what had been left behind into storage. I always felt stretched to my capacity. No matter how hard I tried, I just couldn't maintain a perfect balance between my own life and caring for my mother. Mother and I were both walking a tight rope. As we tried to get safely to the other side, something was always trying to knock us off balance and cause us to fall. I had to constantly remind myself not to neglect my wonderful, supportive husband or my good friends. I needed to keep my safety net mended and not allow it to become full of holes.

One day, the unexpected happened. Allen called and said, "Lee's in the hospital with pneumonia. She's critically ill and is not expected to survive." It took me a moment to collect myself before I could reply. I hadn't even known Lee had been sick. Hearing the distress in his voice, I gently asked a few questions. Allen's voice wavered as he explained, "Lee has an abscess in her lung, and a specialist has been called in. She is going to have surgery tomorrow morning to remove the abscess, but the doctor doesn't hold out much hope for her recovery."

The only thing I could think to say was, "Hold on as best you can. Marie and I will come tomorrow for her surgery, and we will bring Mother with us."

His tone changed, his voice resolute. "Lee said that I wasn't to call you. She told me that under no circumstance was her mother to be allowed to see her. I just thought you should know." His voice broke. "I thought you should know because she might not survive this."

I thanked him for calling me and said, "I do think we should come, even if it is just to support you. I know Mother will want to be there and I plan to bring her. I'll respect Lee's wishes, and she doesn't have to see any of us if she doesn't want to." We made plans for the following day and said goodbye.

I tried to digest what Allen had said, sad and afraid for my sister and deeply concerned for her husband. I didn't know what to do. If my sister was dying, I knew that our mother would walk through the fires of hell to be with any of her children one last time. Could she handle it? I carefully weighed Lee's request and considered what I thought Mother could handle. What would she have done if she weren't suffering from Alzheimer's? I called Marie and we decided to tell Mother the news and gauge her reaction before deciding.

Marie and I met at Mother's apartment, and carefully and calmly explained what had happened. She listened intently. While we were talking, I thought I could see the strong light of my mother's intelligence coming back into her clouded brown eyes. She was unbelievably calm. She took a deep breath and asked, "When are we going to see Lee? I need to be with her, you know. I will find a way to be with her!" She wasn't sad or overly upset; she was resolved, solid, and unwavering, gathering some uncanny strength hidden deep within her. Marie and I breathed a huge sigh of relief. We made plans to pick up Mother the next day, and drive the hour to the hospital to wait with Allen for the outcome of the surgery. I left a note taped next to her phone explaining what had happened, what time Marie and I would be there, and that we would be visiting Lee in the hospital.

My note seemed to work because we didn't get any late night calls. She was ready to go when we arrived the next morning and didn't seem anxious or confused. We ate breakfast together and calmly headed off to the hospital. Mother kept asking why Lee was ill, if she was going to be OK, and repeatedly thanked us for taking her. As always, she asked, "Who is today?"

We drove to the hospital on a bleak, cold, and dreary morning. Marie was driving and I sat in the back seat, watching the landscape rush by. It was nearly spring, but the grass and trees were still wearing their winter browns and the sky was a leaden gray. It was too warm to snow but the clouds held the promise of a cold, hard rain to come. When we arrived, the wind was brisk and uncomfortable, ripping at our coats and making our hair stand on end as we got out of the car and rushed to the entrance. The hospital, although not large, was a modern facility in a rural area of Western Washington. We made our way along the brightly lit hospital corridors, into an elevator, and up to the ICU waiting room where Allen was waiting for us. We each gave him a hug, and he updated us on Lee's condition. She was still in critical condition, and the prognosis wasn't good even if she survived the surgery. Her lung had a huge mass of infection and she tested positive for MRSA. Lee was already in surgery when we arrived, so we settled in to wait for the outcome.

Confused by the unfamiliar environment, Mother couldn't quite remember why we were there. The waiting room was small and cramped. The windows were clouded with steam and spattered with rain, shrouding the landscape outside. She became bored and anxious, so Marie and I took turns taking walks with her, taking her to the restroom, and getting her things to eat and drink. She asked her usual questions. Every now and then, she remembered that Lee was ill and she thanked us again for letting her come.

The surgery took many hours, and as the afternoon dragged on, we grew increasingly worried about the outcome. Finally, the doctor came out and had a long, hushed conversation with Allen. When the doctor left, Allen looked distraught and was crying. "Lee has survived the surgery, but she's still in critical condition. Her doctor said there's still a very good chance that she won't survive. She's been moved to the ICU, and only one person is allowed to see her at a time."

We all agreed Allen should be with Lee, and we would stay in the waiting room unless he needed us. Hours passed, and Lee's condition worsened. The doctor lifted the restriction on who could see Lee, which led me to believe that he didn't expect her to live out the day. We were silently ushered into her room. Lee was unconscious on a bed, a ventilator tube down her throat and taped tightly to her mouth. She looked bloated and unnatural. Her skin was ashen, her head was tilted back, and her eyes were taped shut. Dozens of wires connected her to a series of monitors. The beeping machines and rhythmic pumping and hissing of the ventilator broke the awful silence of the room. Both arms were full of IVs, and we could barely reach the bed through all the tubes and wires. Marie and I stood beside Mother, carefully monitoring her reaction. We had no idea how she would handle this. For all we knew, she would start screaming and run from the room, or worse, attempt to pull out some of the tubes and wires attached to Lee.

It was as if her dementia had washed away. Mother only had eyes for Lee. Her eyes focused, her face softened, and it seemed as if she was literally projecting love from her eyes and encasing Lee in it. She wasn't afraid. She moved as close to Lee as she could get, and gently, lightly stroked the little bit of flesh that wasn't covered by tubes and tape. Quietly, she said, "I love you, my poor girl. Mother's here." Tears streamed down our faces as we watched our mother project her love. We could see the pain etched deeply into the lines of her face as she gazed lovingly down at her eldest daughter, knowing this may be the last time any of us would see Lee alive.

Marie and I also told our sister that we loved her and to keep fighting. Lee was strong, and we hadn't given up hope. If anyone could recover, it would be our stubborn and headstrong sister. If she could hold onto life as well as she did a grudge, she had a good chance of surviving this. When our time was up, a nurse came in and politely asked us to leave. We filed out of the room, mopping our wet eyes, blowing our noses, and trying to catch our breath.

We sat in stunned silence for a few more hours, but Lee's condition didn't change. Mother was exhausted and needed to go home, so Allen promised to call us if we needed to come again. Mother was still subdued on the drive home, not asking her normal string of repeated questions. We were all tired and deflated. I stayed with her until she settled into her nightly routine. Once I was convinced she would be all right, I said goodnight, hugged her tightly, and went home.

The next morning, things were far from all right with Mother. A nurse called me and said, "Your mother was inconsolable at breakfast, and wouldn't stop crying. She told me that her eldest daughter died. Is this true?"

"Lee is gravely ill but is still very much alive. Can you please tell her that? I will come right away to comfort her and leave a note where she can see it." Before I left, I called Allen, who said that Lee had turned a corner overnight, and although she was still in the ICU, she was expected to survive. Mother was in a state of profound grief when I arrived, firmly believing that Lee had died. I told her over and over, "Lee is alive, just very, very sick."

She suffered the repeated tragedy of Lee's death for the next several mornings. Her anguish was terrible to see. She would whimper, "No one should have to outlive their child." I comforted her to the best of my ability and continued to repeat that Lee would be OK. One day, she looked up at me and mournfully asked, "If Lee isn't dead, what made me think she was? Did I dream it?"

"You visited Lee when she was at death's door, but your strong and stubborn daughter met death and told him to go away!" This was an explanation she could believe, and she held tightly onto that story. I repeated it to her every time I was with her. Finally, one day, she started to tell anyone who would listen about her strong and brave daughter who met death and told him to go away.

Despite the suffering and grief it caused her, I wasn't sorry that I had taken her to see Lee. If Lee had died and I hadn't allowed Mother to see her, I couldn't have forgiven myself. However, once that I understood the pain and confusion it caused, I may not make the same decision in the future, especially as her disease progressed. Although her love was strong, it couldn't override her malfunctioning brain. It would be cruel to put her through the daily death of a loved one, forcing her to suffer it over and over. If someone died, I planned to make up a wonderful story about how they went to a faraway, exotic place, whatever I could get her to believe. I hoped we would never have to be faced with that decision.

Weeks later, Lee was not only home again, but back to working nights as a nurse. Although the chasm between Lee and Mother was still there, it seemed to have narrowed a bit since we had rallied to her side. So, I was pleased when my phone rang one day and the caller ID told me that it was Lee. I answered the phone, glad that she was at last making contact.

I didn't even get a chance to say hello before she said, "You won't believe this, but I am back in the hospital."

"What happened?" I assumed she must have been in an accident. It couldn't be too serious, since Lee was the one calling.

In a barely audible and breathless voice, she explained, "I was doing great and was back to work within two weeks of my release from the hospital. I got home from work one night and was having difficulty moving my legs. They just weren't working right. Allen was so worried and insisted I go to the hospital, and it was a damn good thing he did. I just kept getting progressively worse, and the tests confirmed I have a rare disease called Guillain-Barré syndrome." I listened in stunned silence. "Guillain-Barré is an autoimmune disease. My own immune system is attacking the nerves in my body, stripping them of their protective sheaths and resulting in severe pain and paralysis. The doctor tells me I have a particularly bad case. I'm slowly losing all control of my bodily functions. I wanted to call you because I am losing the ability to breathe on my own and will have to be put on a respirator soon."

I was having trouble processing what she told me. My mouth was dry and all I could think to say was, "What can be done for you? Are you going to be OK?"

"Even in a very bad case, it is seldom deadly, just incredibly painful and debilitating. With treatment, I should get better and not have much lasting nerve damage, but we won't know the prognosis until they determine how much of my body is affected. I may have minor nerve damage or I might have long-term paralysis."

"What are the odds?"

She laughed a bit. "Oh, about 1 in 500,000. Lucky me!"

I laughed with her. "I really wish you had won the lottery instead with those odds. You have already cheated death once, so this should be a piece of cake for you!"

We agreed that Mother wouldn't come see her while she was on a respirator, but Lee felt certain that once she was out of the ICU, Mother would be able to come and she would welcome the company. When Allen gave us the all clear, I would bring Mother to visit on our normal Saturday. Instead of going to lunch and the store, we would drive to the hospital to see her. I shared the news with Marie, and because I was busy with work and taking care of Mother, Marie went to help Allen and Lee with whatever they needed.

When Allen finally called and told me that Lee was ready for visitors, I brought Mother to the hospital the very next Saturday. I was a bit worried about how she would react. Lee was still in the ICU on a ventilator, but was able to sit up and communicate. Mother enjoyed the twenty-five-mile drive to the big city of Seattle. It was late spring and the weather was bright and sunny, the sky an impossible blue. The grass and trees had shed their dull browns and were cloaked in vibrant spring greens. The rhododendrons and azaleas showed off their bright colors as we passed them on the freeway. Mother was happy to go for a drive and was excited as we approached the gleaming landscape of the big city. As I turned into the hospital's parking garage, Mother had a frown on her face. "Do I have a doctor's appointment?" I assured her that we were just there to visit Lee. It was a very long walk from the parking garage into the hospital, and I was glad that Mother didn't have any mobility issues. She did complain a lot. "Where are we going and why are we walking so far?" "Who is today?" "Do I have a doctor's appointment?" I continued to answer her questions until we arrived at the ICU and found Lee's room. Mother was quieter and kept close to me, confused but alert. Lee had once again contracted MRSA, so a nurse instructed us to put on gowns, booties, gloves, and masks before entering the room. This unusual request upset Mother, but she calmed down when I convinced her it was necessary to prevent germs from harming Lee.

Lee was in a sterile room with glass doors. A nurses' station was situated just outside the room so someone could always see her and her monitors. The ICU had several rooms like Lee's, all with nurses standing guard over their critically ill patients. Lee was sitting up in bed with a ventilator tube taped to the middle of her throat. Like the last time I saw her, there were several monitors attached to her and IVs in both arms, but this time, she was awake and alert. One of her sons and his wife were in the room, and they were all watching TV.

Mother seemed very pleased to see Lee, and I pulled a chair to the bedside so Mother could sit down. Mother reached out her hand to her ailing daughter; Lee had tears in her eyes as she held it. We stayed for about an hour, and when I saw Mother's head nodding and her eyes start to close, we said goodbye.

We made the fifty-mile round trip visit every Saturday for several weeks. Eventually, Lee was moved out of the ICU and to a different hospital to begin her physical therapy. I continued to take Mother to see Lee while she was hospitalized, as I knew she wouldn't have wanted it any other way. The weeks stretched into months. Mother was content to visit her eldest daughter as often as I would take her, and was always on her very best behavior. She was confused, repetitive, and became easily bored, as I expected, but the love Mother had for Lee seemed to keep her disease in check, at least for a time.

It seemed like Lee had been in the hospital forever, and her progress was slowed by depression. Who could blame her? She couldn't walk, had been in and out of the hospital for the better part of a year, and was away from home and all its comforts. For some reason, keeping Lee clean and comfortable was not a priority at the rehabilitation hospital. We had to constantly nag them to wash her hair and had to insist that the nurse change her soiled diaper before the therapist took her to her daily therapy sessions. Yes, Lee was depressed and so were we all.

Because of Lee's lack of progress, her insurance company informed her that she needed to continue her care outside of the hospital. Lee and Allen were beside themselves. She still couldn't walk, was confined to the bed, and was incontinent. Marie worked hard to help Lee find the resources and assistance she needed. When Marie met with the rehabilitation staff and the hospital social worker, they said that Lee would never walk again, so there was little else they could do for her there. It was this prognosis that led Lee's insurance to cut off funding for her inpatient rehabilitation, despite the fact that her benefits were not yet exhausted. Lee was far from able to manage life at home, but she was set to be discharged anyway. The only other alternative was a nursing home, where we all knew Lee would not do well.

Marie fought to keep Lee in the hospital for as long as possible and insisted that she not be released until plans were in place for in-home rehabilitation. Allen did a phenomenal job of making sure Lee was cared for when she went back home. No one else could have done what he did for my sister.

Once Lee moved back home, which was a considerable distance away, our weekly visits had to end. Mother and I went back to our normal routine. With Allen's care and Lee's sheer determination, she eventually regained the ability to walk with the aid of a cane. She took great pleasure in walking into the rehabilitation hospital that had such little faith in her and proving them wrong.

15 *The Torment of an Avoidable Tragedy*

Mother continued to live in her two-bedroom apartment and held her own for a long time. When she was eighty-one years old, however, things started to change. I came to realize that her apartment was becoming too big for her. She wandered from room to room, not knowing what she should be doing. She put things in the spare room, such as her slippers, and was unable to find them again, causing a catastrophic reaction. Marie and I felt it was time to consider a smaller, less expensive apartment.

We selected a one-bedroom apartment on the fourth floor, also known as the Penthouse, because it had an identical floor plan to her existing apartment, minus the extra bedroom and bathroom. There was no patio, but the large window overlooked a much more active landscape, which we hoped Mother would like. This time, we didn't tell her about the move. We made the arrangements and finalized the plans without her knowledge.

The day of the move went exceptionally well and went off almost without a hitch. Lyle and I took Mother out, while Marie organized the move. Mother enjoyed the day of shopping, and was glad that Lyle was with us. Instead of going back to her apartment, we stopped at my house for snacks, which she liked very much. Meanwhile, Marie was busy helping the moving men transfer all of Mother's belongings from one apartment to the other, and setting them up exactly as they had been. She checked to make sure that the phone and TV were working, and got Honey settled in. When Marie called to say that they were done, Lyle and I took Mother to her new apartment.

As soon as we headed toward the elevator, she stopped us and said, "That's not how I go home!" We assured her everything was OK and that we wanted her to look at a new apartment, one that had a view. She was suspicious and a little angry, but followed us up to her new home. It was amazing how much it looked like her old apartment. Honey slept on her perch by the window, Mother's furniture was perfectly placed, the TV was on, and her newspaper and crossword puzzle were waiting by her chair. Mother knew we had pulled one over on her and was very angry.

Fortunately, her wrath didn't last long. We kept telling her, "The move was your idea. You picked the place and hired the movers. Once you make up your mind, you always do the right thing. We're so proud of you!" Because everything was placed in a familiar configuration, it took less than an hour for her to settle in. I stayed with her the first night to work out any bugs, and the only problem we encountered was that she couldn't find her way to the dining room. She was on a different floor, so she not only had to go down the hall, but into an elevator and find the correct floor. Marie came up with the solution to put signs just inside her door with arrows that told her which direction to go and what button to push in the elevator. We placed a similar sign on the outside of her door. The signs worked beautifully, and soon, she forgot she ever lived anywhere else.

Not long after she moved into her new apartment, I noticed she was having difficulty hearing. Unless I was facing her directly, Mother couldn't hear me and told me to speak up or yelled at me to face her when I spoke. I could hear her TV halfway down the hall because it was so loud. When I knocked on her door, she was unable to hear it and I would have to let myself in, which startled her. Her hearing loss was probably caused by something as simple as too much waxy buildup in her ears, possibly because she never took showers to loosen the wax. The nurse at Dr. R's office attempted to clean her ears, but Mother had been resistant. The doctor recommended that we use a syringe filled with water and hydrogen peroxide to soften the wax prior to her appointment. Mother couldn't remember to do this by herself and wouldn't let me do it for her. I decided not to force the issue, and I will always wonder what would have happened if I had only insisted. Instead, I decided not to upset her. After all, I thought, what harm could earwax do?

Concerned about her continuing hearing loss, I asked the nurse to try to clean her ears again. When the nurse attempted to flush her ear, Mother complained of sharp pain and burning, and I made the nurse stop. She assured me the water was tepid and clean and shouldn't hurt Mother's ear, so I allowed her to continue. Mother put her hand up to her ear and howled in pain. "Stop it! It hurts, goddamn it. I mean it. It really burns! You are hurting my ear!" Even when the nurse stopped, Mother had a pained expression and complained about how badly her ear hurt. Forgetful as she was, if Mother was complaining about pain, it was real and present.

Worried, I asked to see the doctor. I was concerned not only about the pain, but her hearing loss as well. Dr. R gave me the names of few local specialists she recommended, but unfortunately, I had to go back to work and Marie was unavailable to take Mother to a specialist that day. We had to schedule an appointment the next day, when Marie would be available to take her. Dr. R reassured me that her ear was probably just irritated by the water, and the pain should resolve.

The next day, Marie took Mother to a specialist. He was able to clean one ear, but she wouldn't let him touch her sore ear. The specialist gave Marie instructions for Mother to dip her finger in olive oil and rub a small amount in her ear to soften the wax that was obstructing his view of the ear canal. Marie set up the olive oil, and called Mother to remind her about it once a day. I took Mother to her follow-up appointment one week later, and the wax was soft enough for the specialist to remove with little trouble. He said, "Her eardrum is very red and shows signs of trauma. It looks as though a sharp object has scratched it. It should heal soon, and she will be fine."

"If it's so red and looks scratched," I asked, "would an antibiotic keep it from getting infected?"

Looking down his nose at me, he replied, "She doesn't need an antibiotic." He seemed unconcerned and sent us home with no further instructions.

The pain and pressure in Mother's ear only got worse, so I made another appointment with the specialist. He looked into her ear and again was unconcerned by what he saw, but to placate me, he took a swab to test for a bacterial infection and gave us a prescription for antibiotic ear drops. I was more than just a little worried about her poor ear, so I went to her apartment twice each day to administer the ear drops. I lay on the bed with her to make sure she kept her head tilted, and I tried to comfort her and keep her company while the drops worked. Mother was very obedient and did all that I asked without complaint. She would look at me with a child's eyes, wide and trusting. She finished the full course of treatment, and although she seemed a little better, the issue wasn't fully resolved.

I called the specialist's office and gave his nurse an update on her progress. "Mother is feeling better, but she is still complaining about some discomfort. I am worried there is a more serious problem here."

"Her tests came back negative for bacteria, but I will ask the doctor if he wants to continue the antibiotic ear drops." She called me back a short while later and told me that she would call in another prescription. By the time Mother finished the second course of treatment, she seemed to be feeling much better and the specialist recommended no further treatment. I was relieved and thought the ordeal was behind us.

Not more than two or three days after we finished the treatment, Mother's symptoms came back. I was very stressed out because in addition to taking care of her ear, I had two surgery dates approaching to remove cancer from my nose. Lyle had recently been diagnosed with prostate cancer, and had also learned that he would soon be laid off. Marie and Tom had been gone almost a month on an extended vacation, so I had been forced to take a lot of time off work to care for Mother. I was overwhelmed and nearing an emotional breakdown. With everything that was going on, I was less patient with the specialist's inability to get a handle on what was wrong with Mother's ear.

Things came to a head when she called me at work, crying about the pain in her ear. "Why won't anyone help me? I hurt, damn it!"

I called the specialist's office, no longer interested in talking to his nurse, and demanded to speak with him directly. When he returned my call, I was frustrated and upset, crying and nearly yelling. "We needed to get this figured out! This has gone on too long and I'm worried that you're missing something. Don't forget, my mother has Alzheimer's. Something that causes her this much pain and anxiety could advance her disease or trigger her to do something crazy, like wander away to find someone to help her. You can't do anything about her Alzheimer's, but I'll be damned if I let something as insignificant as an ear infection expedite the process and drive her off that cliff." He was responsive and kind, and agreed to take another look later that day.

I took the rest of the day off work to take her back to the specialist, but this time, I insisted she get a CT scan. The specialist still seemed unconcerned, but I was determined to find out what was going on. Even after her month of unresolved pain, the specialist was resistant to order this diagnostic test. I carefully explained my concerns. "Mother is in so much pain, it hurts her to bend over, and when she does, she complains of a swishing sound. I know she is in constant pain because she complains constantly. My mother can't remember more than ten minutes, so if she weren't really in pain, she would forget all about it. This must

be addressed. I won't be put off! This is agitating her and exacer-
bating her Alzheimer's!"

The specialist finally agreed to order the CT scan. I took her
directly to the imaging center to have it done, but our luck ran
out when the scan malfunctioned and they were unable to repair
it. Not knowing how long the machine would be down, they were
unable to tell me when to come back. I called the specialist's office, but the nurse said, "It'll be another two weeks before I can
get you into another imaging center."

I was livid. "You are just going to have to do better than that!
Do I have to take her to the emergency room?" After a lot of arm
twisting, I got an appointment at another imaging center the next
day. It was farther away than I would have liked, but at least she
would be getting the scan. I took yet another day off work for her
appointment, and Mother finally got her scan. That evening, the
specialist called with the results. The scan indicated that there
was a significant amount of fluid and infection behind her eardrum and in the surrounding chambers of her skull. He called
in a prescription for a strong antibiotic and instructed her to begin taking them immediately. I scheduled an appointment for the
next day to discuss treatment options. I was relieved that we had
finally discovered what the cause of her pain and discomfort, but
equally worried about how serious this was turning out to be.

The next day, the specialist showed me the images from the
scan, and it made me sick to think about how badly she'd been
suffering because of all the fluid in her head. He recommended
she take the full course of the antibiotics, and if they didn't resolve the infection, we would need to consider surgery. My heart

froze, knowing what surgery could mean for a person with Alzheimer's: anesthesia, hospitals, horror. I wanted to do whatever it took for Mother to get well, but I was only willing to consider surgery as a last resort.

She took the antibiotics as prescribed, and at long last, she was feeling much better. We returned to the specialist's office for her follow-up visit two weeks later, on her birthday. Marie was still out of town, and Mother and I had plans to meet my best friend, Sue, for a birthday lunch. The specialist looked in her ear, and was pleased with what he saw. "I'm going to puncture her eardrum to see what the fluid behind it looks like."

Horrified, I stopped him and asked why such a drastic procedure was necessary, but he just looked at me with an offended expression. I stared right back at him and said, "What would you do if this were your mother?"

He looked even more offended. "I treat all my patients as I would treat a family member." He proceeded to puncture her eardrum. She screamed in pain and surprise, and I held her hand, trying to comfort her. I was shocked into a numb silence, unable to believe what he'd done.

We were sent home with a reassurance that all would be well, as the fluid he had seen was clear, showed no signs of infection, and that any further fluid would resolve naturally. Feeling violated, Mother and I were both in shock as we walked out of the office. She was trembling. "My ear hurts! I hate that man. You can't make me go back there." I was heartbroken; it was her birthday, she had been so happy, and had finally shown some real improvement, and now this. I just prayed he had not done any more damage and hoped he knew what he was doing. After all, he was a "specialist."

My prayers went unanswered. Mother's symptoms got progressively worse. Looking back, after the specialist punctured her eardrum, he suctioned out her ear with a vacuum, and when wasn't using it, he slung it over a stool. At one point, it looked like it might have touched the floor. I had been so numb with horror and disbelief, that I couldn't reconcile a person in such a position of trust treating us that way. He was, after all, not only a doctor, but also a specialist in his field. What did I know? It wasn't unreasonable to assume that the specialist had opened her eardrum and introduced even more infection. His carelessness and arrogance was a wake-up call for me. I would never fully trust any doctor or medical professional again.

It was time for me to have the cancer removed from my nose. Marie had recently returned from her vacation, and when Mother's ear got worse, she didn't know what to do and took her back to the same specialist. My surgeries were successful and I was back to work within four days. I had to catch up on work for the next couple of weeks, so Marie took over all aspects of Mother's care. The specialist continued to prescribe ear drops and antibiotics, but nothing helped. At one point, he prescribed an ear drop that she was allergic to, and when the pharmacist notified him of the allergy, he said we should just use it anyway. That was the last straw. Marie finally found a different specialist.

When the new specialist looked in Mother's ear, he told Marie that whatever was going on was beyond him, and referred her to a neurosurgeon in Seattle. When Marie finally got an appointment with the neurosurgeon, he recommended surgery to clean out the infection. Neither the new specialist nor the neurosurgeon thought it was an emergency, so the surgery was scheduled for two weeks later. Both doctors thought it was unnecessary to continue antibiotics, and even though Mother's pain required daily narcotics, neither would prescribe her an antibiotic. So, we waited for her surgery date and tried to manage her pain, which was getting more out of control each day.

I stayed with her the night before her surgery. She was not allowed to eat or drink anything twelve hours prior to the surgery, and had to take a shower with a special antibacterial soap the night before and the morning of her surgery. Those instructions were too much for her to handle on her own, so I was there to make sure she followed the rules. Getting her to take a shower was not going to be easy. I asked the staff at her facility to give her a shower, but they didn't have any female aides working when I needed assistance. Helping my poor mother take her showers was one of the hardest and saddest things I have ever had to do. It was difficult and awkward, and because of her disease, she didn't understand and resisted the entire process. After a lot of begging, pleading, and insisting, we managed to complete both showers. We both went to bed feeling exhausted and miserable.

The next morning, Marie came to drive with us to the hospital in Seattle. It had been more than eight hours since Mother's last dosage of pain medication, and she was miserable. She looked strained and pale, occasionally whimpering or moaning. "Why won't you help me? Help, oh help, won't somebody help me?" Marie and I were half-crazy with worry. We drove to the hospital as quickly as we could and checked her in, hoping they would give her something for the pain. Her pain was so intense that she was out of her mind and howling with anger and agony. Instead of going promptly back to the surgical area, we were told that the surgeon was running late and the surgery would be delayed. We had waited so long and been through so much, only to be asked to wait some more. Mother just howled, "Don't they know this is an emergency?" We would have taken her to the emergency room, but didn't think it would help. We waited.

Hours later, she was finally taken into surgery, and Marie and I were moved to a different waiting area. I was so tired from the night before and traumatized by having to witness our mother in so much pain and distress that I remember little about the wait. Marie left her cell phone number with the waiting room attendant and we settled in. We watched other families come and go, and became very worried when a two-hour procedure turned into four hours. Finally, Marie's cell phone rang. She listened in stunned silence as the surgeon updated her on the outcome of the surgery. When the conversation was finished, she looked pallid and horrified. "The infection in Mother's ear was much more advanced than the surgeon anticipated. Her inner ear has been completely destroyed, and he had to remove the bones in her inner ear and part of her skull. She is going to be admitted to the hospital, and an infectious disease specialist will be called in. He said it was a miracle she doesn't have encephalitis. He is nearly finished and will close the wound and call us when she is out of surgery." Marie's voice was even and flat; I think she was in shock. I was devastated. So many questions ran through my mind: How could this have happened? How did it get so far out of hand? Why didn't we push harder when we knew something wasn't right? Will Mother survive this trauma?

Knowing Mother would be in recovery for some time, Marie suggested that we leave to get something to eat. I didn't think it was a good idea. "I think we'll be getting a call soon. Mother isn't going to like what has happened, and they are going to need our help with her." Just as I said that, Marie's phone rang. A nurse in the recovery room called to ask one of us to come and calm Mother down because she was trying to get away. I had no idea where the recovery room was, and they said they would send someone up to show me the way.

Soon, a young man in surgical scrubs came hurrying in our direction calling out my name. When I raised my hand, he waved me over and turned on his heel, expecting me to follow him. "I am so glad you're here. Your Mother is asking for you and she wants to leave. She actually escaped from the recovery room for just a moment. We were able to get her back into bed, but I don't think we will be able to keep her there without your help!"

The recovery room was full of patients in beds separated by curtains and nurses scurrying around, tending to the needs of those just out of surgery. As soon as I saw Mother, I felt sick and sad. She was propped up on one elbow in her bed, her head wrapped in gauze with a large, protruding bandage over her left ear. She was angrily protesting to a nurse. "I need to pee. Why in the hell won't you let me get up? I'm not having it! Where is Anita? I'm leaving, and you can't stop me!" Unfortunately, because it was supposed to have been a short, outpatient surgery, they hadn't put in a catheter. Mother was still coming out of the anesthesia, and was completely disoriented and didn't understand why they wouldn't let her get up to use the restroom.

The nurse impatiently tried to shove a bedpan under Mother. When she saw me, the nurse said, "I don't understand why the doctor wants to admit her for a routine ear surgery." She seemed inconvenienced that she had to attend to Mother at all.

"Her surgery was anything but routine. I suggest you talk to the surgeon if you have any questions." I snatched the bedpan from the nurse, calmed Mother down, and assisted her with the bedpan.

The surgeon saw me helping Mother from across the room and came over. He was tall and seemed very young, almost boyish. With a smile, he told me about the surgery in an oddly animated fashion. "Your mother's surgery was very difficult. She had a tremendous amount of infection and it had penetrated the bones of her inner ear. There was so much infection that some of the bones had actually exploded. I had to remove them, and her inner ear is now completely gone. I did a very good job cleaning out the infection, but it had spread to the surrounding skull. I removed a small amount of skull that was infected. She will be admitted to the hospital and will need to stay for two or three days. Because the infection was in her bones, she will need to be seen by an infectious disease specialist. He should be able to assess her tomorrow. After her discharge, I estimate that she will need to be on an IV antibiotic for at least two months to ensure the infection has cleared. She will be profoundly deaf in that ear, and will probably not have any balance left. She'll feel like a spinning top when she tries to stand. It will take her some time to compensate, and she won't be able to stand or walk on her own." As he rattled on, every word hit me like a sledgehammer. It was like he was pounding me into a hole I couldn't ever hope to crawl out of. He might as well have said, "Your mother will never get her life back. She is going straight to the nursing home. What a great surgeon I am!"

I asked, "How did it get this far? We were assured that this was not an emergency and that she didn't need to be on an antibiotic while we waited. How did it get this bad?"

The surgeon was no longer smiling. "Don't worry. After she recovers, I can give her a cochlear implant and she will be able hear again in that ear."

I was angry at his indifference and the fact that he wasn't the least bit concerned about how her Alzheimer's would affect her recovery. "I couldn't care less about the hearing in that ear! My mother has Alzheimer's. Why don't you understand that? She will no longer be able to live in her home. Everything we have worked so hard to achieve has been destroyed. She won't be able to comprehend what has happened to her. We have to figure out how she will survive this procedure, and you have the nerve to speak to me about another one?"

I stopped to collect myself. My voice was shaking with anger, and I heard my mother's frail and trembling voice behind me saying, "Anita! Anita! What's wrong?"

I heaved a heavy sigh and told the doctor, "Please just call my sister and tell her what you just told me. Let me get back to my mother!" He was no longer smiling but was totally unfazed by my comments.

I was outraged that no one seemed to understand or even care that my mother had Alzheimer's. Why did they not consider her disease when treating her? Ignoring her dementia could lead to her death, regardless of what they did about her ear infection. She might try to get up and fall. She might have become combative and succeeded in escaping the recovery room. She might rip off her compression bandage or pull out her IV and expose herself to another infection. If I couldn't find a way to support her, this ear infection could lead to the acceleration of her Alzheimer's. It just didn't make sense. The nurse wasn't even capable of helping my agitated mother with her bedpan, for God's sake. If it wasn't the doctor's or the hospital's responsibility to understand and treat a patient's dementia, who could I trust to help us? How did they get a pass on this? Doctors aren't allowed to ignore a patient's heart condition, diabetes, or cancer, so why was it acceptable to completely ignore dementia? Are there low reimbursement rates for the elderly, or is it just too expensive to train staff members to handle the special needs of a dementia patient? Whatever the reason, I'm sure it is a financial one.

Marie and I took turns spending nights and days with our mother to advocate for her care. The experience was very similar to her last hospital stay, and we were treated to a symphony of bed alarms playing "Mary Had a Little Lamb." One night, a patient with a traumatic brain injury wandered up and down the halls, trying to get into other patient's rooms while swearing and threatening to kill people. If we hadn't been at Mother's bedside, she would have been entirely unable to comprehend what was happening. We gave her comfort and reassurance and were there to answer her repeated questions. When she asked about Honey, we said, "The vet has taken her home and will bring her back as soon as you are released from the hospital."

Mother always seemed comforted when we told her this. Her voice choked with tears, she said, "That's right, the vet loves her." Marie wrote, "Honey is with the vet" on the white board so Mother could see it. The note reassured her until she forgot, and once again, asked where Honey was.

Mother was in constant pain, but the surgeon was reluctant to prescribe her anything stronger than Tylenol. We had to push for stronger drugs to manage her pain. After all, she just had part of her skull removed and had an infection in her bones, yet it was a constant battle to keep her comfortable. They had been glad to prescribe narcotics while they made her wait for surgery, so they already knew how she would tolerate the drugs. I just didn't understand. When I asked, the only explanation we got was that she shouldn't need it. We pestered the nurses and doctors, and finally, the physician's assistant agreed to give her narcotic painkillers, but only if she asked for them and not on a routine schedule. Even though Mother was in a lot of pain, she couldn't remember to ask, so Marie and I had to keep track of when her medication was due and asked for it before she was in too much pain.

The nurses and physician's assistants were quick to tell us, "If your mother becomes unmanageable due to her Alzheimer's, we will be forced to use chemical restraints to keep her calm." They couldn't write a note to remind her of something, reassure her in any way, or give her adequate pain medicine, but they were all too willing to give her powerful antipsychotic drugs that had potentially devastating side effects and would increase her risk of falling. I wanted to scream with frustration. I tried not to let it get to me and accept that this was just how it was. I could do nothing to change it. I was exhausted and became more cynical with each encounter we had with the healthcare system.

We tried to plan for Mother's care after her discharge, but we were wary of the hospital social worker. We had seen how shabbily Lee had been treated at this hospital. Although their cause was a good one, the social worker worked for the hospital and discharged patients based on insurance and Medicare payments, not what was best for the patient. Their only duty to the patient was to provide information about what options were available. The primary objective of the hospital seemed to be to discharge the patient before Medicare and insurance stopped paying. From my perspective, no one was truly considering the best interest of the patient, and this certainly seemed true for my mother.

Although finding the right transitional care has a profound impact on the success of recovery, the family is given practically no time to make arrangements. I came to call the process of being discharged from the hospital "scraping us off their shoe." We asked about all the options available for Mother's continued care. Marie had already done a lot of research on our rights and insisted that Mother wasn't discharged until we had a workable plan. None of this was easy.

We decided that removing Mother from her familiar setting and separating her from her beloved cat would have a devastating effect on her quality of life. Marie arranged for her to receive her IV antibiotics at the assisted living facility. Medicare and her insurance would only pay for inpatient skilled nursing, so I hired Lee. We paid her what we would have paid a service to administer the IVs. I was able to help Lee out financially in her time of need, and Mother had the added comfort of being able to visit with her eldest daughter twice a day. It was a win-win situation and the only positive outcome of her ordeal.

16 *Another Step Down*

Mother had a peripherally inserted central catheter (or picc line) surgically placed prior to her release from the hospital. This allowed intravenous access on a long-term basis. We arranged for a pharmaceutical company to deliver the medication and supplies. The IV antibiotic had to be administered every twelve hours for the next two months. Lee showed up every morning after working the night shift at the hospital, and came twice a day on weekends and days off.

When Lee wasn't available, we hired a nurse from a local service to administer the antibiotic. Mother was so weak that she was unusually compliant and complained very little. Sometimes she touched the picc line, which was inserted in her biceps and held by a soft, netted sleeve, but she never tried to remove it, and because she was so sick and disoriented, she was easily redirected. I found myself wishing for my cranky, obstinate mother to complain and fuss so I knew she would be OK.

The antibiotic was very harsh on Mother's system, and she soon lost her appetite, developed severe diarrhea, and started to lose weight. She was too weak and too sick to travel, so Dr. R came to her apartment for checkups. She helped us manage Mother's pain medication and prescribed an appetite stimulant to help her regain her appetite. The doctor arranged for a lab technician to come and take blood samples so she could monitor Mother's white count and sodium levels. Dr. R and I worked closely together. I kept her informed about what worked and what didn't, and she immediately adjusted the medication or changed the dose. She was always available and told us to page her, day or night, if we needed anything at all. I truly don't think Mother could have survived without the help and support of her doctor and the in-home care. Dr. R was a godsend and saved our family effort, stress, and worry. After so many bad experiences with doctors, it was a blessing to have a competent, accessible doctor who took our concerns seriously.

Marie and I spent nearly all of our free time taking care of our mother. I spent the night during the weekends, and Marie stayed overnight with her during the week. It was hard on us both, but Mother needed the help. She threw up frequently and needed constant encouragement to take sips of water, a bite of toast, or a sip of broth. Her assisted living facility didn't have the staff available to give Mother the constant attention she needed. We hired a caregiver to sit with Mother during the day, help her up and down, and encourage her to eat and drink. The facility's nursing staff kept the medications for us and delivered them to her apartment. They also took her blood pressure and temperature daily. Marie and I made dozens of batches of chicken soup, and delivered crackers, toast, popsicles, and ice cream, anything we thought she could keep down. I spiked her water with Pedialyte, which seemed to help.

Our efforts were rewarded because Mother did eventually recover. The picc line was removed, her appetite returned, and her health was restored. Life returned to a familiar routine, although she was profoundly deaf in her left ear. She could hear well out of her right ear, so I saw no reason to put her through any more surgeries or procedures. She didn't seem to mind the hearing loss, and life simply went on as before.

This experience taught us how tough our mother really was. She was never dizzy nor did she have trouble regaining her balance. The ear infection, which had lasted for many months, had been slowly destroying her equilibrium, so she had already adapted to her damaged inner ear well before her surgery. Thinking back, I recalled that she had been walking more slowly, leaning against things to put on her pants, or holding out her arm to catch her balance. Like everyone else, I attributed these behaviors to age and dementia, but it turned out to be a common and curable ear infection. I learned from this experience never to underestimate my mother.

Even though I did all that I could, I will always be tormented by this experience, wondering if there was something I missed that could have saved her from this avoidable tragedy. The cost was incalculable: Mother's deafness in her left ear, her suffering, tens of thousands of dollars of her money spent for her care, our time, lost income, lost productivity for my employer, and the additional unknown costs paid by Medicare and her insurance. Thankfully, her Alzheimer's allowed her to quickly forget the trauma of her ear infection, surgery, and lengthy recovery. Sometimes, she remembers the doctor that punctured her eardrum and says, "I'm not going back to him again!"

After Mother recovered from her infection and surgery, there were obvious signs that the ordeal had taken a toll on her cognitive abilities. She was more easily confused and even started to struggle with her cat food ritual. When I visited her, she would ask, "Do you know how I'm supposed to feed Honey? I can't quite remember how to do it. I want to do it just right. It is important to do it just right!"

Now an expert on the process, I gently guided her through the steps, exactly as she had done so many times before. I omitted the banging and swearing, and showed her how to use a knife to sculpt the food into a pointy mound. Mother was overjoyed. "That seems right! I don't know why I couldn't remember that. Thank you!"

She frequently forgot to change out of her raggedy inside clothes when she went down to meals. Some of the staff suggested that I throw her old clothes away so she wouldn't be tempted to wear them. I explained, "It's important to her to wear the same clothes every day because of her dementia. As long as she is decent, we are going to allow her to wear what is most comfortable for her."

Mother often forgot to clean Honey's litter box and starting hiding soiled litter in the cupboards again. I cleaned the litter box every time I visited, and Marie did, too. As long as we kept up with it, she didn't feel the need to hide it. Her ingrained routines became more difficult and she had more bad days than good. She even had trouble winding and setting her clock. Marie and I would find her clock broken or stuffed into a drawer. If it went missing, we looked for it, wound and set it, and put it by her bedside. If we found it broken, we replaced it with a similar clock, knowing she would become agitated if she couldn't find it or it didn't work. She left her apartment less and less, and I worried about her becoming depressed and isolated.

In addition to her normal delusions, forgetfulness, and bizarre and childish behaviors, she began having regular hallucinations, usually right around sunset. The hallucinations were more worrisome than her other behaviors. Mother always had a very active imagination and loved to point out the shapes of animals and faces in clouds, rock formations, or the wood grain of her furniture. One evening, Mother called and said, "Anita, there is a little kitty on top of the building across the street. I'm worried about it and don't know what I should do. It's on the roof and can't get down. It's holding out its little paw to me, begging me to come outside and rescue it. What should I do?"

Very concerned, I asked, "Just exactly how is it asking you?"

"I can see its little mouth moving, saying my name, and begging me to come and help it." This was a new behavior. I had to think fast and find a way to convince her she didn't need to go outside and rescue the cat. "We should leave it for the night, just in case its owner comes looking for it. The weather is warm, so it should be fine. I'll call the Humane Society first thing in the morning if someone hasn't already claimed their kitty." She wasn't sure that was the best idea, but when I convinced her to close her blinds, she forgot all about the imaginary stranded kitty. I didn't sleep well that night. Thankfully, when I called her in the morning, the kitty had been forgotten.

But the little kitty kept coming back. Mother called Marie or me every day, right around sunset, to report that there was a kitty on the rooftop, begging to be rescued. I timed my next visit so I could be with her just before sunset, to see what might be causing this hallucination. As the sun went down, I watched her as she prepared to close her blinds. She immediately pointed and said, "Oh look, right over there. It's a little orange and white kitty. Can you see it?"

I looked and saw light and shadow on a building across the street. "I see it, too," I said. I needed to redirect her without making her feel like she was seeing things. I made a show of looking closely, and then said, "Wow, when I look a little closer, it's not a kitty at all. It's an orange light on the building behind a tree! Would you look at that? If I didn't know better, I would have thought it was a cat. Whew, what a relief! Now I won't have to worry."

I was successful for a while, giving her the same explanation whenever she called about the kitty. Marie always told her the same story, and we hoped that if she heard it enough times, it would eventually stick. However, Mother no longer wanted to accept our explanation, and her hallucination became stronger. "I saw some young bullies climb up a ladder and place a box of kittens on the roof!"

I had to think fast. "I know. How terrible! It's a good thing we called the Humane Society and they came to rescue them." I alerted the staff at her facility and made sure they knew what to say in case she asked about the poor kitty on the roof. I learned that many dementia patients, including my mother, suffer from sundowning, a drastic change in behavior that happens right around sunset. We had taken one more step down into the darkness of her dementia.

I was glad when it was time for our annual visit with Mother's neurologist. I looked forward to discussing her memory changes and my concerns about her hallucinations and sundowning. However, it was a much more difficult visit than it had been in the past. The neurologist had left his private practice and joined one of the large medical groups in the area. His new office was located in a building that housed many different doctors and specialists. It was difficult to find parking, even with a handicap permit. I needed Lyle's help so that he could drop Mother and me off at the front door, while he searched for a parking space. Dropping Mother off alone or walking a long distance were not options.

The neurologist's office was located on the basement level, and we had to walk quite a distance and take an elevator to get there. The trek confused and agitated Mother. When we finally arrived, I sat Mother where I could see her, and stood in line to check her in. The receptionist asked for the usual paperwork and identification, but then insisted that Mother come to the counter and identify herself. Really? I thought. We had seen the same neurologist for almost seven years, yet we had to prove who we were. It was a large clinic and I am sure they had to follow strict guidelines on identification for insurance and Medicare, but it made me feel like we were only a number and our only importance was a monetary one. I let out an exasperated sigh and retrieved Mother. "What are we doing? Are we leaving?" she said hopefully.

"No, they need to take a look at you and make sure you are who we say you are."

She looked disgusted. "Why don't they goddamn know who I am? What the hell is wrong with them? Haven't I seen this doctor before? Do we like this place?"

"It's the same doctor, but he is in a newer clinic. Yes, we like this place. They must have a lot of people pretending to be someone else."

I walked Mother up to the counter, and the young woman looked at her and handed her ID back to me. "Thank you. The doctor is running late, and it could be half an hour to forty-five minutes before he can see you."

Great, I thought, a long wait with my agitated mother. I had lied to her. I didn't like this place at all. I did like the doctor, however, and accepted that we just had to endure the added burden of going through a gauntlet to see him. It made me wonder if doctors ever considered their patients' abilities, comfort, or convenience.

As we sat back down, Mother said, "I don't like it here! Why do we have to wait? Why am I here, anyway? This is an awful place!" Looking down, she said, "Even the carpet makes me mad!"

Surprised by her last statement, I looked down at the carpet and saw that it had a very busy, dark-colored, geometric pattern. Distorted depth perception was one of the hallmarks of Alzheimer's, so I could see why the carpet might cause her to be agitated. I distracted her by kissing her check, holding her hand, and looking her in the eye. "Lyle will be here soon. After your appointment, we'll all get to go have lunch."

"Oh good!" she said. "I'm not ready to go home yet. Do you have time to play?"

I smiled. "Yes, I have time to play!"

Lyle finally found a parking spot and joined us in the waiting room. Mother and I chatted and she kept asking, "Do we like this place?" I noticed an elderly gentleman had arrived to check his wife in, who was in a wheelchair and seemed to suffer from some type of dementia. The man looked a bit confused, frail, and wobbly himself, holding onto his wife's wheelchair for support. When asked to produce his wife's ID, he confessed that they had accidentally been left at home. The young woman refused to check him in, and offered to reschedule the appointment. Distraught, the elderly gentleman looked frustrated but didn't argue. He made another appointment and left with his wife. How sad, I thought. It was hard enough to get my mother here, and she can walk and I had help. Mother sensed my anger and said, "I hate it here. Would you just look at the god-awful carpet? Why can't we leave?"

In addition to the ID and insurance cards, I had handed the receptionist an envelope to give to the neurologist with a detailed update of Mother's condition. I included information about her ear infection, surgery, and long recovery. I also provided the details of her hallucinations. When our turn finally came, the neurologist said, "I'm not concerned that anything physical is causing her symptoms. She seems to have completely recovered from her surgery and her blood work doesn't indicate anything out of the ordinary." He smiled at Mother. "I wouldn't be too worried unless she begins wandering or seeing people who aren't there." I thought it was odd that he made a distinction between imaginary people and imaginary kittens, but I didn't challenge his remark.

Mother looked at me suspiciously, as if to say, "What the hell is he talking about?"

He was impressed with how well Mother was doing after her ordeal. After he performed the familiar cognitive and memory tests, he said, "Although she does have some notable losses, it truly is amazing how well she is doing, especially after her surgery." Frowning, Mother asked, "What surgery? What are you talking about?"

He said, "I'm just impressed by how well you have recovered from your ear infection."

"I didn't have an ear infection. I feel just fine!" She looked over at me and asked, "Did I have an ear infection?" She thought for a moment. "My ear is plugged up, though."

With a wide smile on his face, the neurologist turned to me. "Your mother is the first of my patients who has responded so well to the Aricept. It's doing exactly what it is prescribed to do. Increasing the dosage from five milligrams to ten milligrams should help. Sundowning is very common, and I expect it will continue. Most of my patients experience some form of sundowning, such as hallucinations, agitation, confusion, and sometimes more drastic behaviors." He said directly to Mother, "You're doing great! I'll look forward to seeing you next year."

The neurologist wasn't concerned about her hallucinations or her current living situation, but I was. Worried that she would try to leave the facility because of her hallucinations, I thought it was time to look into the next level of care for her. Eventually, she wouldn't be safe in her current living situation, and I didn't want to wait until the situation was dangerous. Her assisted living facility was able to assist with the tasks of daily living, such as meals, housekeeping, and administering medications, but it wasn't a locked facility. They weren't staffed to handle a person who would wander or became a fall risk. Although not as large as some of the corporate facilities I had visited, it still was a sizeable facility with many residents. I was already unimpressed with their inability to recognize my mother's memory impairment. The staff was minimal and poorly trained, but technically adequate, according to state requirements.

Marie introduced me to Barb, a registered nurse who worked for a company that specialized in the location of care facilities for the elderly. I was wary of this type of locating service, because most make their money from the finder's fees paid by the facilities they recommend. Would she steer her clients to the facility that best met their needs, or to the facility that paid the best finder's fees? My experiences with the healthcare industry had made me skeptical and distrusting, but I was forced to get help because my work schedule was demanding. I met with Barb and told her about Mother's condition, personality, and our requirements for her next home. I entrusted her with the task of helping us find an appropriate home, should her disease make her unable to continue living safely in the assisted living facility. I'm grateful that I trusted Marie's judgment, because Barb provided us with invaluable knowledge and support when we needed it most.

Barb introduced me to Sandra, who helped me hire caregivers. Sandra was a former nursing home director and was active in state politics, supporting the rights and needs of the elderly. I hired caregivers through Sandra's company to visit with Mother, to watch for rotten food, and to dispose of the cat litter properly. I also wanted someone to encourage her to spend more time outside of her apartment, and escort her to facility events, such as music recitals, bingo, or movie night. I knew if she had a friend and confidant, someone who could lead her, she would benefit greatly from the company. I would have loved to spend the extra time with her myself, but I was working hard and needed the income. Lyle had successfully made it through his prostate surgery and was recovering at home, but was unemployed.

I couldn't rely on Marie to fill in, because she was very busy with her own projects and caring for her mother-in-law, who had suffered a stroke and was more physically impaired than our mother. Initially, Marie's husband brought his mother to live with them at their home, but that arrangement was difficult for Marie, so Tom moved her to the same assisted living facility as Mother. Tom's mother needed more care than the assisted living facility could provide, and was soon moved to a local adult family home. It seemed that Tom fully expected Marie to care for his mother, but I saw little evidence that he helped take care of hers in the same way.

Unfortunately, Mother continued to see that darn kitty across the street, and no amount of reassurance satisfied her. She wanted to go out and rescue the kitty at all hours of the night. I alerted the head nurse to my concerns that she was exit-seeking, which is a common but dangerous behavior for someone with Alzheimer's. I knew that by sharing my concerns, the nurse may decide they could no longer care for her and might evict her. The same thing happened to Marie's mother-in-law, when she wandered out of the facility and onto a busy highway. Thankfully, she was returned safely, but shortly after the incident, Tom was notified that they would no longer be able to care for his Mother and gave him two weeks to find a more suitable place for her to live. It seemed we all had our own battles to fight.

The head nurse didn't seem concerned by my mother's behavior. Instead, she promised to watch her more carefully, and added an additional check right around sunset. Unfortunately, an e-mail that I sent to confirm our modified schedule was unclear, and actually communicated that the facility should stop doing their morning checks. I wish someone had mentioned that my request didn't make sense, since I had been expressing concern over potentially life-threatening wandering behavior.

17 *Then We All Fell Down*

Shortly after I expressed my concerns that Mother may wander, I received the call I had been dreading. In mid-October 2012, at two-thirty in the morning, I received a call from a paramedic. I didn't wake up in time to answer the phone, but heard the message on my answering machine and my groggy mind deduced that it must be an emergency. I grabbed the phone and quickly hit redial. I identified myself and the paramedic said, "Your mother has fallen, and it appears that she has most likely broken her hip. She is in a lot of pain, and one leg is shorter than the other. She is stable and alert and asked me to call you." The last part surprised me. I was the emergency contact at her facility, and had assumed they would contact me regarding any emergency. It was odd that Mother would have to ask someone to call me. Why had no one from her facility notified me about her accident? I put that thought aside and carefully listened to where the paramedics would be transporting my mother. Lyle and I hurriedly got dressed and rushed to meet Mother at the same emergency room where she'd had her transfusion years before.

When we arrived, I was relieved to see a large, new, quiet, and orderly emergency room. Gone was the chaos, noise, dilapidation of the past. Lyle sat down and I waited just outside Mother's treatment room until the nurses were done inserting a catheter. She was in pain. I could hear her crying out and the nurses reassuring her that the doctor would be in soon and would give her something for the pain. Mother asked, "Would it be OK if I swear? I know a lot of really bad words and I really want to use them right now!"

"Sweetheart, you can swear as much as you want. We've heard all the bad words and then some!" Mother was being very cooperative, but her voice sounded more like a child than an eighty-three-year-old woman.

My heart ached and I was anxious to get into the treatment room to comfort her. Once the catheter was inserted, the two nurses, one male and one female, allowed me into the room. Mother was relieved when she saw me. Once the nurses left and we were alone, she looked at me forlornly and said, "I have to pee!"

"You have a catheter in. All you need to do is relax. You don't even have to get up."

She became angry. "I know that, but it's not right and I'm going to pee the bed!"

I couldn't find a call button, so I looked out into the hall. I flagged down the male nurse and said, "Something seems to be wrong with Mother's catheter."

He lifted the blanket, checked her catheter, and as he covered her up, he patted her hand. "You need to relax, sweetheart, and just pee. Your catheter is just fine."

After he left, she just kept saying, "I have to go pee. Why won't someone help me?" I held her hand and repeated what the nurse had said. She was disgusted and frustrated. "All right, I'm going to pee the bed and it's not my fault. I don't want to get in trouble!" I could see her relax. "Are you happy? I peed the bed! What in the hell am I supposed to do now?"

She looked as if she could cry. The sheets were soaked. She was laying in urine, with a broken and displaced hip, her leg lying off to the side at a grotesque angle, and she'd had no pain medication. I frantically looked down the hall, but saw no one. It took five minutes for a nurse to come to her aid, but it felt like a lifetime. Mother not only had to be moved to change the bed covers and clean her, but the nurse also had to insert another catheter. I was sick with anguish and worry, but I kept a smile on my face and a soothing tone in my voice. "I love you and I will not leave you!"

She looked up at me, eyes swimming with tears and her voice weak, "Oh good, I'm glad. Please don't go! I don't know what I would do without you!" I thought, New look, same dysfunctional emergency room.

When the doctor finally came, he made us wait for X-rays before he prescribed pain medication, gave her an IV, stabilized her leg, or admitted her to the hospital. Once the doctor had the X-ray in hand, she was finally made more comfortable and moved to a hospital room. Marie had arrived and we were told that surgery would be scheduled later that morning or afternoon, depending upon how many cases were ahead of her. Knowing it would be a while before her surgery, Lyle and I decided to go home to clean up. I looked down at my feet and realized my shoes didn't match, one white and green canvas and the other leather with dark purple trim. I snorted out a quick laugh and briefly smiled as we made our way home.

Shortly after Lyle and I arrived home to change our clothes, wash up, and have a bite to eat, Mother's assisted living facility called. I assumed they were calling to follow up on her status, but the director said, "The head nurse is here with me on speaker phone. This is a call we hope to never have to make. Regrettably, we have lost track of your mother and have no idea where she is. We're calling you to report her missing from our facility." It was mid-October, and although the days were still warm, it was getting quite cold and damp at night. As far as they knew, my mother had been missing since two thirty that morning and could have been dead in a ditch, and they hadn't even notified the authorities.

I was livid, my voice tight and deadly. "I know where she is. Mother is in the hospital. She was taken by ambulance last night at two thirty from your facility with a badly broken leg and a displaced hip. How do you not know about this? I find it hard to believe that a full emergency response escaped the notice of your night staff. I assumed that your staff called 911. If it wasn't a member of your staff, who did? How do you not know about this? More importantly, why did it take so long to report her missing to me? You knew I was worried that she might wander away. I can't understand why you didn't alert someone sooner! If not me, the authorities should have been contacted!"

The director spoke in her familiar firm and authoritative tone. "We have two aides that worked the overnight shift, and our facility meets all state requirements. Our staff didn't report any incidents overnight. They must have been in another area of the building when the paramedics took your mother out. We did all that we could and are required to do. When your mother was absent from breakfast this morning, one of the dining room servers went to check her room. She wasn't there and her furniture was displaced. We searched the building and the grounds. That is our policy and protocol when a resident is missing. After we determined she was not on the property, we contacted you."

"That may be so," I said, with venom in my voice, "but you have a hole in your system and my mother just fell through it!" They promised to investigate and find out who called 911. My confidence in them was lost, but I decided I would let them do their internal investigation and would deal with them later. I had to get Mother out of the hospital alive before I could think about where it would be safe for her to live.

Lyle and I returned to the hospital and joined Marie in Mother's room, which was on the orthopedic floor. Like the emergency room, it was clean, orderly, and state-of-the-art. This floor wasn't just a repository for elderly patients, but serviced all who were getting hip or knee replacements, or who needed to have broken bones mended. Now this must be where the money is, I thought. We stayed by Mother's side as she waited for surgery. We were worried, but if anyone could get through this, it would be her. She was resilient. Once they gave her some pain medication and stabilized her leg and hip, she rested comfortably. The physician's assistant (PAC) came to examine Mother and tell us what time her surgery would be, barring any complications with the cases ahead of her. He was personable and approachable. I hadn't met the surgeon, so I asked, "What can you tell me about the surgeon? Does he have a lot of experience with this type of surgery?

The PAC smiled and gestured toward Mother. "This is our bread and butter!"

I wanted to say, "This is not bread and butter. This is Barbara." Instead, I held my tongue.

When it was time for the surgery, her bed was wheeled her out of the room, and Lyle, Marie, and I moved to the waiting area. Lee and Allen joined us, and we all anxiously awaited the outcome together. After about two hours, the surgery was complete, and the orthopedic surgeon came out and called my name. I reached out to shake his offered hand and thought that if he were as good a surgeon as he was good looking, Mother would be just fine. He was tall with a handsome face that seemed strong but gentle at the same time. His voice was deep and melodious. As he spoke, I was mesmerized. "Your mother's leg was broken and her hip was displaced. I have placed a steel rod in her leg to repair the break, and I relocated her hip. She was dehydrated and low on blood volume, but not so low that she will need a transfusion."

I thought, Or did you just not want to waste a precious resource on an older person? Instead, I said, "My mother has a history of severe anemia and is unable to rebuild red blood cells without iron therapy or other intervention."

He seemed to understand and reassured me, "I'll make sure we support all aspects of her recovery."

I was relieved that we had cleared this hurdle and hopeful that this exceptionally attractive surgeon was an omen of good luck.

Unfortunately, he was just a handsome actor with a bit part in the soap opera our lives were about to become.

I shared the information with my family and everyone relaxed a little, thankful that the surgery went well. Our hopes were high that she would recover from this. As soon as she was transferred to her room, we all went up to see her. We discussed who would spend the night, and arranged for a caregiver to come sit with her. We refused to leave her alone in the care of the hospital for any length of time.

When we got to her room, Mother had already arrived and a young male nurse and a nursing supervisor were working on getting her settled into her room. As soon as Mother caught sight of me she said, "I have to pee!" I was worried about an experience like the emergency room. The catheter bag was empty, so I expressed my concern to the supervisor. She just rolled her eyes and shot me a look that indicated she knew what she was doing. I wasn't convinced. Mother continued to complain about the urge to urinate, but there was still nothing in the bag.

"I am not convinced her catheter is in correctly. She has already had to suffer one accident because of an incorrectly placed catheter, and I'm not going to let that happen again. Can you please just check it for me?"

The supervisor was not pleased, and tersely said, "The only way to determine if her catheter is functioning properly is to do a bladder scan to see if there is urine in her bladder."

"Fine," I said. "Can you please do a bladder scan?"

She ordered the test, but her body language made it clear that she was not happy about it. The bladder scan confirmed that the catheter was properly placed, and eventually, Mother was able to relieve herself. The supervisor shot me a cold look as if to say, "I told you so!"

Mother was glad to have her family gathered around her and was resting comfortably. Just when I was starting to feel that things were going to be all right, the male nurse came in with some pills in a cup.

Lee stopped him. "What are those pills for?"

He looked surprised, and said, "These are her pain medications."

"Can you please hold all oral medications? It would be better if you could give her medication through her IV, at least for tonight. She hasn't had anything to eat or drink for almost twenty-four hours and is still recovering from the anesthesia. Giving her something orally will only make her vomit." Our mother had a very sensitive stomach, so Marie and I both agreed and stood with Lee.

The nurse looked inconvenienced and aggravated, and left in a huff. The supervisor came in shortly after and in a stern voice, barked, "We cannot provide intravenous drugs without doctor's orders. It's something we just cannot do!"

"If that's the case, can you please call the doctor and ask him for the orders?" I repeated what Lee had told the nurse, about wanting to avoid making Mother vomit.

The supervisor grudgingly replied, "I will contact the doctor, if he's still available!" When she returned, she had a syringe and administered the pain medication through the IV. She left the room without looking in our direction.

Later, the male nurse returned with another cup of pills, this time larger pills. Surprised to see more pills despite our request, we asked why he'd brought them. He refused to look us in the eye and continued to approach Mother. "These are her iron and prenatal vitamins. The doctor ordered these to treat her anemia."

I said, "We don't want our mother to vomit. Please hold all oral medications, at least for tonight!"

Lee added, "No oral medications until tomorrow or until she has had something to eat and drink and we know she can hold it down."

The nurse just set his jaw and gave her the pills anyway. Our mouths dropped open in shock. He turned his back on our stunned expressions while he typed information into a computer.

Minutes later, Mother cried out, "I'm sick, I'm sick. I'm going to throw up!"

He didn't move a muscle, and just kept typing information into the computer. I found a basin and held it for her while she vomited up the pills and very little else, her body convulsing with dry heaves. Without looking in our direction, he quietly said, "I will bring something for the nausea," and left the room. The stage was set for a battle. Lee, Marie, and I were angry and upset, and dug our heels in to protect our mother from those who were more interested in policy and pride than common sense and a high standard of care.

I was exhausted. Marie and Lee said, "We can handle this! You're not needed here. We can take care of Mother. Go home and get some rest." They had a point; it had been a long day. Marie was going to spend the night and Lee was a nurse. Mother was in good hands. As Lyle and I left, I could hear them talking loudly about the stupidity of the male nurse and that he had no idea who he was dealing with. I had a sinking feeling that this was only the beginning of our trouble with the nursing staff.

The following morning, I got a call from Marie. "I've just had a conversation with the physician's assistant. He says that Mother will be released in three days because that was all that Medicare and her insurance allowed for this type of surgery. Mother isn't going to be able to go home and will need intensive inpatient rehabilitation. I think I scared him a bit because I let him know that they would have to prove to me that Mother was medically fit before she was released, and that we would have to approve of the rehabilitation facility before we allow her to be discharged. I don't think he liked my tone, but he just kept telling me we had three days and wouldn't listen, so I gave him a piece of my mind. I'm just too upset. I was hoping that you could talk to the social worker. I don't know what the physician's assistant might have said to her, but maybe you could tell her that I'm not a crazy, unreasonable person. We just want to make sure that Mother has the care she needs to recover."

She gave me the name and number of the social worker. "I'm happy to help. I'll call her and let her know that we only want what's best for our mother. You're doing your best and there is nothing wrong with that. It's not your fault that it is so damn hard to arrange appropriate care! We're all tired and stressed out because of what happened last night with the damn nurses."

Next, I called the social worker. I explained our position and she understood. However, she told me, "I will be out for several days, and another social worker will be in charge of your mother's case. You'll need to meet with her." She arranged to have her meet with me later that afternoon.

When I arrived at the hospital after work, I sat down with the social worker, a thin woman in her early sixties. Her face was hard and deeply lined, as if she had spent too many days in the sun or had suffered greatly in her life. She looked angry and tired, and I didn't have a good feeling about our relationship. She handed me a list of approved care facilities, and in a voice that left little room for argument, said, "Your mother will be released in three days. Because you and your sister have insisted, here is a list of facilities you can choose from. There are very few inpatient facilities in our area, and most don't have beds available due to high demand."

"Thank you for the list. Can you tell me anything about these facilities? Is one perhaps a better choice than another?"

She looked at me blankly. "We cannot advise; we can only provide a list of state-licensed facilities in the area. The rest is up to you." I took a brief look at the list, which was short and not very promising. I had wrongly assumed that she would be helpful. I took the list, thanked her for her time, and went to visit Mother.

Marie wasn't with Mother, but a nurse was in her room. I immediately noticed that her oxygen had been removed. I asked the nurse, "Why has Mother been taken off her oxygen?"

Irritated, she said, "She needs to be weaned off oxygen before her release. She has been on room air all day and is doing fine."

I didn't think she looked fine at all. She was slumped in a recliner near her bed. Her feet were up, but her head was down and she was unable to lift it to greet me, barely registering that I was even there. "She looks terrible. Can you please check her oxygen level?"

The oxygen sensor had been removed from her finger. The nurse said in a very condescending manner, "Well, the family is always right. To satisfy you, I will check. You will see that her oxygen level is fine." When she placed the sensor on Mother's finger, an alarm immediately sounded. The monitor indicated that her oxygen saturation was only 84 percent, much too low. The nurse looked surprised and quickly put her oxygen back on. She checked Mother's pulse and blood pressure, and it wasn't long until her oxygen level perked up to 94 percent.

She was able to hold her head up and looked much more alert. She smiled, pleased to see me. "Have I been taking a nap?"

Great, I thought, why don't you starve a person suffering from a brain disease of oxygen. I'm sure that will help! I gave Mother a big hug and replied, "Yes, you were having a little nap." The physician's assistant came into the room to check on Mother. She smiled at him as he examined her leg. The nurse, still concerned, told the assistant, "She is not doing well on room air and became hypoxic. Her O2 sats fell to 84."

The assistant looked unconcerned and was dismissive. "You need to notify the doctor in charge of her care. I'm only here for her orthopedic needs."

The nurse looked me in the eye as she said, "I will chart the problem with her oxygen levels and notify her doctor."

As if things hadn't been bad enough, at the evening shift change I could hear the nurses talking outside Mother's door about the "patient's irregular heart rate and decreased lung capacity." I assumed they were talking about Mother, but that was the first I had heard of either of those conditions. When the nurse came in, I asked, "Does my mother have an irregular heartbeat and difficulty breathing?"

She had a strange look on her face as she said, "Whatever you think you heard, I was discussing a different patient." Later, the doctor confirmed that Mother had indeed developed an irregular heartbeat and her lung capacity was diminished. I was dumbfounded by the treatment my mother was receiving. I stayed until Marie arrived for the overnight shift, and told her what had happened. Like me, she was stunned and angry.

On the second day, the orthopedic surgeon came to evaluate her for her impending release. I asked him, "If my mother has decreased lung capacity, why was she not given any breathing exercises after surgery? Do you know what is causing her irregular heartbeat? Is that normal? Should I be worried? No one seems to be all that concerned, and I want to know why."

The surgeon was surprised. "I ordered lung exercises immediately after the surgery. She should have been given a special tool to blow into that would help increase her lung function."

"Well," I said, "she hasn't received that or anything like it."

He looked perplexed. "I'll see to it that my orders are carried out immediately. I'm not sure what caused the miscommunication, but I guarantee I will talk to the nursing staff about it."

His handsome face no longer mesmerized me. I just wanted him to do his job. "I'm not sure if your assistant informed you, but when Mother was taken off oxygen, her saturation was only 84 percent. When I came to visit yesterday, I found Mother off her oxygen. The nurse told me she was doing fine on room air, and I had to insist that she check oxygen levels. I may not know a lot about medicine, but I do know that levels that low are not good. My mother is already suffering from a brain illness, and the treatment she has received unacceptable. If my mother is discharged too early and boomerangs back here, I will file a complaint with the Department of Health."

He assured me that she wouldn't be discharged too soon. He felt her condition warranted another day's stay, and said he would put in the request. Although I was unimpressed by the quality of care, I was glad to have one more day to determine if Mother was medically fit for discharge. I knew if she were discharged too early, she would only have to be hospitalized again. We also had an extra day to find the best rehabilitation facility.

On the third day, the social worker demanded to know why I hadn't selected a facility yet. I said, "Mother is not doing well on room air, and the surgeon feels another day before discharge is appropriate. My sister and I are still trying to find a skilled nursing facility. We're evaluating all of our options before we select one." Marie had narrowed the search to a few facilities, and was trying to determine if any of them had a bed available. She'd heard that one might be available the next day, and we were holding out hope that it would be free before Mother's discharge.

The social worker was dissatisfied with my answer. "I gave you the list of facilities that had beds available. You have to pick one. Your mother will be discharged according to my schedule, and you must pick a facility immediately!"

I just sighed and smiled patiently. "You might want to check with the surgeon. He feels she is not medically fit for discharge and we have one more day to figure this out."

She had fire in her eyes. "I'll do that!" she said, and turned on her heel and left.

On the fourth day, Mother was still on oxygen, and we hadn't been given an explanation about why her heartbeat was irregular. She still had not yet had a bowel movement. Despite all this, she was going to be discharged. With a malicious gleam in her eye, the social worker said, "All the facilities on the list no longer have beds available. There is only one left, and that is where your mother will go!" It was the worst of the lot, and I knew we would never send our mother there. Marie, who is very prominent in the community, checked with her friends that served on the executive boards or worked in administration at some of the facilities. Many reported that the social worker had called all the skilled nursing facilities in the area and told them that our mother had problem behaviors so severe she required sitters, and that the family was difficult and unmanageable. We had been blacklisted!

Frantically, Marie made some calls and was able to convince one of the facilities that Mother did not have any problem behaviors. Thankfully, they had a bed available. It was close to my home, and we couldn't find a reason not to place her there. Marie promised that our hired sitters were for comfort measures only, and that Mother's Alzheimer's disease made her afraid and a fall risk unless someone was there to comfort her and press the call light for her. The social worker was sullen when she found out we were taking Mother to a facility she had warned about us. She smugly informed me, "Your mother will need to be transported by cabulance because she is unable to get in and out of a car. It will cost around one hundred dollars, and Medicare and insurance will not cover it." She smiled a bit, seeming to take some perverse pleasure in this news.

Prior to her release, Marie and I expressed a final concern to the nurse, as there were no doctors to be found. "Mother has not had a bowel movement in over four days. Why has something not been done about this?"

"She should have had a bowel movement by now. I'll give her a strong, fast-acting laxative before the van gets here. That should take care of the problem." Marie and I believed that giving her a laxative before loading her up in a van was a terrible idea, and refused the medication. Instead, the nurse wrote orders for the skilled nursing facility to begin the laxative upon her admittance, which made much more sense.

Mother was still on oxygen, so I asked the nurse if we were going to get an oxygen bottle to transport with her. "I have no orders to discharge her with oxygen," the nurse said.

"Well, I guess we're not going anywhere, then!" Frowning, the nurse turned and disappeared down the corridor. Soon, an orderly delivered a portable oxygen tank and the cabulance driver arrived. Mother got dressed and the nurse helped her into a wheelchair with the oxygen bottle mounted to the back. The cabulance driver wheeled her out of the room, with Marie, Lyle, and I following behind. He locked her chair safely into the cabulance, which was nothing more than an old van fitted to accommodate a wheelchair.

Marie and I were exhausted from the stress, worry, and the

unnecessary battles to get Mother the care that she not only deserved, but that Medicare and her insurance were paying a lot of money for. We were still reeling from the social worker's inexcusable actions and personal vendetta against us. I had lost faith in all hospital social workers, based upon our experiences so far. I tend to see things in black and white, just and unjust, and I often forget to see the many shades of gray and consider the motivations of others. Perhaps that social worker was burned out, tired of always being the bearer of bad news and being stuck in impossible positions with the families she tried to help. Maybe I'd just crossed her path during a rough time in her life. Something in the system was broken, and I knew it was unfair of me to place all the blame on her. She was near the bottom of the totem pole, as were the nurses. This problem was systemic, a management issue that started at the top and worked its way down. That hospital suffered from a chronic lack of communication, not only with the patients and families, but also between the surgeon, doctors, nurses, and social workers. I did not envy her position and tried to forgive her for the trouble she caused us. I still couldn't wrap my brain around the hostile attitude of the entire hospital staff toward a family that was just advocating for adequate care for their mother. We always tried to be professional, polite, calm, and informed, and didn't ask for anything unreasonable. We made notes of our experiences and planned to file a complaint. I put our hospital experience on the back burner and focused on getting Mother settled into the skilled nursing facility, and hopefully, on the road to recovery.

Mother faced a long road, full of challenges. The odds of regaining a good quality of life after such a devastating injury were stacked against her due to her age and dementia. However, Marie and I were not ready to count her out. We promised each other that we would do our very best to help her recover if she had the will and determination to fight her way back. We knew that our mother would do her part; it was now up to us to do ours.

It felt as if a tremendous weight was lifting off my shoulders as we left the hospital on that bright and sunny October day. I hoped that I would never have to see the inside of that hospital again. I imagined the ads I had recently seen for that very hospital on TV and plastered on city buses, slick ads that showed doctors eager to prescribe this hospital for their patients and even themselves. I thought that maybe it was a good hospital if you aren't elderly or have dementia, but I doubted it.

After all we had been through, Marie and I were no longer willing to be silent or accept the broken system without trying to change it. Our mother had received substandard care and had been treated unfairly. If we don't speak up, others will suffer the same fate and nothing will ever change. Our experiences made me think: What would happen to me if I got Alzheimer's and broke my hip? I have no children and I'm not as financially secure as my mother. Lyle is considerably older than I am, so it is highly likely that I won't have an advocate. If I am lucky enough to achieve old age, I will be at the mercy of a broken healthcare system. Has it ever truly worked properly?

I believe in personal responsibility and expect no one to care for or care about me. It is my responsibility to take care of myself physically, mentally, emotionally, and financially. However, what happened to Mother taught me that even if I do everything right, there are no guarantees. If I became vulnerable, there was a very good chance that I wouldn't receive humane or adequate care. This thought frightened me and ignited the spark to shed some light on the flawed system that failed my mother miserably. I had to let go of my anger over our experiences, unwilling to put what little energy I had into complaining. I hoped that we had just been unlucky; I didn't want to believe that such a substandard level of care is the norm. I didn't want our experience to be swept under the rug of convenience and denial, or worse yet, washed away in the vast sea of Alzheimer's statistics. I had already learned the hard way that what you don't know would hurt you. It wasn't easy or convenient for Marie or me to take action, having so much to deal with already. It would have been easier to walk away and accept that there was nothing more to do. Our burden was already heavy and our sorrow deep.

18 *Into the Welcoming Arms of Our Worst Nightmare*

When we arrived at the skilled nursing facility, where Mother would spend the next three weeks of her life, we were greeted with open arms and a caring attitude, which was a refreshing change from the hospital. The facility was actually a part of a local nursing home with one wing dedicated to skilled nursing and concentrated physical therapy for those who were discharged from the hospital but were too weak or ill to go home. Marie and Mother arrived before us, and when Lyle and I arrived, we were greeted warmly by one of the admission coordinators. She introduced herself and said, "I've already met your sister Marie, and she and I have also spoken on the phone. She told me about your experiences at the hospital. I'm truly sorry about what you've had to go through. This is never easy, even when things go as they should!"

Her kind face and the empathy in her voice made me start to cry. She held out her arms and I sobbed on her shoulder. When I regained my composure, she handed me a tissue and said, "Are you ready to see your mother? I'm sure they have her all checked in by now." I nodded, Lyle took my hand, and we were led into the skilled nursing wing.

I examined the lobby, hallways, and nurses' stations along the way, and it was all as I had imaged it would be: shabby, old, and worn, much like the people who inhabited the building. It was faded and dingy, showing signs of age and hard use, merely a shadow of what it used to be. I took a deep breath and told myself the only thing that mattered was the care that Mother would receive. I hoped that she would benefit from the staff's experience with caring for the elderly and those with dementia. Despite my optimism, I had a sense of foreboding as I walked through that depressing place and to the room that she would call home for the next three weeks.

We were led past a row of elderly patients, all lined up in their wheelchairs against a wall and left to wait. A nurse at the head of the sad procession stood in front of a mobile medicine cart with a computer screen and keyboard. She was busy tapping in information, unlocking and locking the drawers that held medications, and popping pills into paper cups. There were patient rooms on each side of the wide hall, with two beds per room. Pictures of the inhabitants of each room hung on the wall next to the room number. We passed by two Barbaras, a Barbara Jean, and an Alice before we got to the last room at the end of the hall, where I saw a sad snapshot of Mother, another Barbara. Wow, I thought, that picture doesn't even look like her. Next to her picture was a photo of her roommate, Bea. Mother could have been any of the sad and faded people in the mug shots lining the hall, all the hope drained out of the faces in the shiny photos. My hope sunk a little lower.

The admissions coordinator left us as we walked into the dark, narrow room and past Bea, an elderly lady with a large cast on her foot. The curtain was drawn between her and Mother's bed, which was by the window. Mother was lying in bed, with a drab and dingy blanket drawn to her chest. She still was on oxygen, but instead of a modern oxygen tank, she was hooked up to an odd beast of a machine. It was short and squat and was chugging and belching out what I hoped was oxygen. It looked more like a dirty old relic than a piece of medical equipment. I wondered how she would ever get any sleep with that thing rumbling next to her bed.

The room was sparse with an ancient TV perched atop an old and scarred wooden nightstand. A slightly mismatched night-stand sat near Mother's bed with a lamp and a phone. There was a bright fluorescent light over her bed with a pull chain, and a bulletin board with instructions. She was not to bend at the waist, and should always press the call light for assistance with getting up and down.

Barb was there and chatted with Mother while Marie was away filling out more paperwork. She had been providing us with information and moral support throughout our hospital stay and had come to visit Mother to offer encouragement. Sandra, the owner of the company that sent caregivers, arrived a few minutes later. Barb and Sandra promised to see to it someone stayed the night with Mother, even if it was one of them. They insisted that Marie and I go home and get some rest. Mother was exhausted from the move and didn't seem distressed by the idea of us leaving. Marie and I took their generous advice. Marie planned to visit in the morning, and we would make further plans when I got off work the next day.

We left Mother in the care of that sad and dreary place for the evening. It was dark when we left. The weather was forecasted to turn cold with the promise of rain and the long, wet winter ahead. The warmth of the sun had given way to the cold and dark. The forecast mirrored how I felt in the depth of my soul. It was difficult to see how she was ever going to recover from this. I wondered if we had the strength to keep fighting for basic, simple, humane treatment for our mother. We didn't ask for anything other than appropriate care for her condition, respect, and to allow us, her family who loved her, to provide her with comfort, love, and support. The cost of her so-called "care" came at a high price, but the quality of the aftercare she had received so far didn't come close to justifying the cost. We not only had to fight a debilitating disease but also a healthcare system that seemed designed to work against everything we were fighting for. I cried myself to sleep that night, and prayed to God to give me the strength to handle whatever was to come. Lee lived a long distance away, worked nights, and struggled to make ends meet, so it wasn't a surprise when she faded back into her life. It would be a very long time until I saw her again.

I went to work early the next day so I could leave early and meet Marie at the skilled nursing facility. I called Sandra and Barb before I left the house that morning, and we agreed that, much like the hospital, this facility was not prepared to care for the special needs of a dementia patient. During the day, I traded phone calls with Marie and Sandra and we mapped out a plan to hire sitters to be with Mother when Marie and I weren't there. At the end of my workday, I headed over to the skilled nursing facility with a heavy heart. It was less than five miles from where I lived, a small blessing.

I had an awful sinking feeling in my gut as soon as I entered the building. I made my way through the dingy hallway and past the same sad line of elderly patients. Bea's photo was no longer outside the room, leaving a blank space next to Mother's pathetic snapshot, and her empty bed confirmed that she was gone. The curtain was pulled back, and Mother sat in a wheelchair and watched TV with Marie. She looked weak and in pain but smiled at me. I kissed her on the cheek as I asked, "How are things going?"

"I just pressed the call light," Marie said. "We're waiting for the aide. Mother isn't supposed to get up and down by herself. I was told that we always need to call for help when she needs to go to the restroom or get into bed." Mother was uncharacteristically silent, as Marie went on, "She had speech and physical therapy today. I really liked her therapists and Mother did very well. Everyone just loved her!"

Mother gave a small snort as if to say, "Yeah, right!" I smiled, glad for the bit of good news that her therapy was going well. An aide arrived shortly after me, a young man with smooth skin and a broad smile. I later learned that he was from Ethiopia and was training to be a nurse. He wheeled mother into the restroom, and Marie indicated that we should go outside the room to talk.

We went to the family conference and recreation room near Mother's room. It had a sofa and two loveseats in front of a TV, and there was a conference table with eight chairs on the other side of the room. The windows overlooked a yard with a beautiful cluster of trees covered in brilliant orange and yellow leaves that still clung to the branches. The leaves almost glowed with the vibrancy of their color. How beautiful and odd that something dying can look so full of life, I thought. Lost in thought as I looked out the window, I thought of Mother in the autumn of her life. I hoped, like these trees, she would once again come back to life in the spring, but I worried that this was the last time the seasons would change for her. Marie started talking and brought me back down to earth.

We discussed the arrangements I had made to ensure someone was with Mother around the clock. Although Marie was pleased with the physical therapy, she agreed with Sandra and Barb that the facility was understaffed and the aides were overwhelmed. I would visit Mother each day from four thirty until nine o'clock, and a hired caregiver would relieve me and stay overnight for twelve hours. Her regular caregiver would come in the morning at nine, and leave at twelve thirty. Marie would arrive at one o'clock and stay for a few hours until I could get there. After we made our plans, Marie told me that Bea had requested a different room after the noisy and dilapidated oxygen pump had kept her up all night. I wasn't surprised.

We had no reason to distrust anyone. The facility's mission was a good one and the staff seemed caring. Mother would be afraid, a fall risk, and needed to have someone with her almost constantly. Her therapy wouldn't be successful if we didn't support her in this way. The cost of the hired sitters was high, but we felt that this was her only chance to recover. The irony that we had to hire people to care for Mother while she was in a skilled nursing facility was not lost on me. I wondered if the level of care a dementia patient could expect to receive had always been this lacking. Whatever the reason, we knew that the facility didn't have the staff to keep our mother safe. Without someone by her side, I knew exactly how the events would unfold. Alone and confused, she would try to get up on her own because she couldn't remember to press her call light. She would fall and re-injure her leg. Without someone there to explain what had happened and provide comfort, she would become fearful, try to escape, or become combative. These behaviors would lead the staff to give her tranquilizers or antipsychotic drugs to keep her under control, which would only hinder her ability to actively participate in her physical therapy. Without productive physical therapy, she would never leave this awful place. At least we're getting value for the money we are spending, I thought. It was, after all, Mother's money. Her hard work and sacrifice produced that money, and I could think of no better use for it than to support her recovery.

After Marie left, I sat with Mother and tried to orient her to her surroundings. No longer able to remember her fall, she said, "What the hell happened to me that I ended up here? I don't understand."

"You fell and broke your leg, and then you went to the hospital to repair it. Now you're here to get strong so you can go home again."

"I don't remember any of that. My leg hurts and I am so goddamn uncomfortable sitting in this chair!" I could see why – her feet dangled limply, and the footrests on her wheelchair could not be adjusted. I wondered why her broken leg hadn't been elevated. Her room didn't have a recliner, so her options were a wheelchair or a hard hospital bed with shabby covers and a thin, flat mattress. How anyone ever got well here was a mystery.

She wanted to know where Honey was and kept frantically asking about her. I wrote, "Honey is at the vet's house," on her white board next to the name of her nurse and the time dinner was served. "Oh good," she said. "The vet always loved her." Happily, I listened to her old story about the vet's special bond with Honey.

At five fifteen, the nice aide I meet earlier came in. In a singsong accent, he said, "It's time to go to dinner now, Miss Barbara."

Mother frowned and pointed at the white board. "It says dinner's at six. Why are we leaving now?"

"It's my job to get all of my patients to the dining room, and we need to get an early start. Do you need to use the restroom before we go?" She did, so he helped her. When they were finished, he wheeled her out of the room, down the hall, and past the familiar lineup.

We rounded the corner and saw a dining room with several elderly people in wheelchairs pushed up to square tables. There wasn't an aide in sight. The patients sat at the tables alone, waiting. Some had their heads down on the table and slept. Nearly all of them looked drugged or depressed. With sadness, I recognized a woman with her head down and a slack-mouthed, gaping frown. She had lived at the same assisted living facility as Mother. I knew she suffered from dementia but lacked family support. I frequently overheard her son scold or correct her, and I had recoiled at the anger and disdain in his voice when he became frustrated with her memory loss. His cruelty caused her to cry or become angry and hostile. Her peers at the assisted living facility had shunned her because she was difficult and always angry, crying, or acting inappropriately. I even avoided contact with her when I could help it, never quite knowing how to soothe her and having my hands full already. Mother surprised me one day when this lady approached with her fists clenched, looking for a fight. Instead of reacting negatively, Mother gave her a hug, kissed her on her forehead, and said, "You poor dear. It will all work out in the end. Just you wait!"

Sadly, things hadn't worked out well for this poor lady at all. Hoping this wasn't our dining room, I was relieved as the aide wheeled Mother to another dining room down the hall. He pushed her up to a table and told us that the front section was for rehabilitation patients and the back section was for nursing home residents. After he got her settled, he darted off to bring in the next patient.

Mother had an oxygen tank strapped to the back of her wheel-chair, and it gave little puffs of oxygen into her nose through a clear plastic nasal tube, with an intermittent puff and hiss. I heard this same noise throughout the room, an oxygen symphony. It seemed that all the people in the front of the room were in various states of disrepair, old, broken, bruised, pale, and vulnerable. We sat for some time before everyone had arrived and dinner was served.

Mother wasn't hungry. There were only two choices for dinner: a hamburger or a plain turkey sandwich with mayonnaise, both heavy and unappealing. I ordered her a burger but also asked, "Do you have any Jell-O or ice cream?"

The aide looked stressed as he told me, "We're out of Jell-O and ice cream today. The delivery truck didn't come. I can get your Mother some tea or some soup." I requested soup and was able to get her to eat some of the broth, but not much. I ate her burger, which was a huge mistake, similar to the one I had made when I helped her answer questions during her memory test. Of course, no one had told me, but the aides were writing down what percentage of the meal their patients had consumed, as well as what they had to drink. The information about food and fluid intake was used to make treatment decisions. I told the aide what I had done and he showed me how to purchase a meal ticket at the reception desk.

After dinner, the aide dropped her off in the sad line of people, then left to fetch someone else. Mother was angry. "Why the hell did he stop here? I want to go to my room." She was in pain and wanted to lie down. She didn't want to be out in the hall, and I understood why. It was after sunset, and some of the patients were moaning or crying out for help, lost and confused with no one to answer their questions.

An elderly woman with claw-like hands was reaching out for the nurse, tugging on her uniform and yelling, "I have to poop! Someone needs to help me now! I don't want to crap my pants, damn it!" The nurse did a phenomenal job of ignoring her, as if this type of thing happened regularly. Great, I thought, I'll always be visiting at sunset when everyone is sundowning, including Mother. The thought of having to deal with this every night was daunting and my hopes sunk a little further.

At the end of the line, a very tiny woman, dressed in a nightgown with wild eyes and even wilder hair, kept trying to get up and walk away from her wheelchair, but the oxygen tube around her neck tethered her to the chair. The only staff nearby was the overwhelmed nurse trying to pass out medication to the growing line of patients. At the nurses' station, a board full of call lights flashed and beeped. None of the nurses or aides that were darting around paid any attention to the board or the tiny woman. I noticed that the little lady was just about to reach the end of her tether and fall to the floor. I rushed over to her, holding out my arm, caught her before she fell, and helped her back into her chair. The nurse, suddenly interested, thanked me and moved the tiny lady closer to her cart. If I hadn't intervened, would the nurse have allowed her to fall?

I returned to Mother and when she complained, I said, "We need to wait here for your pain medication."

That just made her snort. "What kind of a place is this and why the hell should I have to wait in the hall? I hurt, damn it. I want to lie down!" Mother seemed to be more prisoner than patient in this awful place. We had nowhere else to go. Considering the meager accommodations, this was a costly place to be, so costly in fact, Medicare and Mother's insurance would only cover three weeks and only as long as Mother made progress. If not, the funds would be cut off and it would cost her three hundred dollars a day, not including therapy.

Finally, it was our turn. She took her pain medication and I wheeled her into her room and pressed the call light. She needed to use the restroom and was anxious to lie down. We had to wait quite a while. Not surprisingly, right after the meal, it seemed like all of the patients had the same need at the same time. She kept asking, "Why in the hell can't I go to the bathroom by myself?"

"You're recovering from a broken leg and you need a trained assistant to help you. I can't do it because I might hurt you."

"Why can't you help me? I have to poop and I need to go now!" It seems the laxatives were doing their work.

"Try to hang on. It's too dangerous for me to help you. We have to wait for the aide. You're not allowed to get up by yourself. I'm sorry. I know it's hard to wait." I pointed to the sign over her bed that instructed her to call for help when she needed to get up.

Her reply surprised me. "I won't get up, damn it, but if I'm going to shit my pants or if there is a fire, I will get up and not you or anyone else is going to stop me!"

I couldn't argue with that logic and agreed with her. "If it comes to that, I will definitely help you in either case!" I hugged my surprisingly logical, levelheaded mother and tried to distract her while we waited for the aide.

Thankfully, the aide finally came to her rescue. I breathed a sigh of relief as he wheeled her into the bathroom before she had an accident. When they came out, he helped her into bed so that she could get her legs up. The nurse came in a little while later to check Mother's bandages and give her ice, which seemed to offer some relief. Her pain medications had started working, and although she wasn't overly drugged or groggy, she wasn't complaining as much. After her ear infection and subsequent surgery, I learned that she has a high tolerance to pain medication and if she was in pain, it worked well with minimal side effects. She was lucky in that way.

It was now after seven o'clock, and I turned the TV to Wheel of Fortune, a familiar friend. While we had been away, an unappealing half sandwich had appeared on the table near her bed. I picked it up and examined it. It had pinkish goo oozing out from between the pieces of bread and was wrapped in saran wrap. It was marked, "Deviled Ham – Diabetic Snack." Mother wouldn't have eaten that even if she had an appetite. There was also an ice-filled container of water, so I encouraged her to take small sips. Mother had to go to the bathroom again, so I rang for the aide and waited for him to come. This time, he helped her brush her teeth and wash her face. He put her nightgown on and helped her back into bed.

Once she was settled into bed, she was uncomfortable and exhausted but glad for my company. She repeatedly asked, "Will you stay the night with me?"

"Someone will stay the night, I promise. I need to go home and get some rest, but I have arranged for someone to be here when I go."

She was relieved, but kept asking the question and said that she didn't want to be alone. She finally just looked at me and said, "I don't know if I could survive this without you!"

"You won't have to try. I'll make sure someone is here 24/7!"

I called Marie as we watched TV to give her the update. I was absolutely exhausted when the caregiver came to take over. She seemed nice and I introduced her to Mother. Sandra had already given her information on Mother's personality and instructed her to sit by Mother's side, answer questions, press the call light when she needed assistance, and make sure she didn't feel lost or alone. The sitters had all been given strict orders that they couldn't do the aides' job or interfere with them in any way.

Again, I left my mother in the care of that wretched place and drove home, mentally and physically exhausted. Lyle was already in bed, so I showered, grabbed a glass of wine, climbed into bed, and watched the eleven o'clock news. After I laid my head down, I quietly cried myself to sleep, not knowing what the next day would bring. I fell into a nightmare that would repeat itself many times: Mother was just in front of me, holding out her arms and begging me for help. She was on the edge of a cliff and was losing her balance. I tried to reach out for her, but my arms were trapped and frozen to my sides. I tried to scream for help but no sound came out. My feet wouldn't move. There were people all around, smiling kindly at me, but they wouldn't help. Unable to move or speak, I could only watch helplessly as she fell over the cliff. I awoke with a start, the sheets drenched in sweat and Lyle snoring softly next to me. I started to cry and Lyle woke, gathered me in his arms, and held me until I fell back into fitful sleep.

The remainder of the week was much of the same. I woke up at four o'clock so I could go into work early. I stopped by Mother's apartment during my lunch hour to feed Honey. I had decided to leave Honey at her apartment until I had figured out where Mother would go next. I didn't want to bring the cat home with me and further impose upon my long-suffering husband. When I got off work each afternoon at four o'clock, I went directly to the skilled nursing facility. Marie was there during the afternoon when Mother had most of her therapy, which was a combination of physical, speech, and occupational. The facility was fully staffed during the day, and there were more aides and a nurse practitioner to provide additional care for the patients. Marie spoke to the nurse practitioner, head nurse, and the social worker on a daily basis, all of whom seemed accessible and listened to her concerns. She felt confident in the care that Mother was receiving. Her experience was very different from mine, so different, in fact, that she started to mention that this facility might make a good permanent home. I, however, felt exactly the opposite.

When I arrived at four thirty, it was close to the shift change at five and I saw less of the nurse practitioner than Marie did. I had to rely on Marie to pass on any questions or concerns regarding Mother's care. At five o'clock, it was an entirely different place. The day staff had gone, and the aide staff was minimal. The patients were no longer in their therapy secessions, and all needed help at the same time for toileting, getting in and out of bed, or getting ready for dinner. Unfortunately, when the need was highest, the staffing was slimmest. The few aides that were left had the added job of getting everyone to dinner, serving them, and recording their fluid and food intake.

After sunset, their jobs became even more difficult when the personality shift change happened. Everyone needed even more help because they were sundowning, and becoming confused, agitated, and afraid. Unable to make sense of what was happening, they constantly pressed their call lights, and became angry or wandered away when no one helped them. I noticed that the agitated woman who had to poop and the tiny lady who had been tethered to her wheelchair were both sedated, heads down and sleepy, with drool running off their chins.

The few aides I saw were literally running from room to room, doing the very best that they could. I didn't fault them. I wondered why the patients received the least help when they needed the most. It was just one more thing to add to the pile of things that didn't make sense.

19 *It's Not the Fall That Will Kill You*

During the second week of Mother's incarceration, Lyle left to visit his family in San Diego for ten days. The plans for his trip had been made well before Mother's fall, and he needed to get back home to see his aging parents, both in their eighties, while he could. He was still looking for a job, and once he secured a position, it would be at least a year until he could take any time off. Although he was hesitant to leave me during such a tumultuous time, I sent him away with my blessing. Lyle was the youngest of three brothers, but they had a much tighter family bond than I had with my sisters. His parents were doing well and were well looked after by other family members. Thankfully, we didn't have to worry much for their welfare.

After Lyle left for San Diego, I continued to work and spend as much time as I could with Mother. The weather had finally changed and several big storms were in the forecast. It had been raining steadily with strong, gusty winds. The leaves were ripped from the trees and clogged the drains, occasionally leading to flooded streets. I dreaded my nightly visit with Mother in that awful, depressing, uncomfortable place. Each night at dinner, I couldn't get her to eat anything. At best, she took a sip of a nutritional shake or a spoonful of broth, and every now and then, she ate a cracker, but I knew that wasn't enough. She was getting weaker.

After dinner, it took forever to get someone to help her into the bathroom. The aides knew that Mother was more mobile and that I was capable of helping, so they were no longer responding to the call light. I was left to help her to the bathroom and back into her wheelchair. It was very stressful for both of us. "I don't know why in the hell they won't come to help us!" she complained. I agreed and told her they were shorthanded, which was true.

Every night, another awful sandwich would be left on her table, and every night, Mother didn't eat it. It sat there until morning, when Marie threw it away. Since the weather had gotten cold, the facility started turning the heat on full blast, and the room was uncomfortably hot in the evenings. I had to crack a window to let in some fresh air or it would be unbearable. Mother didn't want her blanket, so I would turn down her covers for her. The first time I pulled her covers down, someone else's toenail clippings fell to the floor. Ugh, I thought. How gross. If that wasn't bad enough, her sheets were full of holes and were so thin that you could see right through them. I asked the aide for clean blankets and sheets, but like our earlier plea for a recliner or a more comfortable chair, our request went unfulfilled.

Due to my age and the stress I was under, my body decided to pick this time to start having hot flashes. They would begin shortly after I arrived at the facility, and as I sat in that god-awful hot room, I would sweat like I'd never sweat before. My face would turn bright red and sweat would trickle down my neck and back. Occasionally, I thought, They're lucky I don't remove all my clothes and run screaming through the building! When I asked about turning down the heat, an aide told me that the thermostat didn't work, and the heat was either on or off. I prayed to God that Mother would be able to get out of this hell as soon as possible. I told Barb to start looking for a place for Mother to live when she was released.

She seemed to be getting progressively worse with each day she spent at the skilled nursing facility. She had cramps every night and it took a long time to get her settled and comfortable. She moaned and complained nearly constantly. Since her admittance, the aides had been putting adult diapers on Mother and she would ask me, "Why in the hell can't I wear my own underwear? Oh God, I feel awful. Why don't I just hurry the hell up and die!" It was torture to see her in this state. I just tried to comfort her, pushed her to take sips of water or a bite of cracker or toast, and instructed our hired sitters to do the same. We asked the nurse for her pain medications as soon as they were due, so she could have some temporary relief.

Marie and I were increasingly disturbed by how little Mother was eating. We brought food from home and picked up fast food, anything to tempt her to eat, but she wouldn't. Marie asked the nurse practitioner to give Mother an appetite stimulant, the same medication her doctor had prescribed when she had lost her appetite after her ear surgery. The nurse practitioner didn't think it was necessary. "Your mother's weight is stable, and her chart indicates she is taking all of her supplements." She did offer a medication we were unfamiliar with, that was also an anti-depressant. Not knowing what the side effects could be, Marie asked again for the drug that we'd had such luck with in the past. Mother was already weak enough, and we didn't want to inadvertently add to her discomfort. The nurse practitioner wouldn't even consider it. "I just don't think an appetite stimulant is necessary because your mother is not losing weight. In fact, she has gained some weight."

Marie and I voiced our concerns daily to anyone who would listen. I met with the nurse practitioner on the rare occasion that she was still there when I arrived, and expressed my concern directly to her. "Mother is eating hardly anything. I can't get her to eat any dinner, maybe a sip of broth or a cracker, and only if I force her. Marie and all the sitters have the same concern and tell me she isn't eating. We can only get her to take small sips of her supplemental shakes. She looks so thin and frail. She has cramps all the time and complains of stomach pain at night."

Frowning, the nurse practitioner pulled out Mother's chart. "Her chart indicates she is taking all of her macronutrients. She isn't losing weight according to our scales. I see no cause for concern here." I wondered what a macronutrient was. Was it a pill they were giving her? I had no idea. I only knew she wasn't eating and was barely taking in any fluid.

She had done so well with her physical therapy, and every one of the therapists enjoyed working with her. She may have been forgetful and repetitive, but she was always willing to try to please those that treated her well and engaged her in conversation. Mother enjoyed teasing and joking with them and making them laugh with her wit. She had made good progress, and was even walking behind her wheelchair and using a walker to get up and down. However, she was starting to experience more pain when she walked, and had increasing difficulty making any progress because she was growing weaker and thinner every day. The nurse practitioner was finally concerned enough to make an appointment with the orthopedic surgeon to determine if Mother had an infection or other problems with the wound site.

Mother was taken by cabulance to the surgeon's office for her appointment. She and Marie were made to wait in an office not set up to care for her and forced to use a restroom that could not accommodate her handicap. Marie reported that Mother had thrown up and had to use the restroom several times during the long wait to see the doctor. She had diarrhea, and it had been horrendous for them both. No one seemed to care about the comfort of a sick, elderly person with dementia. She had to make an appointment and get in line just like anyone else, with no consideration for her age or condition. The orthopedic surgeon, finding no problems with her surgery site, seemed unconcerned and wanted to see her in a month for a follow-up visit.

Concerned about the diarrhea, the nurse practitioner changed Mother's antibiotic. She also ordered a CT scan that was negative for any obvious problems. Mother threw up several times during the cabulance ride, so Marie asked for an anti-nausea medication. The nurse practitioner said that Mother was probably just carsick and didn't think it was necessary.

During the day, I toured adult family homes that Barb recommended. Adult family homes are licensed private homes, regulated by the state. They served just a few residents at a time, and hopefully, could provide mother with the care, security, and attention she needed. The search was not easy. There were a wide range in our area and I only wanted to consider those that were conveniently located, specialized in dementia care, had been in business for some time, and had no complaints lodged against them. Thank God for Barb, who prequalified the homes before I looked at them. I took long lunches or time off in the afternoon to find the right place. They were all good enough, but always had something that discouraged me; some were too far and others just didn't feel like a place Mother could live. My aversion to institutions, like the ones I had visited years earlier and the one she was in now, left me with very few options. She couldn't return to assisted living, the type of place that had already lost her once. Because she was exit-seeking and a fall risk, she needed to be closely monitored twenty-four hours a day in a locked and secure facility. I desperately wanted to find a good place, a place she could actually call home. I couldn't wait to get her out of the hell we had found ourselves in.

One night, things were particularly bad. Mother refused to eat her dinner, and was miserable and lethargic. She looked emaciated, her eyes hollow and her cheeks sunken. I had reached my breaking point. I pushed her to have a bite of toast and a sip of warm water, which she did with much complaint, but then her head tipped forward and she vomited on the table. None of the aides came to help, as they were extra shorthanded that night. One elderly gentleman had literally just arrived from the hospital and no one had even taken the time to dress him. He had been unceremoniously wheeled up to a table, still in his open-backed hospital gown. He shivered and looked lost. I thought, That poor soul was scraped of the shoe of the hospital and dumped here. I felt badly for him, but I already had my hands full trying to clean Mother up. She had only vomited water and the tiny amount of food in her stomach, but it was an awful task nonetheless. One of the aides darted past and I shouted after her, "My mother is very sick. I am taking her back to her room!" The aide just nodded and dashed off.

As I wheeled her to her room, Mother said, "I feel so weird. Something is wrong. I think we should go to the emergency room."

"We're already at a skilled care facility. I'll go get the nurse."

When we turned down the hall and past the line, there was one nurse in attendance, as usual. I caught the nurse's attention and said, "Something seems to be terribly wrong with Mother. She vomited at dinner and wants to go to the emergency room. Can you please check her out?" The nurse stopped what she was doing and checked Mother's pulse, blood pressure, temperature, and oxygen level. "Her vitals are normal. I saw orders in her chart today for some anti-nausea medication. I'll bring it in later. That should make her feel better."

Mother wasn't happy with the nurse's indifference. "I want to go to the emergency room!" She looked up at me with pleading eyes. "I feel so awful. Why won't you help me?"

How I hated to hear that. I was so worried and felt powerless to help. "The nurse just checked you over and said you would be fine. She will bring some medicine soon for your upset stomach."

"She doesn't know what the hell she is talking about!"

I was able to help her into bed and held her hand while we waited for the nurse. She complained about pain in her stomach, and I could hear an ominous gurgling sound coming from her belly. She suddenly sat straight up and said, "I've got to go to the bathroom right now!"

I helped her into her wheelchair and could feel how thin and frail she was, merely a shadow of what she had been before her accident. I pressed the call light and helped her into the bathroom. After she was finished, I didn't flush the toilet because the aides were supposed to be charting her bowel movements. When she stood up, I was shocked by the amount of dark mucus and watery diarrhea in the toilet. Even more appalling was how thin her legs were. The skin on her buttocks and legs hung loosely from her bony frame. Holding her up in an awkward one-armed hug, I pulled the cord for the additional call light in the bathroom as diarrhea started to run down her legs. I needed help. I had to support her because she was so weak, but I also needed to clean her up. I waited, but no one came. Mother started to complain. "Where are they, goddamn it?"

Finally, the nurse came and looked in the bathroom. "I need help!" I said.

She looked blankly at me. "I'll send an aide." She just left me holding my poor mother in the bathroom.

What a fucking nightmare, I thought. Again, no one came, so I sat her back down on the toilet, soaked some clean washcloths in warm water, and set some dry towels nearby. I helped her stand, and slowly and carefully cleaned her up, put her nightgown on, and finally got her tucked into her filthy bed. The stress made her vomit again, and this time, it looked like what had come out the other end. I was beside myself. I held a bag for her to vomit in and saved it to show the nurse.

After an impossibly long wait, an aide finally came to help us. She was young, tall, and blonde, and no more than eighteen years old. She recently finished her training and this was her first job. Like the young man from Ethiopia, her goal was to become a nurse.

"What took so long? Mother has diarrhea and I had to clean her up myself. I am not happy about this. We shouldn't have to wait so long for help. I know you're busy, but when I press that call light, that means I need help now! I don't mind helping with Mother when I'm here, but if I do press that light, I expect someone to come immediately. I want the nurse to look at her bowel movement. It doesn't look right and I'm concerned."

The aide left to find the nurse. The room was getting uncomfortably hot, and I could feel the flush of an all-too-familiar hot flash starting from my belly and working its way up to my face. I started to sweat profusely. An hour went by, and when the aide finally came back, she was alone.

"Where is the nurse?"

She looked guilty and avoided my eyes. "She'll be in soon to give your mother her pills, but she wasn't concerned about the diarrhea." She went into the bathroom, and when she came out, her eyes were wide. "You're right, that doesn't look normal. I'll get the nurse right away."

She came back a short while later, went into the bathroom, and flushed the toilet without a word. Surprised, I asked, "Why did you just flush the toilet? The nurse hasn't been here yet."

"She told me to flush it!" Ashamed and upset, the young aide left the room.

When the nurse finally arrived with the anti-nausea medication, I asked, "Why did you instruct the aide to flush the toilet?"

She smiled patiently. "It was just your mother's chocolate shake. I see no reason to be worried."

"How would you know if you didn't see it? My mother has had almost nothing to eat for days!" I showed her the vomit and said, "It looked a lot like this!"

The nurse examined it. "This is just bile. There is nothing to worry about." She left, and I didn't feel the least bit comforted. I knew my poor mother couldn't take much more of this, and neither could I. The medication began to work, and soon, the nurse returned to give Mother her pain meds. The sitter arrived, but I stayed a little longer to make sure Mother was going to be OK.

I called Marie to tell her what had happened. "Oh my God. I just don't understand it. The nurse practitioner told me again today that Mother's weight is stable. I keep telling her that she's not eating. I have no idea where she is getting information to the contrary!"

"I don't know either and just can't understand why they keep telling us Mother is OK. She's far from OK. I don't believe anything they say. I'll call her doctor tomorrow for some advice and will let you know what she says. We can't let this go on any longer!" Marie agreed.

By the time I left, it was after ten o'clock and it was raining hard with a strong wind. I drove carefully home, exhausted, stressed, and sticky from the anxiety and sweat, thinking only of a hot shower and my bed. When I got home, I went straight to the bedroom, peeled off my clothes and headed for the shower. I had only taken three steps into the master bathroom when, with a slip and a whoosh, I fell and landed hard on my back. My head slammed against the cold floor. Lying naked with the wind knocked out of me, droplets splashed onto my forehead from above – water was pouring in from the vent fan on the ceiling. I thought, Now isn't this just fucking great!

I took a slow, deep breath when I was able. As I slowly stood up, I realized my head had barely missed the corner of the vanity, and I felt grateful that it hadn't been worse. Shaken, I grabbed my robe and went out to the garage for a bucket and some shop towels. I placed the bucket under the leak, mopped up the mess, and took care of the wet towels. My neighbor, Lois, routinely told me to call if I needed anything, and now I desperately needed help. I went to the phone and her. "Lois, I need you if the offer still stands." I told her about what happened.

"Of course, dear. I'll send my husband and grandson over in the morning to put a tarp on your roof. For now, I suggest you just shut the bathroom door, open a bottle of wine, and forget all about it for tonight!" That was the best advice I'd heard all day. Lyle called later, and I told him what had happened but that I had taken Lois's advice and was doing just fine. True to her word, Lois's husband and grandson showed up early the next morning and placed a blue tarp on the roof.

Having to supervise the placement of the tarp, I was a bit late to work the next day. Soon after I arrived at work, Marie called. "I am going in early to visit Mother and try to get a handle on why her condition is deteriorating. I just can't understand why the nurse practitioner keeps insisting that Mom isn't losing any weight. I'm going to ask for that appetite stimulant again. I'll call you later with what I find out."

Marie called me back just before noon, and it was obvious that she was very upset. Her voice shaking with anger, she said, "Before I left to visit Mother this morning, the sitter called to say that the nurse practitioner had been in to examine her. The sitter tried express her concern over Mother's weight loss, only to be told that Mother had actually gained weight. I was so mad that I called the nurse practitioner myself and she told me the same ridiculous thing. I can't understand it! Does she not even look at Mother? How can she not see how thin and awful she looks? I decided to go straight there and make them weigh Mother in front of me, and if they could prove that Mother was actually gaining weight, I would stop complaining." Marie's emotions got the better of her, and her voice broke when she said, "She only weighed 122 fucking pounds! She has lost almost 17 pounds and those morons have been trying to tell us that she's gaining weight!"

Shocked, I collapsed in my chair. "Oh my God. How could this happen? Do you think their scales are off, or are they just that damn stupid?"

Marie snorted. "I don't know, but when the aide saw what Mother weighed, she ran to fetch the head nurse. The head nurse made her weigh Mother again because she didn't believe her. Now we finally have the head nurse's attention, but she can offer no explanation. She called the nurse practitioner and now everyone is scrambling to get Mother some help. They are all assuring me that they'll do everything they can to turn her around!"

My shock turned to anger and confusion. I was astounded. Was there no end to this nightmare? What more could any of us have done? How the hell could this happen? Mother had an advocate around the clock. She was there for rehabilitation and had done her part, just as we had done ours. It seemed the "care" she received at the "skilled" nursing facility was just about to finish our poor mother off. I had no doubt that if Mother died, it would not be her Alzheimer's or the fall that killed her, but the care she had received after.

20 *A Matter of Survival*

After I spoke with Marie, I had to sit and collect myself. Seventeen pounds in three days seemed unimaginable. I was furious. I hoped that the nurse practitioner would finally treat our mother based upon the reality of her condition and not the erroneous information in her chart. Perhaps she would listen to us and give her the medication she needed and that we had been asking for. I had no idea how this could have happened. How had so much weight been lost in only three days? Perhaps their scales were inaccurate or the aides weren't properly charting her nutritional intake. How could the nurse practitioner not have seen what we had been seeing? Regardless, Marie believed that we had their full attention at last. I contacted Mother's regular doctor, and she contacted the nurse practitioner. Tests were to be ordered and her diet changed.

When I arrived at the facility after work, Marie said, "Mother will need IV fluids, which have been ordered. They will start the IV as soon as it arrives from the pharmacy. The dietitian said that Mother was low on sodium and would be given broth and put on a special diet due to her gastric distress." It's about damn time, I thought. Why had no one been concerned about her nausea, vomiting, and diarrhea until now? I had to beg and plead for Jell-O, toast, or soup. We had to force them to weigh Mother in front of us before they lifted a finger to help her.

That night, Mother looked awful and was having cramps in her legs. A nurse prepared her for the IV fluid that had yet to arrive. We went to dinner, although I knew she wouldn't eat. Her mealtime routine and nightly conversation with the other inmates was the only thing that gave her comfort. I didn't force her to eat or drink, having learned my lesson from the night before. She accepted a sip of tea and a spoon or two of broth, but I didn't push it. We returned to her room and waited for her IV. Mother seemed like an empty shell. When the fluids finally arrived, the nurse came in and hooked it up. I prayed to God that things would soon turn around. The room was once again unbearably hot and we were both sweating profusely. Thankfully, the aides were a bit better at coming when I pressed the call light. The night was excruciatingly long for us both. I couldn't shake the awful feeling that Mother was dying. Weak and tired, she fell into a fitful sleep, and when the sitter arrived, I went home and prayed. I didn't want my mother to die in that awful place.

The next morning, we had a meeting scheduled with the social worker to discuss Mother's deterioration and what was being done to rectify it. Marie's meeting with the hospital administration staff to discuss our complaints about Mother's care had been scheduled for the same time. I told her, "I'll meet with the social worker. Your meeting at the hospital is too important. We're lucky they're taking our complaint seriously. I'll be anxious to hear what the social worker has to say about her treatment."

Much to the displeasure of my employer, I left work early to take care of my mother. I had updated Barb and Sandra the night before and about the scheduled meeting. Barb kindly offered to accompany me and I gratefully accepted. Barb was an RN and a former nursing home director, so she was a very good ally. I hoped she could help me get to the bottom of what had happened.

I tried to keep an open mind and focused on what needed to be done to get Mother out of there as soon as possible. Allowing my anger to get the best of me would not be productive. Barb and I went straight to the family room across from Mother's room. The once-beautiful tree outside the window was naked and bare, its limbs dormant for the winter. The leaves were a carpet of orange and gold and were starting to decay.

When the social worker arrived, I recognized him. We had met shortly after Mother arrived. Although I was angry, frustrated, and afraid, I had no reason to distrust him and looked forward to hearing what he had to say. "What happened to your mother is unacceptable, and we are going to do a full investigation. I promise we'll do all within our power to support your Mother going forward." I was greatly relieved to hear this. I had prepared myself for the facility to close ranks and put up a fight.

The dietitian, a cute and well-dressed young woman, came in and sat at the opposite end of the table from the social worker. After introductions were made, he excused himself. "I'll leave you to discuss your Mother's diet and our plan to support her nutritionally. Feel free to contact me anytime if you have questions. Someone will be in touch when our investigation is complete."

He left the room, and Barb and I turned our attention to the dietitian. In a perky and cheerful manner, she said, "I've monitored and charted your Mother's fluid and nutritional intake since her admittance." She wasn't making eye contact as she thumbed through a large file. "According to your mother's chart, I did everything correctly and even instructed the aides to ensure your mother was drinking additional fluids. As soon as we discovered your mother's weight loss, I put additional measures in place to increase her food and fluid intake. We have done and are continuing to do all that we can."

I was thunderstruck. "I'm not interested in the past or what's in Mother's chart. The weight in her chart was incorrect. Her condition was anything but stable. I know she was not eating or drinking enough, and I have witnesses who'll say the same. Telling the staff to make sure she was eating and drinking enough does no good if they don't actually follow your orders. My mother's weight loss and deteriorating condition are proof that your orders were not followed. It wasn't the facility that discovered the weight loss, but the family!" She looked offended. I softened a little and said, "I don't blame you personally for the inaccuracies in the chart. Your actions were based upon the erroneous information about Mother's weight. I'm only interested in what you will do to support my mother and stabilize her condition, now that you know about the drastic weight loss."

She was clearly frustrated. "I don't feel that you've heard me." Once again looking down at her chart, she repeated she had done everything correctly and explained why Mother's weight loss had not been her fault. Barb and I exchanged a knowing look, understanding that the dietitian was only interested in covering her own ass.

We weren't getting anywhere, and I didn't want to hear any

more. "If you're only willing to tell me what you did in the past and are only interested in shirking responsibility, there is no point in continuing this conversation."

She closed her file and handed me her business card. "Please call me if you have any questions. I'll be in touch." She got up from the table and left the room. Wow, I thought. She entirely missed the point of our meeting. I hadn't even known that the facility had a dietitian, especially with all the awful, unappealing, heavy food they had been pushing on Mother. Barb and I hoped that the social worker would eventually provide us with some information that made sense. I was just glad that something was finally being done, and felt the IV fluid would go a long way. After consulting with Mother's doctor, the nurse practitioner finally prescribed an appetite stimulant. I prayed we were not too late.

Barb and I left the meeting room feeling disappointed and went to visit Mother. She was sitting up in bed, attached to the IV. The morning sitter was there and had a relieved smile. "They gave your mother broth this morning and she almost finished it all!" She did appear to be a bit better but still had that awful, sunken look. Her eyes were trying to vanish inside her skull.

A nurse walked in and handed Mother a small cup of clear liquid and some medication. Barb was suspicious. "What are you giving her?"

"This is her MiraLAX, senna, and Doss."

Barb sprang into action. "Oh, no you don't!" She quickly grabbed the cup and pills out of Mother's hand and said, "There is no way you should be giving her laxatives in her current condition!" I agreed. Mother just looked at us, wide-eyed. This didn't make any sense to me, especially with the trauma of cleaning her runny diarrhea still fresh in my mind.

I stepped forward and asked, "Why are you giving her laxatives when she has an upset stomach, hasn't eaten in days, has diarrhea, and has lost seventeen pounds?"

In a monotone, unfeeling voice, the nurse said, "I'm just giving the medications as ordered in her chart. I have no instructions to do otherwise. Your mother has not had a recorded bowel movement in two days, so laxatives are appropriate."

Mother had nothing in her left to shit out. I was livid. Any trust and hope I had in the staff was gone. They were clearly not competent to care for Mother, or any vulnerable person for that matter. I said, "No laxatives are to be given to my mother without my explicate approval for the duration of her stay. I have power of attorney over her care and I am refusing laxatives of any kind. You need to make a note of that in her chart this instant." If they had been giving her this combination of laxatives all along, that would explain almost everything: the nausea, vomiting, cramps, diarrhea, weakness, low sodium, and weight loss. I was sick about it. I had no idea that they had continued giving her laxatives after she'd arrived. This was torture and we had been forced to watch.

I was too angry to be with Mother, so I left the room. Barb stayed behind to smooth things over because Mother had picked up on my anger and was becoming agitated. I was shaking, and started to cry as I called her doctor. I told her what the dietitian had said and that I had just caught a nurse trying to give Mother a potent cocktail of laxatives. She was shocked and dismayed. "I have no idea what they're thinking. It just makes no sense at all.

I do agree that holding the laxatives was the correct thing to do." We decided it would be best to get her out of there as soon as possible. As soon as she stabilized, we would move her to an adult family home and continue her physical therapy on an outpatient basis. The doctor also said, "I'll personally come examine your mother and monitor her progress. We will only send her to the hospital as a last resort."

Next, I called Marie. I said, "I'll ask Sandra to instruct the sitters to verify which medications are being given, refuse any laxatives, and contact us immediately if they try!"

Marie added, "When I'm there each afternoon, I'll ask to see her chart to make sure that they're actually writing down the correct information. I'll be there in about an hour and I'll fill you in on my meeting with the hospital."

Armed with a plan, I had calmed down enough to join everyone in Mother's room. I let the sitter go home, since I had to wait for Marie to arrive. Barb left and I accompanied Mother to lunch. Mother ate very little, but drank a cup of hot tea, which was more than I'd seen her consume in days. She no longer seemed nauseated, and I began to hope that she was on the mend. How would she have felt if we hadn't been there to refuse the laxatives?

When Marie arrived, she filled me in on her meeting with the hospital administration. She had been well prepared, equipped with our copious notes about Mother's treatment, including names, dates, and descriptions of events. Thankfully, the hospital's administrator took our complaints seriously, and several of Mother's nurses attended the meeting. "I emphasized how much we love our mother and how long and hard we have fought to protect her quality of life. I told them exactly what their careless actions have cost us. I think I got through because some of the nurses were in tears and seemed remorseful. Of course, the nurse that made her throw up wasn't there. The nursing administrator promised that she would discuss our complaint with all parties. I just hope something positive will come from this." By communicating our concerns, we hoped to raise awareness of the special needs of dementia patients and the important role family plays in their care. After she finished telling me about her meeting, I went home to rest before my evening shift with Mother.

I did some research on the adult family homes that Barb recommended and was in the process of making an appointment with one near my home when the dietitian called. "We have met to discuss your mother's case. We've determined that our scales are working correctly. The only explanation for your mother's weight loss is post-surgical edema. Although edema cannot explain all the weight loss, we were unable to determine any other cause. I plan to move her to the Bluebird dining room where we serve our most compromised patients. I think your mother will benefit from having an aide available to cue her to eat."

At that moment, I lost what little of my mind I had left. She wanted me to believe that a rapid, seventeen-pound weight loss was due to swelling, despite the fact that her swelling had resolved a week earlier. On top of everything, she wanted to put Mother in the dining room for the catatonic, semi-conscious patients we had passed before our first dinner, just so someone would sit with her to encourage her to eat.

I thought, You stupid moron! Just once, I'd like to say what

I was really thinking. Instead, I told her, "Mother doesn't need someone to encourage her to eat or to feed her. She already has a family member or sitter with her at every meal, doing just that. It's not that she won't eat, but that she can't eat because of her gastric distress. Even when we were successful in getting her to eat a bite of the awful, inappropriate diet you had her on, she would just vomit or shit it out! She's barely able to tolerate soup or toast, but I have to beg for those things. It wasn't until we forced you to recognize her weight loss that you did anything at all to support her nutritionally. For God's sake, I had to stop a nurse from giving Mother a powerful cocktail of laxatives, even after the weight loss was discovered!" My voice dripped with venom, "Do you know what it would do to her mentally to be moved into the dining room for patients who can't even hold their heads up? The only bright spot in her day is her conversations with people at dinner. Moving her to a new dining room makes no sense at all. You are not to move her."

It was like talking to a brick wall. She curtly said, "I feel she will benefit from more cuing. I don't understand why you would refuse my order, but I'm not going to argue with you." In a more cheerful voice, she said, "Feel free to call me if I can support you in any way." I couldn't wait to get Mother out of this terrible place and away from these incompetent, reckless people.

21 *Planning Our Escape*

The adult family home I visited was almost exactly an even distance from work and home and was very convenient to my daily route. The house was in a quiet neighborhood of well-maintained homes. It was a charming single-story home surrounded by a white picket fence. The house was painted a bright shade of blue and had a neatly landscaped yard. It looked promising, at least from the outside. I had already visited several other adult family homes, but they were too far away, the rooms were too small, the layout was confusing, or I had gotten a weird vibe from the caregivers or residents. Barb highly recommended this home because the owners, a mother and daughter, were both licensed practical nurses.

I crossed my fingers as I approached the front door and rang the bell. A young woman answered the door with a broad grin, introduced herself as one of the caregivers, and ushered me into a large living room. The highly polished wood floors were clean, and the room was cheerfully furnished with light blue wing back chairs, a colorful, overstuffed love seat, a large television, and a card table with a half-assembled puzzle on top. A glowing fire burned in the fireplace. Skylights and large windows made the room feel open and airy. The home smelled clean and the scent of homemade cookies baking in the oven wafted through the air. Although it was November and the air outside was brisk, it was cozy and warm inside. Some of the anxiety rolled off my shoulders as I stepped farther into the home. I could definitely visualize Mother living here.

The young caregiver gave me a tour of four available rooms, all of which had neutral carpeting, upscale window furnishings, and adequate closet space. Each room had a window that looked out into a lush yard. I was very interested. The owners weren't available to meet with me that day, so I made an appointment for the following day to discuss a care plan and costs. There were six rooms and they currently had only two residents. I chatted with the residents as they ate their lunch, and they both told me they liked living there very much. One of them admitted that she had done so well that she was planning to move back to assisted living because she missed her friends. As soon as I got back to my car, I called Marie "You have to come see this place right away. I think this is it!"

The following day, Marie stopped by and was just as impressed as I was. We decided that this would be Mother's new home. Later that day, I met with Janice, who ran the home in partnership with her mother, Beverly. Janice, a young woman in her late twenties or early thirties with large brown eyes, told me about the type of care they could provide. I said, "I'm desperate to get Mother away from her current situation. I don't know if she will survive if we don't move her quickly." Feeling overwhelmed, I started to sob uncontrollably. "I don't know how much more I can take. I'm so stressed out by what is happening to my mother. I've had to take so much time off work, and my employer is losing patience. My boss read me the riot act before I came here today, warning me to get a handle on the situation, as if I'm not already doing everything I can! I don't know how the hell I'm going to manage this. I can't lose my job. My poor husband is out of work and recovering from prostate cancer. I can't even support him the way I need to because I'm trying to save my mother. I feel like I'm failing him when he needs me most. I don't know if I can keep this up much longer and still save my marriage and my job." I didn't even try to hold the tears back, and it took me a little while before I calmed down. I felt awful that I had let my emotions run away with me and apologized to Janice for dumping all of my problems on her.

When I looked up, her eyes were wide and full of empathy. She put her arm around me and handed me a box of Kleenex. "I don't mind at all. You have quite a lot going on right now. You certainly don't need to apologize to me!"

She waited patiently as I regained my composure. I continued and was honest about Mother's Alzheimer's, her broken leg, and her need for assistance in getting up and down. I was also afraid she was exit-seeking and would try to leave. Janice said, "We have alarms on all of our doors and motion sensors in the hall. We can put a sensor on her chair and one on her bed that will alert us when she gets up so we can assist her immediately."

I was comforted that they had experience with dementia and could provide round-the-clock care. A large, longhaired black cat sauntered by, and Janice introduced him as Rarri, the house cat. I asked, "I guess Mother won't be able to bring her cat, Honey, with her?"

With an apologetic look and shake of her head, Janice indicated that Rarri wouldn't welcome a new cat. Mother would have to give up Honey, but I had very little choice. I truly believed that this facility was the best place for her, and quality care was more important than her relationship with her cat. I hoped that this new cat would help her get over Honey. The initial cost was five thousand dollars a month, and included all meals and snacks. I would need to buy the sensor pads for her chair and bed, which were two hundred and fifty dollars. The monthly cost would be adjusted if Mother's evaluation suggested that she required more care than anticipated. Janice said that I would need to meet with her mother, Beverly, to finalize arrangements, and their nurse would assess Mother to determine her condition and level of assistance needed. She wouldn't be accepted until the nurse's evaluation was complete, so I scheduled an appointment for the next day.

I called Marie to tell her about my meeting with Janice, leaving out the part about my emotional meltdown. "I'm so glad it went well. We must get Mother out of here as soon as possible. They tried to give her another laxative today! The sitter called me this morning because the nurse tried to give her senna. The sitter refused it, as we instructed. The nurse challenged the sitter's authority, so she called me. I told the nurse, again, that Mother is not to be given laxatives. When I got here, I ran into the executive director. I asked what they were doing about Mother's weight loss and how they intended to prevent it from happening again. He had the nerve to tell me that it wasn't their fault and fed me the same line of nonsense that the dietitian told you! He pissed me off. I told him we didn't accept their explanation. He just threw his hands up and asked what we expected him to do about it. I was so mad and just couldn't let it go! To get rid of me, he agreed to arrange a meeting to discuss what happened. He'll let me know as soon as it's set up."

I was fuming. "There is no way in hell her weight loss was due to post-surgical swelling. It's as if her weight loss is something they've merely misplaced, for God's sake. None of them seem to understand that Mother has suffered harm in their care." I no longer cared that they were shorthanded, underfunded, and unappreciated. They still had an obligation to those entrusted to their care. Mother's abysmal treatment was unacceptable, and I was determined to find out how and why this had happened. If such a thing could happen to Mother, what happened to those without advocates? I refused to let them sweep this under the rug and take no responsibility for their negligence.

Once again, I left work early and arrived at the facility in the middle of the afternoon. I ran into the nurse practitioner as she was on her way out the door. I asked to speak with her and with a sigh, she said, "I only have a moment. I'm on my way out to celebrate a colleague's birthday." We stepped to the other side of the hall so we could speak privately.

"Under no circumstance is my mother to be given any more laxatives. I thought the matter was settled, but I was told that a nurse attempted to give her senna just this morning. I'm very disturbed that our orders were disregarded. I can't understand why you would want to give her a laxative in her current condition."

Looking disdainfully down at me with a smirk, she condescendingly said, "Your mother is on a lot of narcotic pain medication. She needs to be on at least one laxative or she'll become constipated."

I held my ground. "I'm willing to take that risk. She hasn't had anything substantial to eat or drink in a long time. I want her to have the opportunity to retain something instead of just vomiting or shitting it right out. I'm working on getting her transferred to an adult family home to continue her physical therapy on an outpatient basis. I'll worry about constipation if it actually becomes a problem."

She just looked offended and continued to look down her nose at me. "Is that all?" I nodded my head, and she hurried out the door. As I stood in the hall, the social worker approached me. "I've just been informed that a meeting has been arranged for today at three o'clock."

"You can notify everyone that I don't think such a meeting is necessary. Please cancel it. I see now that it wouldn't be productive for any of us." I didn't tell him why it would be unproductive, and I kept my voice polite and friendly. He looked relieved and agreed to cancel the meeting.

When I got to Mother's room, she was sitting in her wheelchair. She was still connected to an IV, but was finally looking much better. Her face wasn't so sunken and her skin didn't look so loose. She appeared to have finally turned a corner. Marie was sitting with her, so I pulled her aside and filled her in. "I don't think Mother will be given any more laxatives, but we still need to be vigilant. I wouldn't put anything past these people. I hope you don't mind, but I ran into the social worker and canceled the meeting. I spoke with the nurse practitioner, who was combative and sanctimonious. Do you really think any of these people will consider changing their position? They're just going to close ranks and will do anything it takes to cover their own asses. They must know that their actions caused Mother harm, but they have an obligation to their company to minimize damage and protect themselves from a lawsuit. I have no intention of suing them, but they must be scared."

Reluctantly, Marie agreed. "What's the next step? Where do we go from here?"

"Our first priority must be to get Mother out of here as soon as possible. After she has been released, I'll ask for a copy of her chart and look for discrepancies between her condition and the charted information. If I find a smoking gun, I'll file a complaint with the state and leave it up to them to investigate and take corrective action. I don't know what else I can do. First, we need to concentrate on getting Mother well."

At that point, Mother gave me a weak smile and asked, "Who is today?" My heart fluttered with hope.

That evening was a repeat of so many that came before: answering Mother's repeated questions, eating dinner with the weak and broken, passing the long line of confused, sad souls, waiting for medication in the hall, sitting in the stifling and dreary room, and waiting for help. Mother's pain was subsiding, and she no longer suffered from cramps and nausea. Disgusting sandwiches no longer appeared in her room; instead, they were replaced with Jell-O, broth, salty chips, and popsicles. I could almost see the light at the end of the tunnel. I was glad when the long and emotional day was over, and the sitter arrived so I could go home. Lyle had returned from San Diego, and I looked forward to the comfort of his steady, calm presence and warm embrace.

The next day, I met with the nurse from the adult family home. I was looking forward to learning the results of her assessment and beginning the process of transferring Mother out of that horrible place. Marie was already working on moving her furniture to the adult family home. Dr. R had convinced the owners that Mother would pass their test, and we wanted to move her as soon as possible. The nurse was already talking to my mother when I arrived. Mother happily told her, "I have an old kitty whose eyes are as green as grass. Her name is Honey, and the vet is taking care of her because they love her so much." It tugged at my heart to hear her talk about her beloved cat; I knew she would probably never see Honey again. She wouldn't be able to understand why she could not bring Honey home, so reuniting them would only cause her sorrow.

I introduced myself to the nurse and shook her hand. "Your mother is delightful. I'm sure she will be a good fit in her new home. We will be glad for the opportunity to care for her as soon as she has been released and is ready for transfer."

I was elated at this wonderful news. I called Marie, and she then notified the social worker, who said that he would begin the release paperwork. He arranged for a hospital bed, wheelchair, and walker to be delivered to the adult family home. A physical therapist would visit her twice a week for outpatient rehabilitation. Dr. R came by and confirmed that she would be safe to discharge as soon as her IV was complete. We had a plan of escape, and it appeared we would get her out alive and on the road to recovery. She had one day left for her IV therapy, and then we would be free of this god-awful place.

I went to the assisted living facility to collect Honey and bring her home with me. Marie had already removed the furniture Mother would need at her new home, and the apartment was nearly empty. It didn't take Honey long to settle in at my house. She craved attention after being alone in the apartment for almost a month. I had been feeding her once a day and some of the staff had been going in to pet her, but the poor kitty missed being the center of my mother's universe. I was glad to have one less errand to run each day.

The move date was set and our plans were in place. I contacted the assisted living facility to terminate her lease. I hadn't spoken to the head nurse and director since shortly after Mother's fall, when they called to tell me of the findings of their investigation. Apparently, none of their staff had called 911. The fire department had a key to the facility and had silently let themselves in without notifying any of the overnight staff. The director concluded their staff was not at fault, but asked the fire department to pull the emergency cord in the resident's room when they are called in the future. I took their explanation with a grain of salt, still upset that they had waited so long to call me and hadn't notified the authorities when she went missing. I really didn't believe anything anymore.

When I called the director of the assisted living facility to tell her of my plans to move Mother to an adult family home, she responded in an all-too-familiar tone. "It's up to the head nurse to decide if your mother is fit to return to our facility or not. You won't be entitled to a refund or be able to break the lease unless our nurse does the assessment."

I was floored. They were trying to stick me with an assessment fee or make me pay a penalty for breaking her lease. "My mother cannot return to your facility. She is a fall risk, needs constant care, and is exit-seeking. If you need an assessment, I will not pay to have your nurse do it. Mother's doctor will call the nurse and tell her that your facility is not capable of providing the care she needs. You knew that my mother was exit-seeking and having hallucinations, and you lost her. I fully expect to be let out of the lease."

Calm and professional, she said, "It's still not my call to make. I will pass the information on to the head nurse and have her call you with her decision."

I called Dr. R and asked her to fax a letter to the assisted living facility with her determination that Mother would not be safe living there. She was happy to help and said that she would follow up with a phone call. The head nurse called me the next day and informed me that she had determined Mother was no longer safe living at their facility. We were released from her contract without penalty, as long as her belongings were removed by the end the month. Finally free from the assisted living facility, and nearing the end of our stay at the skilled nursing facility, I looked to the future with hope.

22 *A Life Still Worth Living*

Moving day arrived, Mother's furniture was in place, and they were expecting her at the adult family home. I planned to meet Mother and Marie after work. Marie was at the facility completing the discharge paperwork, and would follow the cabulance in her car. I couldn't wait to leave that horrible place and never return. The only hitch in our plans came when the skilled nursing facility officially discharged Mother first thing in the morning, well before she was actually scheduled to leave. She hadn't had a bath or been cleaned for days, and Marie wanted her to begin her new life clean and comfortable. She asked the staff to bathe her, but since Mother had been discharged, Medicare would no longer reimburse them for their time. That was the last straw for Marie. She raised hell until someone cleaned Mother up and got her dressed and ready to go.

I went to the adult family home ahead of them to make sure Mother's TV was working, she had a newspaper, and her room was ready. When the cabulance finally arrived, Mother was unloaded and wheeled into the home, two of her daughters by her side. Pleased to see me, she asked, "Why are you here? What is this place?"

"This is a special rehabilitation facility to help you get your strength back." Beverly, one of the owners, helped her with her coat and wheeled her to the dining room table to get her a hot drink and something to eat. Confused by the strange surroundings, she kept asking, "Where am I? Why am I here? Where is Honey?" Marie was tired, worried, and overwhelmed, and left shortly after bringing Mother in. I stayed behind to comfort her and answer her repeated questions.

The home was a new and different environment for Mother. She was used to a more institutional setting, one with many residents, a large dining room, and a very rigid schedule. Even the skilled nursing facility, as awful as it was, had begun to seem like home. Although her new home was clean and cozy with soft lighting and a cheerful fire, it was nothing like she was used to. She quickly became anxious. "When am I going home to see Honey?" she asked.

"You are home, at least for now. It's only temporary until you get much better."

She found no comfort in my words. "Are you going to stay with me? Am I ever going to get Honey back?"

Reluctantly, I said, "I can't stay long because I need to get home and make supper for Lyle. Honey is staying at the vet's house while you're getting better. They love her very much, so you don't need to worry about her."

"I don't want to stay here! I want Honey back!"

I felt so tired and sad. "It'll be all right. I promise that I will come and see you when I get off work tomorrow. In the meantime, if you need me, I live nearby."

Beverly stayed close to Mother and gently reassured her that she would be there to take care of her. Mother started to fret. "You can't leave me here! I don't want to stay. Please don't leave me here by myself."

I knew she was in Beverly's capable hands, but my heart ached for my confused, frightened mother. "You will be safe here and will be well cared for. I would never leave you if I thought differently."

Mother started to cry, and in a pitiful voice, said, "But I don't know my way around here. I'll be lost because I have no focal point. How will I know where I'm supposed to go? I'm scared. Please don't leave me here!"

I thought, Oh my God, my poor mother realizes that she will be completely lost without a point of reference. I held back tears as I hugged her tight and reassured her that she would be fine. "The caregivers will be able to help you find your way. I promise I'll be back tomorrow."

Beverly showed me out, and as I made my way to my car, I thought about how sad, traumatized, and afraid Mother was. On top of that, she was thin and frail because of what happened to her at the skilled nursing facility. It was harder than I had anticipated to leave her, but I knew that I had to let her adjust without me. I needed to allow the staff at the home to do their jobs and get her settled in. I had Lyle to consider, my neglected job, and I had to reclaim my own life.

Although Barb cautioned me to stay away, I knew I would never fully trust anyone again because of our experiences. I no longer needed to hire sitters, because she would receive more concentrated care. I would always stay involved, and I planned to return to our old, comfortable routine. No, I thought, I will never stay away. My mother had no voice, and I had no trust. I prayed that I had made the right decision and had placed her in the right home, and that this wasn't going to be just another total disaster. When I went to sleep that night, I knew that someone would be watching over my mother, and Beverly promised to call if there were any problems. Mother was finally away from the dirty, toxic environment at the skilled nursing facility and had come home to a clean and comfortable place with caregivers that seemed to be competent. For the first time in ages, I slept well and without nightmares.

Unfortunately, Mother didn't adjust well to her new home. She wasn't sleeping, had become very anxious, and gave the staff a hard time. She mourned losing Honey every day, and if I didn't leave a note where she could see it, she would be inconsolable. Beverly said that I should talk to Dr. R and consider putting her on a sedative and antipsychotics to alleviate her agitation and help her sleep, but I considered drugs to be a last resort. How could she have any quality of life if she were drugged into a stupor? I had seen what medication could do; I pictured Mother with a vacant stare, a slack, open mouth, and drool running down her chin. She was already a fall risk and I wanted to avoid giving her something that would make her balance even more precarious. The thought of another trip to the hospital or skilled nursing facility was un-imaginable.

I contacted the Alzheimer's Association for advice. The coun-selor suggested that if she continued to be agitated and battled insomnia, she would be uncomfortable and unhappy. I didn't want her to be comatose, but her life would be terrible if she were perpetually fearful. With the help of her neurologist and Dr. R, Mother started taking a low-dose anti-anxiety medication, lorazepam, and a mild antidepressant, trazodone. Her doctor visited regularly, made herself available to the home's staff, and watched Mother carefully for side effects. Once again, this wonderful doctor made a tremendous difference in our lives, saved us from unnecessary stress and worry, and helped keep my mother safe, healthy, and comfortable. The neurologist adjusted her dose of antidepressant only once, and soon, Mother was feeling a little better.

Though her depressed state was manageable, things didn't truly improve for a long time. She complained that she was bored and couldn't find her way around. She didn't understand why she had to use a walker or have assistance using the bathroom. She left her walker behind several times and fell, but didn't hurt herself because someone was always nearby to help. She still frequently told me that she wanted Honey back. She stopped asking, "Who is today?" Instead, she moaned, "I wish I was dead!" Getting used to her new living arrangement was almost as hard on me as it was for her. Although I could finally sleep at night, her mental decline and unhappiness caused me a great deal of heartache.

I gave her caregivers as much information as I could about her habits, likes and dislikes, routines, and triggers. We worked closely together and came up with ideas for cues that would help her. I put a white board in her room with important information, such as what day it was, when the next meal would be, and when I was coming back. We learned if we wrote too much information, she would read to the bottom, forget what it said at the top, and have to read it again. This cycle made her distressed and usually made her cry. It was torture for me to see her this way.

I tried to stay calm and wasn't afraid to change tactics if something didn't work. I went back to my normal visiting routine but no longer called her daily, as she didn't need reminders for medication and just seemed confused by my calls. She no longer had her own phone, but the staff always called me if she wanted to talk and encouraged me to call if I needed to. I missed my daily calls and mourned the loss of our frequent communication. Mother was more agitated after my visits, but I kept them up anyway. Eventually, she calmed down and our old routine gave her comfort once again. I still had many trust issues and questioned everything they did at the adult family home. I'm sure I came close to driving them crazy.

Mother was still very weak and hadn't yet gained any weight back, but her weight had stabilized and she was doing well with physical therapy. Other than her unhappiness with the living arrangements, she was doing well physically. She no longer needed a wheelchair, she could get up and down on her own, and she was almost completely weaned off her pain medication. Mother was causing a great deal trouble for the staff at her home. She needed constant reassurance, followed the caregivers around all day, and kept forgetting her walker. Because the staff hadn't learned all of her triggers, she often pounded the walls and threw things in her room in fits of anger, scaring the caregivers. Beverly decided to wait for her to adjust before taking on any more clients.

Before long, Thanksgiving was upon us. Mother was still too

weak to come to my house for Thanksgiving, so Marie and I decided to have a family holiday at the adult family home. They were down to only two residents, and the other woman was going out for Thanksgiving dinner. Marie, Tom, and his mother, Maggie, joined Mother, Lyle, and me for our first holiday after her fall. Marie prepared turkey, potatoes, and stuffing, and I brought vegetables, olives, snacks, and dessert. The caregiver working that day helped us heat up the feast and serve the meal, and then left us alone to have an intimate family gathering. It was nice to be together, and although Mother was still not eating much, she seemed to enjoy having her family around her. We finally had reason to hope she would be able to regain some quality of life, which would truly be something to be thankful for.

By the time Christmas arrived, Mother was strong enough to eat Christmas dinner at my house. I hid Honey and her cat paraphernalia away in a back bedroom, knowing Mother would become obsessed if she saw her again. She still asked about Honey daily, and still needed a note to calm her down.

Marie and I decided to make Christmas all about the mothers, both of whom were living in adult family homes and struggling to survive. I set up two comfortable easy chairs in front of the fire in our family room. Marie splurged on gifts and wrapped them in festive packages. All the gifts were for the mothers, and we served them their meal and showered them with presents and attention. Mother was still very thin and didn't eat much, but she and Maggie enjoyed the attention. They laughed and smiled like a couple of young children, expressing looks of joy and surprise as they opened each present and held them up for the camera. As

I watched Mother, smiling and happy, I thanked God that she had survived her ordeal and the careless people who tried to take her from us.

Finally, Mother was stable enough that I called the skilled nursing facility and requested her complete chart. I wanted to determine what had gone so terribly wrong and why the information in her chart hadn't reflected the reality of her condition. No one could dispute her significant weight loss, but their lame attempt to explain it away as post-surgical edema made no sense. A seventeen-pound weight loss could not be solely explained by the reduction of swelling. Mother had weighed 136 pounds prior to her fall. When her swelling was at its worst, the facility charted her weight at 140 pounds. By the time Marie forced them to weigh her, she weighed only 122 pounds.

Although I was angry, disappointed, and frustrated, my motive was not revenge. I felt compelled to find out what happened and why. If this happened to my mother, it most definitely could happen to someone else, someone without an advocate watching over things. No matter what I found, I didn't intend to sue the facility. There were already far too few facilities able to care for the ever-increasing number of patients coming out of the hospitals, and as bad as the skilled nursing facility was, it probably wasn't the worst. A lawsuit would be costly, and would take time that I didn't have to spare. Even if I found enough evidence to sue them, I didn't think a lawsuit would hold accountable those who were most responsible: the people at the top, the facility doctor (whom we never saw), the director, and the executives. The bigwigs set the policies that created the problem, but also had the power and means to insulate themselves from legal culpability. In the end, the only ones who would benefit from a lawsuit would be the law-yers. If I found something tangible and provable, my plan was to report it to the state. I hoped the state would investigate and prevent this from happening in the future. The skilled nursing facility would take the state much more seriously than they would take me. They would be unable to make the problem disappear if they had to answer to the state. Once again, I couldn't have been more wrong.

As much as I hated to, I went back to that awful place to pick up her chart. That night, I sat at my dining room table with a large glass of wine to fortify me and read my mother's chart, from the hour of her admittance to the hour of her discharge. As I read, her experience unfolded before my eyes. There was not one smok-ing gun, but many. It was painful to read. I couldn't believe that they had willingly given me this file; the errors in her chart were so obvious and egregious.

Her chart painted a clear picture that explained why she would writhe in discomfort, complain about cramps, and feel sick to her stomach. I found three major errors that contributed to Mother's swift decline. First, she was wrongly charted as being incontinent, perhaps as an excuse to put her in an adult diaper. This unnec-essary measure was demeaning and made her uncomfortable and distressed. Next, the dietitian incorrectly charted Mother as overweight. Last, Mother had been given a strong laxative when she was admitted, and given senna and Doss twice a day thereaf-ter. Despite having regular bowel movements and taking a strong antibiotic, the nurse practitioner added a third bowel medication,

MiraLAX, several days into her stay. Eventually, her diarrhea became so serious they suspected she had C. diff, a bacterial infection that causes severe diarrhea and inflammation of the colon. The laxatives were withheld when they suspected C. diff, but only for a short time. I was baffled by the logic that led to prescribing laxatives for a patient experiencing diarrhea, nausea, and vomiting. I was so horrified and shaken by her chart that I had to stop reading.

After I finished reviewing the chart for the first of many times, I called Marie. She was as shocked as I was. She said, "I had a few conversations with the nurse practitioner that I didn't tell you about. Just before we discovered Mother's weight loss, I'd been asking what we could do to make her more comfortable. She told me that it was common for an elderly person to deteriorate after a traumatic injury, and that statistics show a majority of elderly patients who break a hip do not survive. She had the gall to say that if Mother had another accident, we should consider 'not putting her through this again.' "

"Like we had a choice? What were we supposed to do? Shoot her like a horse with a broken leg? Or better yet, just let her stay in excruciating pain with a broken leg and displaced hip? Why the hell didn't you tell me this before now?"

Marie sighed. "Because I knew how angry it would make you."

I was increasingly convinced that I needed to file a complaint with the state. I had the chart and witnesses to support my claim. First, I called Sandra. I asked if she would take an objective look at the chart as a former nursing home director, and tell me how best to make my case to the state. I wanted to do this right and

not just out of anger. She agreed to help even though her involvement didn't benefit her. Many of her client referrals came from
that facility. She had nothing to gain and everything to lose by
getting involved.

The next day, I copied the chart, marked the entries I felt were
problematic, and sent it off to Sandra. She was appalled. "Oh my
God, Anita, there are so many violations in your mother's chart,
I don't even know where to begin. I've shown it to Barb and she
agrees. As state-licensed professionals and mandatory reporters,
Barb and I are obligated to report our findings to the state. I just
wanted to let you know before we do. Your mother suffered real
harm at their hands. I'm so sorry this happened. You're doing the
right thing, and Barb and I will support you anyway we can!"

She gave me a phone number to call and a place to start. I
contacted the state and was given an address to submit a written complaint. Soon, the state investigator assigned to Mother's
case contacted me. "I'm the caseworker assigned to investigate the
complaint you made on your mother's behalf against the skilled
nursing facility. We've found sufficient cause to investigate your
complaint. I would like to ask you some questions regarding the
complaint you've filed. Do you have the time to discuss this now?"

Relieved that my complaint had been taken seriously, I told her
about our experiences. My voice broke and I started to cry. Retell-
ing the details brought the horror and sadness of our experience
back to the surface. I struggled to maintain my composure, but
I got through it and then gave her the contact information for
Marie, Sandra, and Barb.

She kindly said, "I assure you we will do a thorough investigation. I will personally visit the facility unannounced and will determine if any corrective actions need to be taken. Once the investigation is concluded, I will send you an official report of my findings. In the meantime, if you have any questions, please feel free to contact me."

I felt satisfied after I hung up. I had done my part and was confident that our experiences would be held up to the light. I hoped that something positive would come out of Mother's nightmare. Marie called me several days later to inform me that the investigator had also contacted her. The wheels of justice were finally turning.

Several weeks later, I received a letter from the state. As I read it, my outrage grew into something with a life of its own. The report was short and not very thorough. An investigator, not the one I had spoken to, had gone to the facility during the daytime hours when they were fully staffed and running smoothly. The nurse practitioner, dietitian, and director all had been interviewed, and several other charts had been reviewed. The report indicated that no violation was found, and no citation was issued. A brief paragraph explaining their findings asserted that the facility was responsive and listened to the family. Mother's weight loss was attributed to the family's refusal of an appetite stimulant. It was also noted that the dietitian recommended the resident be transferred to the assisted dining room for increased cueing, but the family refused. There was no mention of the continued use of laxatives or the facility's unwillingness to recognize Mother's weight loss.

I let out a primal scream of frustration and wadded up the let-

ter in my hand. I paced back and forth in my living room, trying
to make sense of what I had read. I was crying and muttering to
myself when Lyle came home. Seeing the crumpled letter in my
hand, he wisely went to the back room to watch TV until I had
calmed down.

I called Sandra and Barb. Both were surprised and outraged,
and told me that no one had responded to their mandatory re-
ports, and no one had called them regarding mine. None of us
could believe that this had been handled so carelessly. Based
upon the investigator's findings, I could only assume she hadn't
reviewed my copy of the file or considered my account. She hadn't
been to my see mother's condition for herself. I suspected that she
had taken the facility at their word and gone through the motions
to close the case. I was angry enough to do whatever it took to
force the state to take our case more seriously.

I had to wait almost a week before I was calm enough to call
the district supervisor in charge of my mother's case. After I detailed our experiences, I said, "I don't think the investigator assigned to our case considered my side at all. She's not the one who
initially called me, and based upon her report, it appears she took
the facility staff's account at face value. I have written proof and
witnesses to dispute everything that the facility is claiming."

The supervisor agreed that the findings were one-sided. Another complaint was opened. Again, I described the errors in
Mother's chart and recounted our story, and sent it to the district
supervisor. Again, the investigator I originally spoke with called
to say that she was going to do a thorough review and would contact me with her findings. Again, I received letter that fully exon-

erated the facility of wrongdoing and placed most of the blame on the family.

My anger and frustration grew, and I couldn't understand what I was missing. Each time a complaint was filed, all the facility had to do was point a finger back at the family. Everything the facility said was taken as the truth, even though they had no facts to support their version of events. I started to wonder if there was a political motivation or something else happening behind the scenes. No matter how much information I provided, the state was unable or unwilling to find fault with the facility.

Still, I refused to give up. I was so stressed and angry that my blood pressure was out of control. I wasn't eating or sleeping well, and even Lyle, my staunchest supporter, wanted me to give up. I could not. The spark had been fanned into a flame and I couldn't let what happened to my mother be swept under the rug so that they could do the same thing to the next unfortunate soul who was forced into their care. I sat down and started to write Who Is Today? I didn't want to succumb to the negative, angry emotions that were taking possession of my soul. Mother's ordeal had to come to light somehow, so why not write about it?

I called the district supervisor again, sharing my anger and frustration with the system. I said, "I cannot let something so obviously wrong be casually brushed away as if it had never occurred. I still have nightmares about our experience. Every time I see my mother's emaciated, withered body, the horror of what happened is fresh in my mind. My mother was given no choice but to go to that awful place. She was supposed to get skilled care, and instead, she was neglected and suffered harm. If what happened to my mother isn't considered a problem, we should all be afraid. I hope you never have the misfortune of being forced into such a facility!"

She agreed. "I suspect that you would've been satisfied if the facility had taken responsibility for their actions and promised to do their best to prevent something like this from happening in the future."

"Yes, I would have, but they're going to have to recognize that they did something wrong before they can correct it. Would it help if I sent my copy of the chart, the one I've been basing my complaints on?" She said it would and opened a third complaint. This time, when I sent my written complaint, I included the chart, an outline, and a spreadsheet with inappropriate actions and corresponding dates.

The supervisor later called and said, "Although everyone in our district office agrees that what happened to your mother was not right, we're hesitant to cite the facility. We've found several violations. However, it's our opinion that any citations written would not hold up to an appeal, and an appeal would be likely. The facility has a near-perfect record and will fight hard to defend it. I'm not ready to give up just yet. I plan to turn the case over to a different county, who will have an unbiased investigator review the complaint and visit the facility."

A new complaint was filed. I thought it was an odd process, but unwilling to let the matter go, I agreed. All the information was transferred to a different county for fresh eyes. I was more convinced than ever that there was political motivation at work.

I went through all the familiar steps with the new investigator, and this time, she did find fault with the facility. Her investigation summary report read:

Failed Provider Practice Identified. Citation(s) Written.

The facility failed to ensure the named resident's medication regimen remained free of unnecessary medications when a third bowel laxative was added, and without informing the resident's representative, and without adequate assessment and indication for the medication's use. The facility had dietary assessments and interventions implemented, however, the named resident experienced significant weight loss while residing in the facility during a change in condition. In addition, the facility held several vitamins and a diabetic medication on numerous occasions without notifying the ordering physician.

Citations were issued by the state against the facility. A written response from the facility was required and would go into their permanent record. Almost six months after my first complaint, I received notification that the facility had addressed all of my concerns. I felt great relief and satisfaction when I read the procedural changes that prevented giving laxatives in excess and required informed consent for laxative use. However, the facility still refused to admit that they had done anything wrong.

It was a small victory that had taken months and a tremendous amount of effort to achieve. I have no way to know if the facility continued to follow the new procedures after the state closed the investigation, but the effort was worth it. The conditions we encountered can only exist if we allow them to continue without complaint. It wasn't easy and I almost gave up many times. Even if this small slap on the wrist helped only one person, then it was well worth the effort. When Mother is no longer on this earth, I plan to volunteer for the Washington State Long-Term Care Ombudsman program so that I can advocate for the rights of those, like my mother, who are vulnerable and have lost their voice. The faces of those we left behind still haunt me. When I read an obituary for someone who has died from complications of Alzheimer's or a fall, I always wonder if that really was the cause.

It was finally springtime. The days were longer and the flowering trees exploded with pink and white blossoms that showered the lawns and roads with their delicate petals. I returned to my normal Monday, Wednesday, and Saturday visits with Mother, although I hadn't yet started taking her out. I didn't want to risk a fall, and decided to wait until her strength returned. Then one Saturday morning, she looked over at me and asked, "Who is today?"

Hearing that question brought tears to my eyes and real joy into my heart. "Why, Saturday, of course! Our day to play."

"Oh good," she said. "Where are we going to play?" She looked at me and frowned. "Why are you crying?"

I smiled through my tears. "I'm just having an allergy attack. Would you like to go out to lunch today?"

"Well, I sure as hell don't want to stay around here! It's so quiet and there is nothing to see and nothing to do. Where are we going?" We began to go out every Saturday like we had so many times before.

As her health improved and she regained her weight and strength, we reestablished a familiar routine. I visited three times a week, but it didn't seem to be enough for her. Lee had only been to visit Mother once since she had moved into her new home, and even her calls became less frequent. Once Marie was confident in the care Mother was receiving, she came to visit less and less as well. Eventually, her visits dropped to once every other week, to take her out for a wash and set or to fill in for me on the rare occasion that I go on vacation or take a break.

Mother needed more stimulation than the adult family home could provide. Her brain might have been dying, but her wit was still sharp and her sense of fun and adventure was still intact. The caregivers provided excellent care but had others to look after, some who were very sick and on hospice. The home reached its six-resident capacity and the caregivers could no longer spend all of their time keeping Mother occupied. Once again, I hired a sitter to visit with her, engage her in conversation and activities, and take her out for drives or an ice cream cone. This seemed to be the magic formula for Mother and she started to flourish. I knew that things were truly going to work out when I walked in to hear her telling her companions all about how she had worked for Bill Gates. I was so glad to hear her talking about Bill again, although I thought it was weird that she could hold onto her delusions better than reality.

More than a year has passed, and although she is confused, forgetful, childlike, and impulsive, my mother is still in there. She is still intelligent, kind, witty, and loving with a wicked sense of humor. Some days, she will ask, "Are you Anita?" It's an unsettling question, but one that doesn't surprise me. She has learned how to navigate her way around her new home, is quick to smile and joke, and will tell her repeated stories to anyone who will listen. She tells me how clean it is and that they keep track of her, which gives her great comfort. She often asks about Honey, but is reassured when I tell her the story. I say, "You're both just a couple of old sweethearts and are getting the care you need to be happy!"

She loves to pet and talk to Rarri, and is fond of small stuffed animals. I have filled her room with stuffed animals that she calls her friends. She points to them and smiles as she tells me, "You can't feel sad with those around!"

I'm preparing for the inevitable, but I know I'll never be ready. She'll get worse until one day, she forgets who I am. She may become incontinent, start to wander, or become combative. She may fall and we all may become victims of a careless system once again. I don't think we will experience these issues because her adult family home shows her such devoted care and attention, but there is no guarantee. Eventually, Mother will die. This seems to be the beginning of the end. I hope I'll be ready. All I can do is to help her live her life in comfort and peace until it's her time. I will take the time I'm given and cherish each moment I have with her.

Our journey has been humbling but enlightening, and has made me a better person. I no longer resent the time I spend caring for my mother; instead, I celebrate every opportunity to make a difference in her life. I still have moments in which I'm overwhelmed by sadness or weary of the constant effort. Our trials have made me more cynical than I would like to be. I had to learn the hard lesson that life isn't fair, but that I also have the power to make a difference.

My reward for all of my effort and sacrifice is the joy that I feel each time I see the smiling face of my fragile Mother and hear her sweet voice say, "I'm a lucky old sweetheart, heavy on the sweet!"

Who is today? Today is the day I have Mother to hug, to love, to laugh with, and to care for.

References

I found the following resources helpful in lighting my path. I encourage you to utilize these references, but also to do your own research, as there are many resources available to those that seek them.

Alzheimer's Association
24/7 Helpline: 1-800-272-3900 (toll-free)
www.alz.org

Books

Frank Broyles, *Coach Broyles' Playbook for Alzheimer's Caregivers: A Practical Tips Guide* (University of Arkansas, 2006)

Nancy L. Mace and Peter V. Rabins, *The 36-Hour Day: A Family Guide to Caring for People Who Have Alzheimer Disease, Related Dementias, and Memory Loss* (Grand Central Publishing, 2012)

When I'm frustrated and wish that my life could be as it was before Alzheimer's disease came to call, I read a poem I found in *Coach Broyles' Playbook*. This poem always makes me cry, but sets my heart and my feet back upon the path I will travel with love until the end of my mother's life.

Do not ask me to remember.
Don't try to make me understand.
Let me rest and know you're with me.
Kiss my cheek and hold my hand.

I'm confused beyond your concept.
I am sad and sick and lost.
All I know is that I need you
To be with me at all cost.

Do not lose your patience with me.
Do not scold or curse or cry.
I can't help the way I'm acting,
Can't be different 'though I try.

Just remember that I need you,
That the best of me is gone.
Please don't fail to stand beside me,
Love me 'til my life is done.

– Author Unknown

65799128R00183

Made in the USA
Charleston, SC
05 January 2017